A QUEST FOR ADVENTURE

David Horton's Conquest
of the
Appalachian Trail
and the
Trans-America Footrace

by
David Horton
&
Rebekah Trittipoe

A Quest for Adventure

Library of Congress Catalog Card Number
97-61968

ISBN: 1-890306-05-3

Front Cover: Day 22 in Western Colorado
Photo by Regis Shivers

Warwick House

Publishing

720 Court Street
Lynchburg, Virginia

ACKNOWLEDGMENTS

There are three special people needing to be thanked for their part in getting this book into print. Maureen Kruse, David's secretary at Liberty University spent many hours transcribing the audiotapes made by David during the Trans-Am experience. With an approaching deadline, Maureen approached her unenviable task with diligence. We thank her for her efforts.

Secondly, we want to thank Nancy Horton for her work on this project. We recognize her quintessential role in reading, editing, suggesting changes, and helping with the layout and content selection for the book. Nancy also had the "pleasure" of transcribing many of the Trans-Am tapes. Most of all, however, we appreciate her willingness to persevere with us until the conclusion of the project.

Gary Trittipoe's input into this book must also be recognized. Gary was always willing to read and critique the book as it was being written — line by line, chapter by chapter. He is also credited with taking many of the photos found in the latter chapters of the Trans-Am portion. Without Gary's support, this book would not be what it is today.

There were many meetings of the Hortons and Trittipoes to discuss content and logistics. This called for the sacrifice of time and energy from our spouses. Both Gary and Nancy offered their unique perspectives and enabled us to put together this story. We really do appreciate their patience with us and with the entire project.

~David Horton and Rebekah Trittipoe

DEDICATION

I wish to express my deepest thanks to the hundreds of people who supported both the Appalachian Trail speed record and the Trans-America Race. There is no way that I could have accomplished either of these feats had it not been for so many people who gave in so many ways. There were those who supported the efforts financially. There were those who served as crew. There were those who constantly encouraged me with prayer. There were those who wrote and sent me care packages. There were those who provided necessary goods and services. All of these people were an integral part of my adventures. I am humbled by it all.

But most of all, I wish to express my thanks to those closest to me: Nancy, my wife, and our children, Brandon and Allison. I know that my absence from them caused hardship in their lives. While I was following my dreams, they were living in day-to-day reality. I was not there when they needed to talk or make decisions. I was not there to participate in church activities. I was not there to go out as a couple with our friends. I was not able to even give much verbal support via the phone lines. I realize that I did make life more difficult for everyone. Therefore, it behooves me to give the biggest round of applause to my family. Fulfilling my dreams of the Trail and the Trans-Am would mean nothing without them. I am forever indebted and appreciative.

~David Horton

TABLE OF CONTENTS

Preface 1
Introduction: The Setting 4

PART I
FROM GEORGIA TO MAINE
Chapter 1: Preparing For the Trail 11
Chapter 2: Week 1 on the A.T. 22
Chapter 3: Week 2 on the A.T. 28
Chapter 4: Week 3 on the A.T. 34
Chapter 5: Week 4 on the A.T. 40
Chapter 6: Week 5 on the A.T. 48
Chapter 7: Week 6 on the A.T. 58
Chapter 8: Week 7 on the A.T. 67
Chapter 9: Week 8 on the A.T. 82
Chapter 10: From Maine to Mundane 96
Appalachian Trail Statistics 100

PART II
FROM SEA TO SHINING SEA
Chapter 11: Preparing For the Great Race 105
Chapter 12: Week 1 of the Trans-Am 111
Chapter 13: Week 2 of the Trans-Am 124
Chapter 14: Week 3 of the Trans-Am 134
Chapter 15: Week 4 of the Trans-Am 143
Chapter 16: Week 5 of the Trans-Am 155
Chapter 17: Week 6 of the Trans-Am 166
Chapter 18: Week 7 of the Trans-Am 178
Chapter 19: Week 8 of the Trans-Am 191
Chapter 20: Week 9 of the Trans-Am 201
Chapter 21: The Final Day 214
Chapter 22: From Racing to Recovery 219
Trans-America Footrace Statistics 222

A Quest for Adventure

PREFACE

"Once a man has made a commitment to a way of life,
he puts the greatest strength in the world behind him. It's something
we call heart power. Once a man has made this commitment,
nothing will stop him short of success."

– Vince Lombardi

David Horton grew up in rural Marshall, Arkansas, one of three children born to Ezra and Lois Horton. While attending elementary school, David's childhood days were filled with a mix of studies, farming chores, hunting, and fishing. High school found him a member of the basketball team and the quarterback for the football team, despite his lean frame. But I am told that even in those early, formative years, David was a young man filled with a passion and drive for life, athletics being an important part of that life. He always wanted to be the best and worked hard to achieve that end.

It was that same incentive that took David to the University of Central Arkansas in Conway, Arkansas. College to David was like freedom is to a prisoner. The nickname of "wild man" soon became his trademark as he enjoyed, and perhaps even abused, his new found autonomy. He met and married Nancy Paladino in 1971 and discovered the pressures that multiple roles such as student, husband, and provider produced. However, he was a hard working student and disciplined himself through Bachelor and Master degrees in education (1972 and 1973 respectively), with math and physical education being his selected teaching fields.

The next phase of his life found him in the teacher/coach mold as he took a teaching position in Bee Branch, Arkansas, at Southside High School. His intensity was found in the classroom as well as on the basketball court. In fact, in those days, his intensity was just a little too much as far as the referees were concerned! But no one could dare claim that he was devoid of zest. He loved to teach and was naturally gifted in that area. However, after three years of teaching secondary education, higher education soon

1

beckoned him to the University of Arkansas in Fayetteville, home of the Razorbacks. So, with his wife and two kids by his side, he completed his doctorate of education in 1978.

Not only were those years in Fayetteville important educationally, it was there that a professor urged his students to "practice what you preach." That is, to teach about fitness is not reasonable without living out fitness. Striking a chord in David's mind, he hit the streets with his running shoes on. At first, running wasn't exactly loads of fun. In fact, it was tiring and hard work. But that did not stop him. In 1979, having moved to Lynchburg, Virginia, to teach at Liberty University, he chose the JFK 50-Miler in nearby Boonsboro, Maryland, to test the waters of ultrarunning. He placed twenty-fourth in a time of 7 hours, 43 minutes and 16 seconds. And the rest, as they say, is history.

In the ensuing years, David has been relentless in his pursuit of excellence. As of mid-summer 1997, he had over one hundred ultra race starts, eighty-seven finishes, and thirty-eight wins. His cumulative mileage exceeds 70,000 miles. And as a contributor to the sport, he has served as the race director of the well-known 50-Mile Mountain Masochist Trail Race, the Blue Ridge Odyssey multi-day event, and the Holiday Lake 50K. Additionally, it has been his encouragement and training example that has encouraged many a would-be ultra runner into actually becoming one. This author speaks from personal experience.

It is possible there are others who have made parallel accomplishments. However, David's vision and quest for adventure sets him apart from the crowd. Hidden in the dry statistics of 101 ultra starts are two very significant events that arguably represent additional 116 ultras. (Since an "ultra" is technically any race over the standard marathon distance of 26.2 miles, each of the 116 days of David's "quests" was an ultra.)

In 1991, Horton set foot on Springer Mountain in Georgia to begin chasing the Appalachian Trail speed record, which stood at 60.5 days. Fifty-two days, nine hours, and forty-one minutes later, David stood atop yet another mountain, Katahdin, in Maine. His relentless pursuit of the record carried him over 2144 miles of trail, solitude and isolation being his constant companions. But despite the grueling nature of the feat, another dream of adventure and challenge was growing even before the realization of his accomplishment had set in.

June of 1995 found Horton standing not on a mountain, but on a beach, Huntington Beach, California, at the outset of another ultra; an ultra that consisted of sixty-four straight days of vicious racing against the world's best, comprising a total of 2906 miles. After the sixty-fourth day of racing over desert, mountains, flatlands, hill and dale, Horton would be owner of the third fastest time ever in the world for the transcontinental crossing.

This book attempts to let the reader experience through the written word the essence of each of these journeys. You will be struck by the enormity of these tasks. You may even cry in relating to David's many times of utter despair and desolation. But then you will rejoice at the high points, the times of athletic excellence, and the times of philosophical and spiritual breakthrough. Forrest Gregg once said of Vince Lombardi, the legendary coach of the gridiron, that "He made us realize that if the mind is willing, the body can." David lived those words.

Catch the vision and live the dream!

~Rebekah Trittipoe

INTRODUCTION

The Setting

*One of God's greatest miracles is to enable ordinary people to do
extraordinary things.*

— *Author unknown*

The day was like so many other East Coast summer days.
Even with the dawn of the new day, the oppressive heat could
be felt and would continue to build with every passing moment.
The cock-a-doodle-doo of the roosters would sound muffled in
the heaviness of the early morning air. The combined effect of
heat and humidity would make it feel as if there were a monster
on your chest, fighting you for every breath and stealing away
your energy. The newscasts warned people of the heat, encouraging inside activity and discouraging long exposures to the elements. Seeking to protect them, even dogs and cats would be
given refuge inside air-conditioned walls by their owners. Those
traveling the highways would do so in climate-controlled vehicles. Local ice cream and soda shops would do a booming
business on this day. Tempers would easily be ignited by even
the smallest of irritations. Children would beg their mamas to
turn on the hose or go to the local pool. Mothers, too hot and
tired to argue, would agree. Productivity in the work-a-day world
would have to be guarded since motivation is inversely propor-
tional to the rising temperatures. Farmers would consider postponing their chores until evening, choosing rather to pass the
time at a local diner discussing the price of corn. But off in the
distance, a small band of runners would be seen, stretched out
along Route 30 in rural Pennsylvania and making their way ever
closer to New York City.

To most of those ten runners, today would be just like so
many days before and many days that would follow. They would
start running before dawn, unreasonably hopeful that the sun's
rising would be somehow postponed, if only for the day. They
would forge on ahead, barely pausing every two miles when food

and refreshment would be offered to them. They would don hats and sunglasses to provide a buffer from the sun. They would douse themselves with water and place ice cubes under their hats to externally cool themselves. Day's end would find them 47.1 miles further from Huntington Beach, California, and 47.1 miles closer to finishing their transcontinental crossing in New York City. Their feet, though weary from the millions of steps taken before, would move, without faltering, toward the goal. They would not move to the right or to the left. No deviation from the prescribed course would be taken, for this would mean wasted energy. They would reach today's finish line, shower, eat, rest, and prepare themselves for more of the same before the rising of the next sun.

But to one runner, today would be forever set apart from the other sixty-three days of the race. Today he would find himself at the intersection of his dreams, forcing him to pause from the relentless pursuit down the highway to ponder his life's choices. As the tractor-trailers roared by, this lone runner would seek the refuge of another trail, another journey, if only for a moment.

The date was August 14, 1995. The race was the Trans-America Footrace, the modern equivalent to the trans-continental Bunion Derbies of 1928 and 1929. The runner was David Horton, experienced and celebrated in his sport of ultra-running. The day had begun at 3:55 a.m., just as fifty-eight previous days had begun. Horton turned off his alarm clock, hurriedly donned his shorts and singlet, pulled on his socks that had been washed out the night before, slipped on his running shoes and sought to break the fast with cereal, coffee, and a donut. At the stroke of 5:00 a.m., Horton and the other runners were on the start line, listening for, and perhaps even dreading, the word "go." In fact, many of the runners likened the start to a funeral: an event they had to attend but didn't have a clue how they could again survive. But the soon-vacated start area in the parking lot of an old, fly-infested, and unairconditioned gymnasium in McConnellsburg, Pennsylvania, was a clear sign that each of the runners, including Horton, had accepted yet another challenge the race offered. The trials and triumphs of previous days found Dusan Mravlje, a Slovenian "soldier" whose job it was to train and race, to be in first place overall. In second place was Florida's Raymond Bell, who had won the race in 1993. David Horton found himself solidly in third place overall, closing in on a weakening Bell, but being chased by Australian Patrick Farmer (also a Trans-Am veteran and second place finisher in 1993) and the small but mighty Japanese runner from New York City, Nobuaki Koyago.

The day's stage required that the runners traverse and conquer 47.1 miles within the required time of 15.7 hours. Failure to do so would negate the previously run 2627 miles and would force retirement from the race. There would be no exceptions to the rule. The course, marked by flour arrows at turns, would follow along Route 30 in Pennsylvania. So, the runners ran one hundred yards down a gradual slope before turning right at the arrow to begin a three-mile, 14-percent-grade climb. The heaviness of the air due to a torrential downpour during the night made the climb even more formidable. Horton, uncharacteristically running halfway up the incline, was caught by Koyago, Mravlje and Farmer when he finally decided to begin power walking. The Slovenian threw verbal barbs at Koyago, the winner of the previous three stages: "Hey, don't you think the pace is a little slow? This hill is child's play!" Whether the sarcasm had any impact on the Japanese runner is unknown, but the crest of the mountain saw Nobuaki Koyago in the lead, running like a man possessed. He proceeded to build a one-mile lead on the next runner, Patrick Farmer, by mile fourteen. At day's end, Koyago would cross the finish line with a full three-mile lead.

Meanwhile, Horton would struggle. Cautiously running down the backside of that first mountain, the professor from Liberty University would be passed for the first time by the runner in eighth place overall. The effect of being passed served as a mental cattle prod. Horton gained ground, regained his position, and was running steadily. With the humidity remaining high and the temperatures climbing with the rising sun, all ten runners pressed on. Horton did enjoy posing momentarily at mile thirty for a photo with some running friends from his hometown of Lynchburg. But after another half mile of running, Horton took his first five-minute break of the entire race. It was at the 30.5 mile point of this day's stage that the route intersected the 2144-mile Appalachian Trail.

"Here I stand at the crossroads of life," stated Horton into the video camera. After a brief thirty-yard run into the coolness of the forest, he returned to the shoulder of Route 30 to record his thoughts on videotape. Although drowned out at times by the roar of the semi-tractor trailers, David began to recall the moment four years prior when he passed this exact spot. It was in the spring of 1991 that he found himself standing atop Springer Mountain in Georgia, at the beginning of his Appalachian Trail adventure. In pursuit of the speed record on this south/north continuous trail, he ran day after day in the quietness and solitude that the trail affords. Over mountains, through valleys, across grassy meadows, he went. Few were the encounters with the mainstream of humanity. And, little did he realize that when he followed the trail out of the woods, across Route 30 and reentered the woods on the other side, that he would have a déjà-vu experience when his west-to-east Trans-Am race would intersect his route.

Two races. Two challenges. Both grueling but both very different. The first was a race against time in terms of days, the elements, and the roughness of the terrain. The second was a race against time in terms of hours and minutes, against other competitors and the redundancy of thousands of miles of pavement. However, there was a common foundation to the two events. Both were incredibly difficult. Both required conquering the severe bouts of depression that invaded the mind of this endurance athlete. Both required conquering the mentally debilitating and physically crippling injuries associated with running mile after mile, day after day. Both required the mental toughness and fortitude that so few in our society possess. And both require an unquenchable quest for adventure.

Horton did conquer the Appalachian Trail in 1991 and set a speed record yet to be broken. On this particular day in 1995, Horton would continue his Trans-Am run within five minutes of his encounter with the A.T. He would finish in the heat, humidity and peak of the tourist season in Gettysburg, only to prepare himself for the next day of racing. And on the fifth day hence, he would cross the finish line of all finish lines in New York City with the third fastest time ever recorded in the world.

This is the story of those quests.

PART I

FROM GEORGIA
TO MAINE

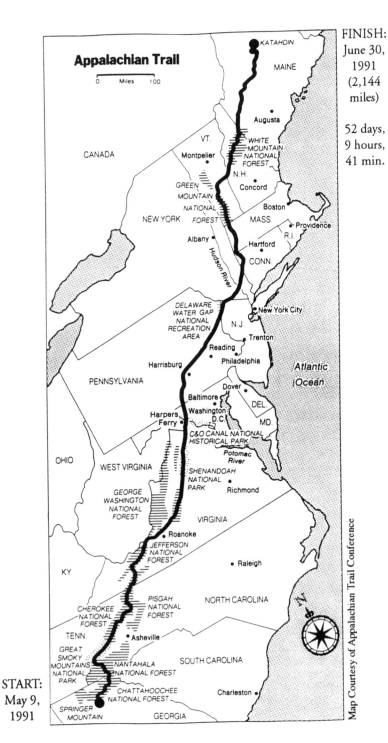

Appalachian Trail

0   Miles   100

KATAHDIN

MAINE

FINISH:
June 30,
1991
(2,144
miles)

52 days,
9 hours,
41 min.

Augusta

VT.

WHITE
MOUNTAIN
NATIONAL
FOREST

CANADA

Montpelier

N.H.

Concord

GREEN
MOUNTAIN

NATIONAL

NEW YORK   FOREST

Boston

MASS.

Providence

R.I.

Albany

Hartford

CONN.

Hudson River

DELAWARE
WATER GAP
NATIONAL
RECREATION
AREA

New York City

N.J.

Trenton

Reading

Philadelphia

Harrisburg

PENNSYLVANIA

Dover

Baltimore

DEL.

Harpers
Ferry

Washington
D.C.

MD.

Atlantic
Ocean

C&O CANAL NATIONAL
HISTORICAL PARK

Potomac
River

OHIO

WEST VIRGINIA

SHENANDOAH
NATIONAL
PARK

Richmond

GEORGE
WASHINGTON
NATIONAL
FOREST

VIRGINIA

Roanoke

JEFFERSON
NATIONAL
FOREST

KY

Raleigh

PISGAH
NATIONAL
FOREST

NORTH CAROLINA

CHEROKEE
NATIONAL
FOREST

TENN.

Asheville

GREAT
SMOKY
MOUNTAINS
NATIONAL
PARK

NANTAHALA
NATIONAL FOREST

SOUTH CAROLINA

START:
May 9,
1991

CHATTAHOOCHEE
NATIONAL FOREST

Charleston

SPRINGER
MOUNTAIN

GEORGIA

N

S

Map Courtesy of Appalachian Trail Conference

10

CHAPTER 1

Preparing For the Trail

"Remote for detachment, narrow for chosen company, winding for leisure, lonely for contemplation, it beckons not merely north and south, but upward to the body, mind, and souls of man."
-A. T. sign near Springer Mountain

"You have to have dreams to have dreams come true." That is one of the mottos I live by. Everyone has dreams. Some dreams are for money, fame, cars, relationships, physical achievements, and the like. It is easy to have dreams of grandeur. Taking the steps necessary to make a dream come true is the hard part and one that most never attempt. In the spring of 1991 I took the first step to make one of my dreams come true.

As an instructor of physical education at Liberty University in Central Virginia, I challenged students every day to have dreams in every area of their lives. I would explain that my three lifetime goals were to: 1) run the 2144 mile Appalachian Trail, 2) bike across the United States, and 3) run across the country in a competitive stage race.

In 1987, an article came out in *USA Today* about the 50th anniversary of the Appalachian Trail (A.T.). The A.T. was officially opened as a footpath from Georgia to Maine in 1937. The distance as indicated by the 1991 *Appalachian Trail Data Book* is 2144 miles. Reading the article reinforced the idea I had several years prior — to go the distance.

As an ultrarunner living close to the A.T., I would often meet thru-hikers as I was out on training runs. Normally, an average thru-hiker will take five to six months to complete the journey, averaging around fifteen miles per day. Many hikers are either fresh out of college or recently retired. I was forty-one years of age at the time, which did not place me in either category.

Being a college professor allows me to have the summers off. To make extra money, I have worked for trucking companies for the last twenty-plus years. I normally work on the dock as well as drive to pick up and drop off freight. In late 1990, I was driving a truck for Consolidated Freightways when I started thinking once again about the A.T. The more I thought about it the more I knew I wanted to run the A.T. Somewhere on that drive a mental decision was made: "I *am* going to do it!" Then came the big question, "How?"

For the next six weeks I started to formulate a plan. However, my first major obstacle was to obtain my wife's approval. This was going to be difficult. I just had to wait for the right moment.

I had mentioned to Nancy a few times before about my desire to run the A.T. She had never taken me seriously. But never before had I actually made that decision. Knowing that I had to have a good rationale for doing the A.T., I started planning in earnest as to how I would pull it off. I knew that logistically I could not take five months to complete the distance. So, being a competitive ultrarunner, I began to think in terms of a speed record. Contact with the Appalachian Long Distance Hikers Association led me to Warren Doyle, the group's founder. He told me that the official record was sixty-four days, although the unofficial record set by Ward Leonard of Salt Lake City, Utah, in 1990 was 60.5 days. There, it was settled. I had to do the Trail in less than sixty days. Although my friend,

Ward Leonard, former A.T. record holder, and David finally meet on Apple Orchard Mountain, October 8, 1995.

Dennis Herr, also had interest in doing it, he could only spare about forty days. I told him he was crazy thinking in those terms.

In early September of 1990, I went to the Groundhog Fall Fifty-Mile Run in Punxsatawney, Pennsylvania. Dr. Gary and Millie Buffington directed the race. Gary is an emergency room physician in Florida and the creator of Conquest™ replacement drink. He was very encouraging when I told him of my plans and said that he would supply me with all the Conquest™ I would need. He thought he and Millie could help in the task of crewing me. This was to be the snowball that got the whole process going to make my dream a reality.

I sought the help of Robin Carroll, an instructor at Liberty University and director of Liberty Expeditions. Robin is very knowledgeable with regard to backpacks and wilderness expeditions. He thought he could get the Kelty Company to furnish me with a pack.

As time passed and I shared my dream with more and more people, it dawned on me that I had better talk to Nancy before she heard of my plan from someone else. If this happened, I knew the plan would be doomed. So, on a Sunday night in September I told her there was something I wanted to talk to her about. Her response was, "Oh no, what is it you want to do now?" I told her to have a seat and listen to my entire plan before she said anything. I carefully laid out all the details on how I was going to do the Trail in sixty days and how I would keep expenses down. After listening to all the details, she just looked at me in silence. After a few minutes she said, "I know you've talked about the A.T. for a long time, and you know I'm not concerned about the cost. My major concern is about the length of time you'll be away from us. I can't believe you would choose to leave your family for that long to achieve your selfish desires." Well, at least she didn't say, "NO"! Nancy continued, "You've already made up your mind, and I guess you would do it whether I said yes or no." She probably had a point. But after a few days of further discussion, she grudgingly gave her approval. She wasn't happy about the whole thing. But I had her permission and that's all I cared about. Full speed ahead!

From Nancy's point of view:

"You've got to be kidding! No way! Only in your dreams! I can't believe you would consider leaving your family for a month, much less two!" These were only a few of the choice words I had to say when David first approached me with the idea that he wanted to run the A.T. the summer of 1991. Well, let me tell you, his announcement went over like a lead balloon! To be perfectly honest, I hated the idea. I was totally against it. Yet, down deep, I knew that this was a tremendous desire of his. I knew he wanted to do this with his entire being. I finally just had to ask the Lord to give me a better attitude and help me to be more supportive. This was probably the hardest thing I did.

I was told that the best outdoor store around was Rockfish Gap Outfitters in Waynesboro, Virginia. Owned by Matt and Dorothy McCall, the store is a favorite amongst hikers, located just three miles off the A.T. The McCalls helped me to make equipment selections. These included a Blue Kazoo sleeping bag by North Face™ with a Sierra™ design bivy sack. A Mountainsmith™ Bugaboo was also selected as the best pack for my needs. Most thru-hikers carry dehydrated food and a small stove. I really didn't want to take a lot of time cooking and knew I did not want to carry a stove and fuel. I had to constantly think about keeping my load as light as possible. Fortunately, Gary Buffington came to the rescue with the food problem. He had been in contact with the Star Food Processing Company which produces meals ready-to-eat (MREs). I called them, and after some discussion, they agreed to supply me with the meals that I required.

Other important advice about the A.T. was obtained from Bill and Laurie Foote of Lynchburg, Virginia. They had thru-hiked in 1987. I was fortunate to attend a lecture and slide presentation of their trip. Later, I met with them in their home, and they were invaluable sources of information.

More importantly, Bill was the first non-ultrarunner who actually thought I could do it. Although my running friends had confidence in me, most hikers I met were skeptical. Even in a survey of LU's faculty conducted by Dr. Dale Gibson, only 50 percent thought that I could make it. So, Bill's opinion about my chances was taken to heart.

Now, I had to figure out how much distance I could cover each day and where I would spend the nights. The best source for planning is the Appalachian Trail Conference (ATC) headquartered in Harper's Ferry, West Virginia. Jean Cashin, who was in her twentieth year of service, was most helpful and encouraged me to pursue my goal. I was able to obtain three invaluable pieces of written information. Dan Bruce, a five-time thru-hiker, wrote *The Thru-Hikers Handbook*. It contains information about planning, trail towns, resupply points, and a myriad of other tidbits of useful information. *The A.T. Data Book* is published each spring. It contains a lot of information, but specifically indicates the closest post offices to road crossings along the A.T. This is vitally important in determining where you are going to mail your supplies. Then, there is a series of ten guidebooks and maps covering the entire A.T. If you want to know where you are and where you are going, these are important to have! Based on my research, I figured I needed to average thirty-eight miles per day to achieve the goal.

Hikers on the A.T. stay in tents, shelters, hostels, and motels. The basic shelter is no more than a three-sided wooden structure. There are approximately 230 shelters, positioned usually within a day's hike of each other. The hostels provide bunkhouse type amenities for $6-12 per night. Though the motels have beds and showers, they almost always force the hiker to actually leave the trail, adding more travel and time to and from the trail. My plan was to stay in as many hostels or hotels as possible since I felt I could sleep and eat better, factors that could and would influence my running.

Starting the figuring from Springer Mountain, the southern terminus of the A.T., I mapped out where I would be at the end of each thirty-eight-mile segment. If there were no facilities nearby, a day might require more or less miles than thirty-eight, making up for the deviation the next day. As things turned out, this plan actually projected a fifty-six-day schedule, allowing me to take off a day or two if needed.

The part of the planning that concerned me the most was the physical preparation that would be necessary. I knew how to train for ultras, but 2144 continuous miles was quite another thing! All my reading and research did not tell me how to cover that distance in fifty-six days. My physiology books stated that it takes forty-eight hours to replenish your glycogen stores after three hours of continuous endurance exercise. (Glycogen is the fuel preferred by the body but is quickly depleted and slowly restored.) I queried exercise physiologists if it was really possible to train for such an event. They all had the same opinion: "No." I told them I thought you would have to use the first two to three weeks of the event itself to get in shape. They agreed.

I called Warren Doyle, who at that time had thru-hiked eight times, to ask how long it takes for this adaptation to take place. His response was, "About ten thousand miles." I said, "No, no. How long does it take each time you start?" He confirmed my thinking by answering that it would take two to three weeks. But he also offered that the single most important thing on the trail was "adaptability." As I thought about it, I knew I too would have to develop this trait in order to succeed.

My spring break at LU was in March of 1991. Since the beginning of my quest was a mere two months away, I thought this would be the perfect time to train on the trail. I did not really want to do it alone, so I suckered my good friend, Dennis Herr, a.k.a. "Animal," into accompanying me. I had a four-day run planned out that would have us cover thirty-seven miles per day. This seemed like it would be a good dry run of what was to come.

To make a long story short, we started out at Catawba in the late evening, where the A.T. crosses Route 311 in Virginia. It was fifty degrees with a hefty wind. My twenty-pound pack felt really heavy. Off we went into the woods, our tiny flashlights piercing the darkness, headed for the Boy Scout shelter one mile down the trail. It was tough sleeping on hard wooden floors with the sound of scurrying mice surrounding you. And it was cold! In the morning, it quickly became apparent that running with a pack was not easy. No matter how I adjusted the straps, it was never just right. It definitely was not made for running.

I had hoped to cover the distance each day in ten to twelve hours. This would translate to three miles per hour in rough terrain and four miles per hour in easier terrain. The first day took us thirteen hours, twenty-three minutes. This was not good! However, we could at least be consoled that forty-five minutes of those thirteen-plus hours were spent off trail when a fellow runner, Doug Young, met us and whisked us off to Burger King. That evening, we ate some MRE's. Funny how they taste better at home than when you're in the woods, tired, cold, and hungry.

On the second day, we woke to several inches of fresh snow. Despite the cold, the day was a little better than the first, due in part to another runner, Roger Hall, meeting us with pizza, ice cream, and Coke™. Dennis had to leave that evening, so I trudged into the woods after supper, feeling lonely and uncomfortable.

The third day of my trial run was hampered by ever-present nausea. There was little I could eat and keep down. I also ran out of water and resorted to eating snow. The overwhelming thought was, if I can't handle four days, how can I handle fifty-six days?

My spirits were dropping out of sight. I knew I could not make it to the conclusion of the fourth day (Rockfish Gap), so I plodded on a bit ahead of schedule for the third day to the Tye River. There I hitched a ride to a store, called my wife, and had her come fetch me.

In three days I had covered 122.4 miles, just over forty miles per day. It was much harder than I had anticipated. I was filled with uncertainty. I knew I would have to make some adjustments in my approach. My confidence was shaken, but not shattered.

Part of my regrouping was a new backpack from Kelty, White Cloud™, obtained for me by Robin Carroll. It was lighter and more adaptable to running. In April, I started out on another trial run, starting from Rockfish Gap and heading north. After the return of troublesome nausea, two hikers, who graciously shared a hot meal with me in the evening, saved my day. However, it was depressing when the nausea continued to torment me the next morning. I wanted to quit. I told myself I did not have to do this. I stopped after just thirty miles, postponing my connection with Animal, who was to meet me, by several hours. When we did finally connect, I even told him I would write letters telling everyone that the run was off. No way, José! It's over. It's finished! Animal listened patiently, but then tried to convince me to at least give it a try. He also reminded me that if I backed out now, it would be exceptionally difficult to get any support in the future. Despite my repeated "no, no," his final words encouraged me to sleep on it and make no decisions until tomorrow. I started my long drive home.

Things did seem different in the morning. I had to give it a shot. I had told so many people of my plan it would be too embarrassing to back out. Of course, I called Animal to tell him about my change of heart. And, I had *Ultrarunning* magazine run a small ad describing my upcoming adventure and soliciting volunteers to help me along the way. I was surprised at the many calls that began coming in. With help along the way, it would mean that I would only need to carry a small fanny pack rather than a full-size pack. This was good!

In early April, I received a phone call from Scott Grierson, age 24, of Bass Harbor, Maine. Scott and Joe Ballant of Florida were also planning a speed record attempt. Scott said he wanted to ask me some questions. I felt it only fair if he returned the favor by answering my questions. I knew of his hiking greatness, but at six feet, two inches and 220 pounds, he seemed more like a bear than a hiker. As it turned out, we both had plans for a fifty-six day hike/run. However, he was to start on May 7, two days before my start. They planned to walk sixteen to seventeen hours per day. I even suggested they wait two days so that we could proceed together. That, he would have to think about! In the end, the pair stuck with a May seventh departure, telling me they would be waiting for me on the top of Katahdin with a bottle of champagne (or Coke™, since I don't drink alcoholic beverages).

As the time drew near for me to depart, I became more and more anxious. Earlier, it had seemed like a great adventure, full of fun and excitement. Now, it seemed scary and unattainable. Enough people had volunteered so that I would only have to carry my pack three or four days. But even so, it was increasingly hard to concentrate on finishing out the semester. I could not avoid gazing at the 2.5-by-4-foot map of the A.T. that hung on my wall. Nancy still wasn't sold on the idea, stating, "I hope you're successful and achieve your goal, but I hope you're miserable while you're out there, wishing you hadn't done this, and that you miss your family terribly." She did agree, however, to produce a weekly newsletter, sending it to those people who were helping to support my efforts.

I finished my final exams on May seventh and prepared for the trip on Amtrak that night. For me, it was a very solemn occasion. It was so strange. I didn't know how to act. Maybe the challenge ahead of me was more than I was capable of achieving. Other than my wife and son, Brandon, the train station was deserted. Or so I thought. Out from the shadows popped friends and colleagues. I couldn't believe they had come, and yet it made me feel even lonelier. It was as if I was leaving forever. Final hugs and kisses were so hard and yet I climbed aboard the train.

▲

A different perspective:
    When we all met at the train station to see him off, I noticed a very definite change from his normal personality. He had nothing to say. No excitedly recited details of the trail! I saw a very different side of him that evening. I could see that he was being faced with all the pressure and apprehension of leaving his family and the difficulty of his goal. I could also see the fear of letting us all down who were so sure and confident that he could succeed.
                            ~Kendra Fleming, David's secretary

▼

All during my preparation, I continually looked to God for direction. I knew I was not able to do this thing on my own power. The Lord would be my strength. He had opened all the doors and made all things fall into place. I would now depend on Him as never before. I decided to keep a log of my journey and His direction and guidance.

Nancy adds:

David left for Georgia on May 7th. What a big day for him. What a sad day for me. I had the biggest lump in my throat as I waved to him from the train station. I was wondering if he felt as sad as I did at that moment. Would he be all right? What was I to expect for the next two months? Would I be able to handle it? What if he doesn't succeed? Will he be able to handle such a big disappointment? Questions, questions, questions...

From the log - May 7 - I feel lonely. Leaving my friends and family, the darkness seems to envelop me making me very small. A sign on a church billboard asked the question, "Are you sure you are headed in the right direction?" That seems so appropriate. I feel nervous and anxious about what lies ahead. "And I will do whatever you ask in my name, so that the Son may bring glory to the Father. You may ask me for anything in my name, and I will do it." John 14:13,14 (NIV)

Gary and Millie Buffington with David on Springer Mountain the day before his start of the A.T.

May 8 - Slept very little on the train.... Gary and Millie Buffington met me.... Beautiful cool day.... It seems foolish to think that a person could go over 2000 miles to Mt. Katahdin.... After dinner I feel more relaxed.... I look forward to tomorrow and whatever the future holds. Philippians 4:13 — "I can do all things through Christ who strengthens me." II Corinthians 12:9 - "For my strength is made perfect in weakness."

▲

From the mailbox:
There are times in our lives when we are drawn uncontrollably to some dangerous source of misery.

~ Suzi T.

▼

CHAPTER 2

Week 1 on the A.T.

"A runner must run with dreams in his heart..."
— *Emil Zatopek*

DAY 1 - MAY 9 - 37.1 MILES - 8:44

"Started on Springer Mountain, GA at 6:54 a.m. Foggy at the start and all day long. Rained pretty hard in the morning...off and on in the afternoon. Didn't even feel the first 15 miles. Had to make myself run slow. Blood Mountain was much easier than I thought. Toughest section was from Neels Gap to the end. Felt a little nauseous at the end. Stopped at 3:36 p.m. Early on in the day I felt very confident...as the day wore on my confidence faded. It is going to take a lot of hard work. I'm depending on you, God. Stayed in the Days Inn in Helen. Neat town. Modeled after a German town.

It was hard to believe that I was actually chasing my dream. It seemed so easy. But, it also seemed impossible to think that a person could run all the way to Maine.

During the day I would see other hikers. They would ask me if I were out for a jog or training run. I would just say, "Yes." If they asked where I was heading, I would say, "North." I didn't want to tell them where I was going or what I was doing. It seemed so foolish.

As I was signing the register in the Walasi-Yi Center (a hostel owned by Jeff and Dorothy Hansen) at Neels Gap, a young lady said, "You must be Dr. Horton." I had never seen her before in my life. Later, I learned she was Scott Grierson's girlfriend. Small world.

Everyone who hikes the A.T. has a trail name. Scott's was "Maineak" and Joe Ballant's was "Gator." I wasn't sure what my name would be. But when people started exclaiming, "Oh, you must be the runner!" I figured "The Runner" would be an appropriate name.

DAY 2 - MAY 10 - 45.3 MILES - 11:53 - CUM. MILES 82.4

Started at 6:00 a.m., finished at 5:55 p.m. I saw a turkey, a fox, and a deer, which snorted at me. Felt good most of day. Last 8-10 miles got difficult. Long day. Didn't get to eat until 9:00 p.m. Felt nauseated 2-3 hours after run. No views. Rained and foggy all day.... Gary and Millie are a godsend. Their help is super.... Didn't see a single hiker the last 30 miles but did run into Roger Ruit of Buena Vista, VA.... He's been out 64 days.... I have to start sleeping better. Woke up at 2:07 a.m. and didn't go back to sleep until 4:45 a.m. Got up at 5:00 a.m.

The nausea factor was present again. Gary gave me something that helped alleviate the problem. I didn't really want to go forty-five miles today, but there were no road crossings the last 15.6 miles. A little bit later I heard that Maineak had gone 50.7 miles the first day.

The climb out of Bly Gap was very steep. However, I was rewarded with a trail that was tunnel-like through very dense rhododendron. I did reach the Georgia-North Carolina border. Mentally, this was very motivating, knowing that I had one state down and thirteen to go.

DAY 3 - MAY 11 - 38.9 MILES - 8:55 - CUM. MILES 121.3

Best day yet. Felt good all day. Really no bad times. Overcast and nice most of the day. Heavy shower in the afternoon.... I think this is the first day I started getting used to the trail. Ran too hard last five miles (49 minutes). Started having fun and enjoying it today. I hope and pray to have many more days like today. Thank you Lord for a wonderful day.... Stayed in Franklin.

It was very motivating to be in a second state today. The nausea wasn't a problem, and I began to entertain the notion that perhaps I could finish what I had started.

DAY 4 - MAY 12 - 41.5 MILES - 10:31 - CUM. MILES 162.8

Rain as usual late in day.... Toughest section yet from Wesser to Stecoah Gap.... 3:18 for 13.1 miles.... Stayed in Tuskeegee Motel.

This was to be my first indoctrination of what was to come. Tough climbs and descents were to be constant throughout the day. Wayah Bald and Wesser Bald were just a warm-up for the big mountains later. There was a long 6.5-mile descent into Wesser, during which I slipped and fell on the slippery rocks in a very steep section. This would actually be the first of many falls. Shortly thereafter, the fog lifted and I was treated to a view of mountain after mountain. But the section between Wesser and Fontana Dam proved to be as tough and difficult as they say. Additionally, many of the trail markings were very old and indistinct, compounding the difficulty of staying on the trail.

When I first beheld Fontana Dam, I broke into tears. This was the first major landmark that I had achieved on this adventure. I was actually realizing, and partially succeeding, in chasing my dream of many years. The dam is spectacular. In the background behind the lake lie the majestic Great Smoky Mountains that represent the challenge that lay ahead.

Gary and Millie Buffington had to leave today, and my new crew of Karl and Kathy Henn took over. Changing of the crew

David crosses Fontana Dam.

would be repeated many times, and it was always a bittersweet experience. But changing crews is probably a good thing, since I cannot imagine that anyone could put up with me for the entire time.

DAY 5 - MAY 13 - 37.8 MILES - 10:01 - CUM. MILES 200.6

Rain every day.... Very muddy, very rough footing.... The day took longer than I thought it would and it wasn't a fun day. Glad to be through for the day. I look forward to a shorter day tomorrow. Stayed with Karl and Kathy Henn at the Oakmont Campground in a tent. Slept better than any other night so far.

The Smoky Mountain National Park is the most visited park in the United States. I probably saw more thru-hikers in this section than anywhere else. The first road access after Fontana Dam is at Clingman's Dome at 30.3 miles. This necessitated my carrying a lot of food and supplies in my backpack. This was the first time, but not the last, that lack of access was a real problem.

Although the ATC and many hikers do not recommend it, I would use the water out of springs to mix with my Conquest™ powder. This has been my practice for years, and I have escaped without any repercussion. Personally, I think that if water is flowing out the side of a mountain, the chances of contamination are very slim.

During the last three miles before reaching the Dome, a veritable flood of rain was coming down. The trail was very steep, washed out, and inundated by the flow of water straight down the mountain. However, I did take a side trail up to Clingman's Dome, topped with an observation deck at 6643 feet. This is the highest point on the trail. I've heard that the views are great, but you couldn't prove it by me! I couldn't see one hundred feet in front of me.

DAY 6 - MAY 14 - 30.8 MILES - 7:15 - CUM. MILES 231.4

It rained as usual — six for six days.... Very muddy and wet...horrible footing...no views.... My right shin started hurting a little around 11:00 a.m. Hurt a little worse as the day went on. Tried to take it easy. I am a little concerned about it. I'm taking aspirin. Kathy and Karl came and fixed supper for me at the shelter.... I feel lonely and anxious. Lord, help me deal with this problem. People are praying for me.

The continuing rain was starting to get old. I had developed several blisters due to the fact that I had only one pair of shoes with me and they did not dry out overnight. When my right shin started hurting a little, I did not worry too much about it. However, when the pain failed to abate, it definitely became a concern.

Staying at the Davenport Gap shelter, my recourse for bathing was a freezing cold stream by the ranger station. After the Henns left, I found myself alone in the shelter. It was my opportunity to again pour out my heart to God, asking for His help and sustenance through this time. I came to realize that I really was

The crew's view:
There we were, hiking up to Davenport Gap Shelter in the Smokies to bring David Horton his pack and cook him dinner. Karl was in front carrying David's white, densely packed pack. I was in the back carrying a backpack full of dinner, Conquest™, Cokes™, and breakfast. Our sons, Davy (7) and Kyle (5) were between us carrying packs also full of food. Just think, it took four of us to carry enough dinner for David!

I spied David speed walking toward me. "Hello, David! How are you?" I held out the bottle of Conquest™, he grabbed it, and kept briskly walking uphill, drinking a little. "I'm off schedule. Hard going today!" he answered me. He reminded me of the Mad Hatter in *Alice in Wonderland*. He seemed unable to stop. He also seemed disappointed with his time, obsessed with time as he is.

~ Kathy Henn

never alone for He had said, "I will never leave you or forsake you." I went to bed around 8:00 p.m. only to be rudely awakened by a man and three women entering the shelter area through the wire fence and gate surrounding it at 9:30 p.m. So much for being alone.

DAY 7 - MAY 15 - 35.4 MILES - 8:36 - CUM. MILES 266.8

Davenport Gap to Hot Springs. Right shin has been very sore all day. Took 6-8 aspirin and two Tylenol #3™. Hot and humid. First day it didn't rain on me. It started raining just after I finished. Got down mentally during the morning but hung in there and felt mentally good after I finished. Stayed at the Alpine Court, Room #1. Ate a good meal at the Trail Cafe.... Linn Finger helped me today and brought me a new pair of Air Pegasus. Great to have dry shoes! Next two days will be interesting, as I don't have anyone helping me and I must carry my own pack and fix my own meals.

It was on this day that I called Gary Buffington and told him about the pain I was experiencing in my shin. He suggested icing it to help alleviate the inflammation. This would be the first of many nights sitting with a bag of ice on my leg.

▲

The crew's view:

I was immediately impressed with his focus and sense of urgency. This was not a walk in the woods. This was a race!

[The next day] I bumped into Doyle Carpenter who informed me that the intrepid runner had spent the night in his camper and was already on the trail. When I asked about his shin splint problem, Doyle just shook his head and matter-of-factly said, "He won't make it — no way!" When I saw David at the next intersection, I had to agree with Doyle's assessment.... It goes without saying that this is one time I am glad I was wrong.

- Linn Finger

▼

CHAPTER 3

Week 2 on the A. T.

"What does not destroy me makes me stronger."
-*Source unknown*

DAY 8 - MAY 16 - 34.8 MILES - 11:54- CUM. MILES 301.6

Hot Springs to NC 212. Walked all day. Rain late in the afternoon. Right shin sore...tendonitis...shin splints.... Downhills really hurt. Mentally down during the day. Doyle Carpenter met me about 6 miles from the end. Picked my spirits up. Carried backpack until I met Doyle. Lord, please help my leg to get better.

As I look back on things, this was one of my worst days, if not the worst. This was probably the day that marked the start of a major decline.

My original plan was to go only 32.7 miles to the Flint Mountain Shelter. With immense pain in my shin, carrying my pack, and knowing there was no real need to hurry, I decided that I would walk all day. The flats and uphills presented no problem. However, the downhills were excruciating. Additionally, every time I would urinate, it would be bright red with blood. My knuckles and wrists became swollen with fluid, forcing me to continually loosen my watch. Then, to add insult to injury, a cold rain started to fall. My spirit had turned grayer than the skies.

I had not been expecting Doyle to jump out of the bushes at twenty-eight miles. Gary Buffington had called him the night before, describing my plight, and talked him into helping out. It was the levity of the moment and the welcome relief from carrying my pack that urged us on 2.7 miles beyond my original intent. He graciously drove me into Erwin, Tennessee, where we each inhaled a pizza. Unfortunately, the only hotel in town was at capacity and so we slept in his pickup truck back out near the trail.

DAY 9 - MAY 17 - 38.9 MILES - 11:22 - CUM. MILES 340.5

NC 212 to Indian Grove. Right shin a little better but down-hills really hurt, especially down to the Nolichucky River.... Very hot.... Stopped 45 minutes at the river then walked the last 7.1 miles. Fingers got real puffy again...some blood in urine.... Doyle helped me again today.

With Doyle accompanying me, I did not have to carry my backpack. The walking from the day before seemed to have helped since I was able to run just a little bit. However, I would have hated to have anyone see me because I was so slow. Doyle's experiences with shin splints were not encouraging. Both he and the lead runner developed shin splints so severe that they were both forced into retiring from a 1000-mile Trans-Texas race. He was encouraging me to take off a day or two or maybe even quit. However, I said, "As long as I can still move forward, I can't quit! It's too early in the run. Too many people are counting on me. I'm not going to quit now." This was a cumulative test of everything I had done in my life, both physically and mentally.

On the downhills, I had to force myself not to cry each time my right foot hit the ground. But finally down at the river after a long downhill, we took our shoes off and soaked our legs in the cool water while waiting for my next crew to show up. When that did not happen, I decided that I had to walk the next seven miles lest I fall off my schedule. Though Doyle protested wildly since my leg was swollen, inflamed, and the cause of much pain, I persisted. Knowing that three miles were uphill and four miles were relatively flat, I thought I could accomplish the task. Looking back, quitting is usually a mental decision rather than a physical decision. I needed to cover the territory and "fight."

Eventually, my crewman, Geoff Elijah, did find me, bearing special anti-inflammatories sent by Dr. Buffington. Just knowing that the medicine was available made things seem a little bit better.

DAY 10 - MAY 18 - 36.4 MILES - 11:11 - CUM. MILES 376.9

Indian Grove to Elk Park, NC. Shin better.... Did well most of the way until 2-3 in the afternoon. Balds on Roan Mountain

29

were spectacular. Prettiest place I've been. Hard rain on top. Emotionally I broke down after supper. Lonely, no money, shin has tendonitis. Lord help me. Stayed in dumpy hotel.

Before my trip had started, I had sent a detailed itinerary to friends who would be helping me. Included in that letter were the addresses of the twenty-two mail drops at which I could receive cards, letters, and goodies. Meeting me at the base of Roan Mountain, Geoff handed me the mail that he had picked up at the post office. Eating the chocolate chip cookies sent by friends Rick and Nancy Hamilton, I read each letter carefully. They were very motivating, urging me to continue on. Those people had so much faith in my abilities. Needless to say, I felt the pressure to live up to their expectations.

Many mountains were just under six thousand feet in elevation, and the cookies and letters seemed to make the climbs easier. I surveyed the beauty of God's creation that not even the rain could mask. The Hump Mountains were equally spectacular. There were views in every direction. I felt tremendous joy.

It's a good thing that I experienced a high early in the day because the night proved to be a disappointment. I was out of money, my shin still hurt, I was feeling lonely and sorry for myself. Phoning home to Nancy was difficult, because all I could do was cry. I felt bad about this because I knew she would worry.

DAY 11 - MAY 19 - 33.2 MILES - 10:01 - CUM. MILES 410.1

Elk Park to Watagau Road. Nice day. High temperature was 63 degrees. Very clear with great views.... White Rock Mountain, Fire Tower, Laurel Falls were spectacular.... Shin okay until noon then sore the rest of the day. Mentally felt better. Ate at Western Steer and staying at Comfort Inn in Elizabethon, TN.

North of US 19E on the A.T. was an area of vandalism in 1990 and 1991. Through the law of eminent domain, the ATC had bought a 1000-foot right-of-way through the land of several property owners. Some of the owners did not want to sell but were forced to do so. One shelter had been burnt down and sev-

The wife's view:

Before David left, he asked me if I would do a "progress" report each week. David would call me and let me know what was going on. He wasn't feeling good. He didn't want to talk. He was having some very serious physical problems, which were also affecting him mentally. This disturbed me more than he could have imagined. He was hurting, and I couldn't do anything to help! As a mother, you always feel helpless when your children become sick and you can't do anything but cradle them in your arms and give them that special attention that they need. My husband is like a child in that sense as well. When he feels bad, he wants a little special attention and love. He wasn't getting this on the trail. I could feel his loneliness and depression on the phone. But, I was helpless to do anything but pray.

-Nancy Horton

eral rangers accosted. Fishhooks were even hung across the trail at eye level, and trip wires had been run along the ground. I felt a bit uncomfortable traveling through this area. Thankfully, I experienced no difficulties.

DAY 12 - MAY 20 - 31.1 MILES - 9:57 - CUM. MILES 447.2

W. Dam Road to Damascus, VA. Started raining at 7:30 a.m. and rained most of the day.... Cool 55 degrees...wore jacket. Terrain was easiest yet. Shin was better today.... Spirits were great.... Nice to get to Virginia.... Left shin getting a little tendonitis.

This was exactly what my right shin needed — an easy day. The trail was very smooth and not all that hilly. However, favoring my right leg had now produced the same problem in the left leg.

Mentally, it was uplifting to reach my home state of Virginia, although it was a bit imposing knowing that one quarter of the A.T. lies within its boundaries. Doug Young met me a few miles from the end of the day. Doug was a colleague at LU and is an excellent ultrarunner. I was grateful that he would be helping me for several days.

Geoff, Doug and I pigged out at a Bonanza Steak House for dinner. Theoretically, since you burn about one hundred calories per mile, I would require an average of 3800 calories plus 1200 to 1500 more for basal metabolism. That's a lot of food! The average hiker loses about thirty-five pounds during the course of the hike, but I knew that I could not afford to lose much off my original 155 pounds. So, consuming five thousand to six thousand calories per day became a task rather than a pleasure.

DAY 13 - MAY 21 - 41.1 MILES - 11:24 - CUM. MILES 488.2

Damascus to 603. Beautiful morning... 55 degrees at the start with a high of 70 degrees. Beautiful scenery until I got on Whitetop Mountain (2nd highest in Virginia). Foggy on Mt. Rogers (the highest mountain).... Trail trashy after that.... Both shins were hurting.... Quads feel beat up too. Used ice packs for three hours on each leg.... I'm glad tomorrow is a shorter day. Stayed in Marion, VA.

Twenty years ago today Nancy and I were married. To say that I had an understanding wife to let me be on the trail on this occasion is an understatement. Even though she wasn't thrilled with the whole project, she really had been very supportive and a source of great strength.

One of the highlights of the day was to spy two herds of wild ponies on Mt. Rogers. These ponies were basically very friendly and would even approach for a handout. Several of the females had small foals with them. An attempt to get close to a foal lying by the trail was quickly abandoned as the mother charged at me.

DAY 14 - MAY 22 - 35.4 MILES - 9:09 - CUM. MILES 523.7

Mt. Rogers to Groseclose 617. Second easiest day...ran well all day with no low periods. Shins didn't hurt too much until the last 3.7 miles. Last 3.7 miles were through fields — hot and not nice. Very pleased with the day. Nice to see Nancy after two weeks. Stayed

*at Village Motel. I'm a quarter of the way through. With the Lord's
help and a lot of friends, maybe I can make it.*

This day had been a special day for me because Nancy had
come down to spend the night. I don't know if it was the fact that
she was coming, but the day was easy, and I finished very early.
That also allowed me to ice down my shins for a longer period of
time. Nancy had brought a home video which our friends, Mike
and Phyllis Hall had helped put together. My son, Brandon, was
playing basketball with Mike, and Allison, my daughter, was prac-
ticing her flag routine for color guard. The Hall's three kids were
all running around, making it look like a giant circus. With the
Halls temporarily living in our home, perhaps it was a good time
for me to be away.

CHAPTER 4

Week 3 on the A.T.

*If you run hard, there's the pain — and you've got to work your
way through the pain.... You know, lately it seems all you hear is
"Don't overdo it" and "Don't push yourself." Well, I think that's
a lot of bull. If you push the human body, it will respond.*
-Bob Clarke, NHL Hall of Famer

DAY 15 - MAY 23 - 38.2 MILES - 10:32 - CUM. MILES 561.7

*Atkins 617 to Laurel Creek 615. Ran well early.... Beautiful
view from Chestnut Knob Shelter.... Very rocky stretch from Walker
Gap to Jenkins Shelter.... Got very hot in the afternoon - 85 degrees or more.... Stayed at Big Walker Motel in Bland.... Right
shin is better but left is getting worse.*

I would try to keep track of Maineak by checking the registers
at the shelters. At one shelter he had left me a message reading,
"Hey Prof. Horton, I hear you gained five miles on me. What do
you think about all the rain we've been getting? Good luck to
you." It was a surprise that I had gained any ground based on the
problems that I was having. It goes to prove that you never know
what can happen.

The last 2.5 miles of the day proved to be interesting, with
twenty-two stream crossings. In places the streams were forty to
fifty feet across. However, the pleasure akin to a kid finding a
mud puddle soon disappeared as the continual sloshing slowed
the progress of a runner wanting to be finished.

DAY 16 - MAY 24 - 38.5 MILES - 9:56 - CUM. MILES 600.2

*Laurel Creek to Woodshole. Real nice trail and terrain for the
first 20 miles. Nasty uphill at 20. Got real hot in the afternoon
and I slowed down... nasty terrain from there on in. Right shin
okay but left shin pretty sore. Ate at Pizza Hut and then stayed at
Woodshole Hostel. Spirits very good. Maineak still two days ahead.*

The hostel that I stayed at is near Sugar Run Gap in south-west Virginia. It is an old log homestead discovered by Roy and Tillie Wood in the 1940s. Opened to hikers in 1986, it consisted of an 1880s log home and barn converted into bunkhouses. Tillie was still running the place and told me that Maineak had been there two days prior.

It was really nice talking to other hikers and listening to their stories. However, I still felt very uncomfortable telling them about my efforts. My task still seemed impossible to accomplish.

Doug Young left, and Roger Hall and Janet and Greg Comfort arrived at 2:00 a.m., spending the night in their truck. When I awakened my new crew, they were really glad to see me - especially since it was only 5:00 a.m.!

▲

More crew's views:
    When Greg called and said he and Janet wanted to also help on that weekend, we decided to pool our resources.... We stopped in Roanoke and got doughnuts at Krispy Kreme, figuring on giving David something different the next morning. But they ended up a little flat after Janet slept on them!

~ Roger Hall

▼

DAY 17 - MAY 25 - 41.6 MILES - 11:30 - CUM. MILE 642.0

Sugar Run Gap to USFR 156. Trashy running to Pearisburg and after Pearisburg.... Left shin hurt from the start.... Felt fairly good last few miles.... We ate at Country Cooking in Roanoke and slept in the back of their truck.... Slept awful.

This had been one of those days that wasn't a lot of fun. The terrain was tough and boring, and I was in pain from my left leg. At day's end we tried to find a hotel without any luck. So, it was back to the trail. The Comforts and I started out by sleeping on the ground, but the gypsy moth excrement was like steady drizzle

The crew's view:

David made his bed in the bed of the pick-up, Greg and I decided to sleep in our sleeping bags on the ground, and Roger chose to spend the rest of the night in the cab of the truck. It was a tough night for all. David didn't sleep well because he couldn't get comfortable on the ridges of the bedliner in the truck. The gnats and mosquitoes were so bad that Greg and I slept with pillowcases over our heads. Roger had to stand watch, with gun in hand, as a group of young men and women, seemingly in drunken stupors, parked next to the pickup to continue the party they had obviously started earlier that night. With the pillowcase almost suffocating me, I stayed awake listening to the sounds of the forest at night. One of the noises in particular disturbed me. I decided to tell Greg that there was something unusual and worth investigating. But undeterred, Greg rolled over, seemingly unconcerned about the bear that I perceived was about to devour us and more concerned about the sleep of which he had been deprived. I picked up the flashlight that I had laid next to me and pointed the light in the direction of the snorting sound coming from the pitch-black night. The light penetrated the darkness, and the animal snorted once again and was gone. Upon wakening at 4:30 a.m., all agreed that it must have been a ferocious deer to have put such a fright in me.

David wasn't in a great mood because he hadn't slept much the night before. Reluctantly, he stepped onto the trail at about 5:00 a.m.

~Janet Comfort

on us. And it was so hot! I then tried the back of the truck but to no avail. To make the night special, a bunch of drunks drove up to our spot, stopped, and got out. Thankfully, they walked on by and caused us no real trouble.

DAY 18 - MAY 26 - 39.5 MILES - 11:04 - CUM. MILES 681.5

USFR 156 to 311. Tough day... lots of climbs and descents. Very hot and humid with temperature 85-90 degrees.... Animal met me and ran the last 13 miles with me. That lifted my spirits. We ate at The Home Place and they talked me into driving back with them to Lynchburg to spend the night at home. I had planned on going to the Catawba shelter to cut down on the next day's mileage. Right shin is recovered.

What do I mean about tough climbs and tough descents? A tough climb and descent to me is usually one thousand feet or more. It can be less if it is very steep. The entire A.T. has a total gain of over 465,000 feet with an equal amount of descent. This figures out to be over eighty-eight vertical miles. This would be comparable to starting out at sea level and making sixteen round trips to the top of Mt. Everest.

Nancy and the kids met us for dinner, and they did convince me to make the hour and a half trip to spend the night at home. Regardless of the drive back the next morning, it was nice to have all the creature comforts of home, if just for one night.

DAY 19 - MAY 27 - 39.5 MILES - 10:41 - CUM. MILES 721.1

Catawba to the Peaks of Otter Overlook on the Blue Ridge Parkway. Shins felt fine until noon, and then the left shin started hurting just a little. Right shin has crepitus but doesn't hurt. Left Achilles Tendon started hurting around 18-19 miles. Got a pretty good rain at 1:15 p.m. to cool things off. Day did pass quickly. I think I was 61 miles behind Maineak yesterday morning. Stayed at home again for the night.

Mentally, it made me feel much better to get to this familiar section of trail. McAffee Knob and Tinker Cliffs afforded some of the best views in Virginia. The Knob is a large anvil-shaped rock that juts out into space, overlooking a magnificent valley. Going by Bobblett's Gap Shelter brought back memories of Animal and me running through the snow two months earlier.

DAY 20 - MAY 28 - 37.9 MILES - 9:59 - CUM. MILES 759.0

Peaks of Otter Overlook to 812. Shins did not hurt today. Right one is normal size and left shin is decreasing in swelling. Left Achilles very sore early but seemed to get a little better until Petites Gap, then it hurt all the way in, especially walking uphill. Got very hot and humid.

Just as my shin problems were going away, my Achilles starting hurting. I guess the Lord didn't want me to get too self-sufficient.

I stayed at home that night for the last time. This was the third night in a row to sleep in the comfort and security of my own bed. It was really sad leaving home in the morning knowing that it would be another month until I was back. Nevertheless, it was not hard for me to go back to the trail. The challenge was laid out before me, and I had to conquer. I was exactly on pace, and the thought of quitting never entered my mind.

Thoughts of a colleague and friend:

Perhaps the most significant observation that shocked me was your sharing of thoughts about death and the difficulty you were having on the trail.... As I sat and tried to encourage you, it was difficult because you constantly referred to how you could fall and die on the trail without any means to help yourself.... Oh, were you ever down!... Frankly, there was no way you were going to quit that race. I knew then that you would either finish or die in the attempt.... As I left your house that night, I was scared for your safety since it seemed to me that any common sense that you ever possessed was being drained, and hopelessness and recklessness were overtaking your mind.... It prompted me to pray for you on a consistent basis.

~Alan Rabe

38

DAY 21 - MAY 29 - 39.3 MILES - 10:59 - CUM. MILES 798.3

812 to Crabtree Meadows. Tough day, lots of hills... Little Rocky Row and Long Mountain.... I was worried about my Achilles but it did seem to loosen up going up Long Mt. and miraculously did not hurt the rest of the day. Last 14 miles the left shin got pretty sore.... Hot and humid.... Nancy and Rodney Laughon brought up chicken and we ate it at Crabtree Meadows. Stayed in a tent pitched by a babbling brook.

The hot weather continued to make progress difficult. The day before I thought both of my shin problems were behind me, but I was wrong. That left shin was not doing so well.

I was delighted when my wife Nancy and Rodney brought fried chicken, all the fixings, and Breyers™ chocolate ice cream. I don't think I've ever tasted better food in all my life. It really hit the spot.

Nancy and I had trouble saying good-bye that night. We knew it would be a month-long separation and that there were to be many rough times ahead. It was sad and a little frightening for both of us.

Chapter 5

Week 4 on the A.T.

The good Lord gave you a body that can stand almost anything.
It's your mind you have to convince.

- Vince Lombardi

DAY 22 - MAY 30 - 40.5 MILES - 11:58 - CUM. MILES 838.5

Crabtree Meadows to Jarman Gap. Longest and hardest day.... 95-98 degrees with humidity to match.... Very rocky footing.... The Priest and Three Ridges as hard as ever.... Died late in the day due to the heat... left shin hurt bad and right quad was extremely sore.... Excruciating just walking downhill at the end. Ate at Gattis and stayed at Animal's house. Extremely beat up and very low. Worried about tomorrow.

The misgivings I had felt the night before played out on this day. Not since the early trials of shin splints and bloody urine did I feel so low. I moved like an old and broken down man, badly out of shape. I hated it that Animal and his family had to see me in such a condition.

For the last eight miles I had been in Shenandoah National Park. The gypsy moths had eaten all the leaves off the trees. The forest looked like it was in the dead of winter, all bare and naked. Unfortunately, it was not only ugly, but it made the travel more difficult. With no shade, the temperatures became nearly unbearble.

DAY 23 - MAY 31 - 36.9 MILES - 9:55 - CUM. MILES 875.4

Jarman to Swift Run. In the morning I was still beat up. I said, "Lord, it is up to you. I don't see how I can do this." He answered my prayer. I ran/walked 16.4 miles in 4:05. I took two Tylenol #3™ at 8:15 a.m. because the pain in my right thigh was so bad. Finally, at 8:50 a.m. (16.4 miles) I decided to walk the rest of the day. So I did. I made good progress and my spirits rose again. Still very hot. 92-93 degrees but a nice breeze was blowing and it felt better than yesterday. It is good to be finished early. Killed a rattlesnake after Pinefield Hut. Stayed at Neil and Donna Hayslett's house in Massanutten Village.

There are always major turning points in your life that you can see only after the fact. This particular day was one of those days. The previous day had taken a tremendous toll on me both physically and mentally. The pain from the day before was still present and would not be relieved by medication. Although it was really a tough mental decision because my progress had been so slow for the first sixteen miles, my decision to walk the rest of the day actually was the best thing for me. I was able to make good progress and as a result, my mental outlook changed dramatically. It was what I really needed at the time. This day would prove to mark the beginning of my recovery from my physical ailments as well.

Just after noon this day I came face to face with something that could have drastically altered the rest of my trip. I had been walking in some tall grass just past the Pinefield Hut when I noticed something lying across the trail. I looked at one end and saw the diamond-shaped head and at the other end were the unmistakable rattlers. I threw some rocks at the serpent, hitting him with the second rock and setting off his "rattle show." Chills ran down my spine as he lay in the trail challenging me. I then found a large stick with which I proceeded to kill him. I know that some people have mixed emotions about killing snakes. I personally only kill the poisonous ones. I sure would hate to get bitten by a snake that someone else had let get away.

DAY 24 - JUNE 1 - 43.0 MILES - 12:07 - CUM. MILES 918.4

Swift Run to Elk Wallow. Neil Hayslett ran the first 17 miles; Roger and Sue Hall ran some after that. Nice rain from 2:00 - 3:30 p.m. Really cooled things off a lot. I thought a lot about those doing the Old Dominion 100 right now. I was able to run slowly down hills. Left shin doing pretty good. Right quad was still sore but better than yesterday. Roger killed a 3-4 foot rattlesnake. 1/4 mile later we saw another one.

41

The crew's view:
After we separated on the trail that morning, I thought of David daily and began to pray for his progress. I also began to pray for me: not that I would be instantly healthy or that everything in my life would be smooth sailing, but for me to be able to accept those things I couldn't change and to work towards God's goal for my life. I looked forward each week to receiving David's updates. I drew inspiration from the fact the he was actually getting stronger as he relied on God for his maintenance.

~ Neil Hayslett

This day marked the beginning of my second month on the trail. May seventh seemed so long ago!

The day was a sharp contrast to most of my other days. Most of my ailments seemed to be subsiding, and I had someone to run with nearly all day. It was really good to have that companionship. The company took my mind off of any pain that I was experiencing. The previous nine hundred miles were virtually run alone.

The snake encounter of the previous day and the two additional incidents reminded me of the potential problems that can be encountered on the trail. Any tall grass or rocky areas now made me nervous. This was another area of my journey where I had to place my trust in God to protect me from harm.

With the Old Dominion 100 being run on the same day, many of my thoughts were of those runners on a parallel ridge just thirty miles away. I had run the OD 100 seven times previously at that point, winning three times. However, I was not envious! I was much more content to be where I was on the Appalachian Trail headed toward Maine.

DAY 25 - JUNE 2 - 40.1 MILES - 10:41 - CUM. MILES 958.5

Elkwallow to Paris, VA. A little unmotivated at the start. Nice running in the last section of the Shenandoah Park.... We saw lots of deer, including three little fawns. One of the fawns was by the trail at the National Zoo. Sign by zoo said, "No trespassing. Violators will be eaten."... Right quad better. Left shin is healing but still got sore the last 2-3 hours. First day I've felt like a runner in a long time. I think Maineak picked up some miles in the last few days. Not as hot but still humid. Nancy and Rick Hamilton took me to their house.

Physically and mentally I was getting better. It felt so good to feel that I was actually deserving of my trail name, "The Runner." And seeing all those deer, over twenty, also lifted the spirits.

It was great to have the Hamiltons pick me up and take me to their home in Boonsboro, Maryland. I would be taxied back there to sleep for three nights in a row. This made it much easier to get the adequate food I needed as well as the opportunity to thoroughly ice down any remaining injuries. I was so grateful for their help.

DAY 26 - JUNE 3 - 43.5 MILES - 11:36 - CUM. MILES 1002.0

Paris to Crampton Gap. Took 23 minutes to go to ATC headquarters. First 20 miles terribly rocky, overgrown, straight up and straight down.... After that, things went well. Took two Tylenol #3™ going up Weverton Cliffs and felt spaced-out by the time I got to the top.... Saw a 6-foot black snake.... One mile along the towpath I ran 8:46. Pleased with the day. Glad to be over 1000 miles. Saw no hikers today and only 2 or 3 yesterday — none were thru-hikers. Maineak left his card for me at Crampton Gap.

Early in the trip I had passed a lot of thru-hikers. I later heard that there were over one thousand hikers who started at Springer Mountain, Georgia, in the spring with hopes of making it to Mt. Katahdin before winter. In the last few days I had not seen any thru-hikers.

The first twenty miles were very rocky and overgrown. The trail had obviously not been cleared recently. It seemed to be a never-ending series of abrupt climbs and descents. I thought the day would be mentally depressing, but I was wrong. I actually began to feel better after the first twenty miles. Why? I'm not sure. Maybe it had something to do with reaching Harper's Ferry, West Virginia. This is the psychological halfway point for hikers. Or, maybe it had to do with the fact that I was leaving Virginia, going through West Virginia and into my sixth state, Maryland. Or, maybe it was because my shins, Achilles, and quads were all getting better. In retrospect, it was probably a combination of all of the above factors.

As I crossed the Shenandoah River Bridge going into Harper's Ferry, I noticed three wild ducks playing around and at ease with nature. I sure didn't feel at ease today. I felt as though I was challenging Mother Nature to see how quickly I could get to Mt. Katahdin.

I took time out at the river to let Nancy Hamilton take me to the ATC headquarters. Jean Cashin took my picture and put it in a book with the rest of the thru-hikers. They had beautiful T-shirts of the A.T. on sale and I wanted to buy one. However, I felt as if it would be cheating to get one before I finished the entire trail.

My day was scheduled to end at the foot of Weverton Cliffs. When I got there I felt good and told Nancy I was going on to Crampton Gap, 5.9 miles north on the A.T. Finishing at Crampton Gap, I noticed one of Maineak's cards thumbtacked to a post be-

---

The crew's view:
    David was doing an "ultra" a day, and the crewing was as tiring and dreamlike as a real race a day. The rush and wait, the 4 a.m. starts, the backroads with few people make the experience surreal and wonderful. The world becomes non-existent, and the rush and wait, jog back, is all that exists. There is a freedom in no real contact with the "real" world that sharpens your senses for the unexpected fantastic beauty of the trail, woods, fields, streams, mountains, roads, and towns.

                                                              ~ Rick Hamilton

side the trail. No message, but I knew who the card was meant for... ME. This extra mileage was the first time since day eight that I had gone beyond my scheduled stopping point. It also put me over one thousand miles, which mentally made me feel that I was making real progress. Only 1142 miles to go. Boy, did that still sound like a lot!

From this point on, my pre-arranged schedule went by the wayside. I would add forty miles to the point where I had ended the day before and see if it came close to a road crossing. If it didn't, I would look to see if the next road crossing was within a few more miles. Therefore, scheduling became a day-by-day regimen.

DAY 27 - JUNE 4 - 43.0 MILES - 11:47 - CUM. MILES 1045.0

Crampton Gap to South Mountain, PA. Beautiful day with temps in the 70's, low humidity and a nice breeze. Best weather yet. Joe and Nancy ran 33 miles with me. Moved very well, shins and quadriceps hurt very little. Basically ran all day. Best day yet and I really enjoyed it. No tough climbs and only a couple of rocky sections.

This was one of those special days that I had prayed for so earnestly. Great company, great weather, felt great, and made great progress. One of the highlights of the trip was getting to meet, run, and fellowship with new people. That morning I had met Joe Robeson, a retired principal of the Boonsboro, Maryland, school system. Joe and I had much in common and we shared some very special stories from our youth. I didn't even think about the miles that we were doing. Hills came and went as we ran on. The rest of the day was to be no different as the fellowship continued, even after the miles were completed in my seventh state, Pennsylvania.

DAY 28 - JUNE 5 - 52.8 MILES - 12:17 - CUM. MILES 1097.8

South Mountain to Carlisle, US 11. Great weather. Fifty-five degrees at the start and 75 at the finish, low humidity with a nice breeze. Rick Hamilton helped me. Terrain was very easy, especially as I came into the Cumberland Valley and Boiling Springs area. Boiling Springs was a beautiful little town. Passed the halfway point of the trail at 11:10 a.m. Biggest mileage day and longest time on the trail in a single day. Didn't work very hard, just cruised. Left and right shins did not hurt.... Right quad was a little sore but not too bad. Stayed in a motel on the edge of Carlisle.

Rick Hamilton was the only one who was free to help me because Nancy and Joe had other commitments. So, the day was completely different from the previous day because I had to run solo throughout the day. At first it was lonely, but later the loneliness that I had learned to live with for the earlier one thousand miles seemed natural.

Rick followed me to the sign indicating the halfway point on the A.T. I figured that if I could hold this pace I would finish in a total of fifty-five days, therefore achieving my goal. That gave me something new to think about during the times of solitude and aloneness.

I had heard a great deal about Pennsylvania and its rocks. It was purported to be terribly rocky in some sections. But if this day was what they called rocky, I figured that I had nothing to worry about. The terrain was very flat as we reached the Cumberland Gap and Boiling Springs area. I ran through pastures, fields, and hedges as I passed farm after farm. I felt so good and the terrain was so easy that I felt as if I could run forever. Finally, Rick said, "I think it's time to stop. It's getting late and you've gone over fifty miles." We had checked the Boiling Springs register that indicated (we thought) that Maineak had done fifty miles in this area. If he did it, there was no way I wasn't going to go the distance as well.

During this time I was checking every trail register to try to figure out how far Maineak was in front of me. In Pennsylvania, I started reading registers that Maineak had been there the day before. I knew I was gaining some ground on him and this really got me psyched.

That night Rick and I stayed in Carlisle, Pennsylvania. We were able to find an Italian buffet with some of the best pasta dishes that I had ever eaten. It would have been interesting to see how many calories I consumed. This would be the only pasta buffet along the entire trail.

Thoughts from a colleague and coach:

I understand enough about work to know that doing the entire Appalachian Trail is an inconceivable amount of work. Compressing all this work into fifty-three days is even more incomprehensible. I know that a highly trained body and extremely focused mind are capable of tremendous accomplishments. However, I cannot understand the physiology of recovering from injury while continuing such a strenuous work routine. Any doctor or trainer will verify that injuries require rest, and ignored injuries will become debilitating.... Of all the things about this feat that are inconceivable and incomprehensible, this healing must be the most unexplained factor.

~ Brant Tolsma, Ph.D.

CHAPTER 6

Week 5 on the A.T.

*Man can only enjoy that which he acquires
with hard work and toil.*

- Author Unknown

DAY 29 - JUNE 6 - 51.6 MILES - 12:40 - CUM. MILES 1149.4

Rt. 11 to Green Point, PA. Saw a beautiful swan in the morning.... Very rocky stretch into Duncannon.... Beautiful view of Duncannon from Hawk Rock.... Last 15-mile stretch was very ugly.... Tired in the afternoon but pleased with the last 2 days.... Longest time out yet.

The early miles went by easily as I continued across the Cumberland Valley on gently rolling terrain. But I had learned many things while on the A.T., many coming into play over and over again. I learned that "things never stay the same"! If the trail is rocky for awhile, sometimes it gets better and sometimes it gets worse. If the trail is steep, sometimes it levels off, but sometimes it gets even steeper. Things never stay the same.

How true this was for the remainder of Pennsylvania. The last ten miles into Duncannon were extremely rocky. It was very difficult to walk, let alone run. There were sharp, pointy rocks embedded in the ground that constantly threatened the good health of my feet and toes. Ramming my foot into these rocks on several occasions sent waves of pain up through my shins.

The rocks were so bad in Pennsylvania that they have named different rocky sections as Rocky I, Rocky II, Rocky III, and Rocky IV. This ten-mile stretch was Rocky I, and it lived up to its name. It made me wonder what Rocky II, III, and IV had in store for me.

Dave DeKok of the *Patriot News* in Harrisburg, PA interviewed me for an article in his newspaper as I passed through Duncannon. He told me that Maineak had arrived at the same spot two days earlier, looking very strong. He reported that Maineak had been questioning why I had not tried to make up any ground on him.

I told Dave that I had some problems and was doing the best that I could. What I did not tell him was that I had done fifty-two miles the day before and that I knew I was closing in on Maineak. I did not want Maineak to see that in print. I wanted it to be a surprise when I came up behind him on the trail. Call it a "pride" thing.

In the summer of 1990, as Jeff Hood and Molly La Rue were hiking the A.T., David Crews took their lives in a murderous act. This happened while they were sleeping in a shelter near Duncannon. When DeKok interviewed me, he asked if I had stopped at that shelter. Actually, I had seen the sign for the shelter but had not remembered the gruesome event that had taken place there in the woods. In retrospect, I'm glad I didn't.

I arrived at PA 325 and completed 36.5 miles early in the afternoon. Rick Hamilton and I discussed whether I should stop there or go on. The next section, Rocky II, was fifteen miles in length until the next road crossing. Since I felt pretty good, I pressed on. Rocky II was even rockier than Rocky I. Progress was slow, the section was boring, and it was anything but pretty. I did not encounter any other person. I was grateful when Rick's Suburban finally came into view. Less than one thousand miles to go. Still sounds crazy, doesn't it?

DAY 30 - JUNE 7 - 41.3 MILES - 10:07 - CUM. MILES 1190.7

Green Point to Windsor Furnace Shelter. Started at 4:51 a.m. — 44 degrees at the start.... A very rocky day.... Bonnie and Harry Boyer and Harry Smith helped me. We had a good time. Saw a rattlesnake, but Bonnie wouldn't let me kill it.... Also saw a black snake.... Run was easy overall.... Very little effort and never really got tired.... I think I'm getting in very good shape. The day seemed short.

My 4:51 a.m. start was my earliest start while being on the trail. In the first eleven days of this adventure, I had started at 6:00 a.m. In the next eighteen days I started after 6:00 a.m. only once. In the last twenty days, I started before 5:00 a.m. every morning. Part of the reason for this was to avoid running so much in the heat of the afternoon. The coolness of the morning was much preferred.

I also finally felt that I was approaching a higher level of fitness. I had hoped and anticipated that this would happen, but now I was very relieved that it was a fact. I did not experience any ill effects of running multiple days of fifty-plus miles.

My three new crew persons, Harry Smith and the Boyers, all runners, joined me for their turn at chasing me over hill and dale. We spent the night sleeping back in Auburn, Pennsylvania, at the Boyer's home.

DAY 31 - JUNE 8 - 41.6 MILES - 10:17 - CUM. MILES 1232.3

Windsor Furnace to Little Gap. Rocky as usual, big ones and little ones.... Some nice views, but they didn't seem to mean much.... Saw two black snakes.... Very nice view after Lehigh Gap.... Very rocky like I think Katahdin will be.... Got very hot by the end of the day (86 degrees) but not too humid.... Top of left arch started getting sore the last 10-12 miles. Bonnie, Harry and Harry ran with me.... A little depressed at the end of the day.

The rocks continued to rear their ugly points. I found myself feeling sorry for the hikers who spend three times as long as I did in these rocky sections. It must seem like hell to them.

As rocky as the trail had been, it really got serious as I started to climb out of Lehigh Gap, near Palmerton, Pennsylvania. This was classified as Rocky III. *The Thru-Hikers Handbook* states if it's a sunny day, the heat radiating off the rocks will make you think that you're in a scene from Dante's *Inferno*. It made me think this

▲

The crew's view:
Looking back, you have to believe that somebody was watching over David through those rocks. All it would have taken to end it would have been one missed step or unseen snake.

~Harry Smith

▼

50

is what it would look like after an atomic war. However, the view from the top was fantastic, even though the countryside resembled the Badlands, devoid of vegetation. The former zinc-smelting plant was the culprit. It no longer belches fumes, so the ridge is ever so slowly being reclaimed by greenery.

Bonnie and Harry Smith had taken turns running with me throughout the day. When I got to the last section, I was a little down mentally. It seemed as though this was a common occurrence throughout my journey. I asked them to let me go the last section alone. Halfway up the climb out of Lehigh Gap, I sat down and talked to the Lord. I said, "Lord, thank you for the heat, hills, rocks, good days, bad days, shin splints, quad pains, and everything else. Thank you for all the help you've given me in allowing me to live out my dream." I needed that time alone with my Creator. I then pressed on.

I estimated that I was drinking 1.5 to two gallons of Conquest™ per day. When you drink that much, you can figure out what will happen. I decided to count how many times I would urinate on this day. (When you're exhausted, it's amazing what you'll think about!) I covered almost forty-two miles and urinated twenty-one times: once every other mile. I guess you could say I was well hydrated.

DAY 32 - JUNE 9 - 41.1 MILES - 10:41 - CUM. MILES 1273.4

Little Gap to Mohican Road. Took on Rocky IV.... Stretch was worse yet.... Could hardly walk.... Sharp rocks.... Glad to get out of PA and into NJ.... Ray Cimera and Dick Hearn helped the last ten miles.... Hot at the end of the day, and then had to take on Rocky V.... I look forward to fewer rocks.... Top of left arch hurt some but not much.... Spirits good.... Maineak is only one day ahead.

I had now been on the A.T. for one month. It seemed like a lifetime. It did not seem possible that the A.T. could go all the way from Georgia to Maine, with me following the two-inch wide white blazes the whole way.

This was my last day in Pennsylvania. Praise the Lord! I had been anticipating leaving this state more than any other state that

The crew's view:
I was amazed at how well David was holding up under the constant pounding. I ran about twenty miles each day I was with him and was pleased at how I held up after running Old Dominion 100 one week before. I could not fathom putting in the miles he did day after day.... On my long drive back home I thought about the faith David must have to continue on with such conviction and fortitude. I have always tried to set a good example for my own children and students I teach, but David is one of life's examples for all of us to follow.

~Michael Ranck

I had passed through. I was so tired of rocks! Maybe they should rename the state "Rocksylvania."

The last fifteen miles of the day (Wind Gap to Delaware Water Gap) were perhaps the most tedious underfoot than any section of the A.T. It is rumored that the locals come out every spring with chisels and files to sharpen each and every rock. This was the infamous Rocky IV, and it was a knockout. The worst yet. When I finally left Pennsylvania by crossing the Delaware River Bridge, I looked back and screamed, "Good riddance, Pennsylvania. You can have all your rocks!" I would never have to run on the A.T. in Pennsylvania again!

Dick Hearn and Ray Cimera from Wayne, New Jersey were waiting for me on the other side of the bridge. Ray was the first person to volunteer to help me on the A.T., but we had not met before this day. Dick made my day by having some Ben and Jerry's™ ice cream waiting for me. I wolfed it down on that hot Sunday afternoon.

Ray and I covered the last ten miles of the day to Mohican Road. This section was Rocky V, but was not as bad as the previously encountered Rockies. We passed Sunfish Pond, the first glacial pond encountered as you head north. I saw more day hikers on this section than I had seen in the last two to three weeks combined. Being a southern boy, I would speak to everyone we passed. Some would return the greeting, but some would glare back with a, what's your problem, bud? expression.

That night Harry Smith and I stayed at Ray's house. Ray and his wife cooked us a great meal of spaghetti and meatballs with ice cream for dessert. As was my custom, I tried to get in bed by 8:00 p.m. since I would usually rise by 4:00 a.m.

My watch served as my alarm clock. I thought I heard my alarm ring, so I jumped out of bed, trying to rouse Harry at the same time. He just rolled over. Nevertheless, I started to dress, and Ray came out of his bedroom to ask if everything was okay. I said that it was and he retreated to his room. I really could not understand why Harry wouldn't budge when I again told him it was time to go. So I glanced at my watch to tell him exactly what time it was in an effort to hasten his awakening. Much to my surprise, it was only 9:30 p.m. I had been in bed only for an hour and a half. This made me feel a little silly as I lay back down to sleep. However, it does illustrate the point that I had no problem getting out of bed in the morning. Perhaps this was the easiest part of my day.

DAY 33 - JUNE 10 - 45.9 MILES -11:34 - CUM. MILES 1319.3

Mohican Road to Wallkill Road. Harry Smith ran with me all day. Ray Cimera and Dick Hearn helped and ran with me.

The crew's view:

When Dave got to us at about 3:00 p.m. he had already run thirty-seven miles. He looked as fresh as I did and I had not yet run. He was very cheerful and talked to all the hikers going up and down the trail (Sunday hikers). He was joking with them. It was then that I started to feel that this man was no average runner. He was not wasting any time at aid stations — sometimes as little as thirty seconds — and then he was gone. He was on a mission.

-Ray Cimera

First 18 miles were very rocky (Rocky V)... after that it was better.... Ran pretty strong all day.... Left shin and Achilles did not hurt.... It got real hot in the afternoon — 90 degrees.... We were out in the open around the sod farm at the end of the day. Spirits were very good.... We saw two wild turkeys near High Point.... There was a memorial on High Point similar to Washington Memorial.... I think I was only 41 miles behind Maineak as of yesterday... 56.4 miles ahead of schedule.

Every day saw me exceeding my goal of thirty-eight miles per day. I knew that sooner or later I would catch Maineak. Despite the rockiness of the first third of the day, my good progress kept my spirits high.

When we had entered New Jersey, we saw many signs warning hikers to stay away from raccoons. It turned out that the incidence of rabies in raccoons was very high that season. As fate would have it, we encountered a huge raccoon right in the middle of the trail. Ray, Harry and I yelled, screamed, threw rocks, and waved our arms trying to scare the animal back into the woods. I guess we were such an odd sight that he could only stand transfixed, staring at our antics. Finally, he must have grown tired of the game as he sauntered away and ran up a tree at his own pace.

The Thru-Hiker Handbook also posts the following warning: "Assuming you are the first person on the trail each day, you will have to eat two extra Snickers™ bars during your hike to have the additional energy needed to break all the spider webs you encounter stretched across the trail from Georgia to Maine." I knew I needed at least the two extra candy bars because I was constantly waging battle with those cobwebs. Sticky spider webs are not the most pleasant things to have stuck to your face and glasses every morning!

DAY 34 - JUNE 11 - 42.8 MILES - 11:36 - CUM. MILES 1362.1

Wallkill Road to Arden Valley. Hilly all day long.... Short steep uphills and steep, rocky downhills.... Got very hot and muggy in the afternoon.... Last 7 miles through Harriman State Park were very pretty.... Went through cave on A.T. (Lemon Squeezer)....

*Stayed with Steve Feller at night.... 59 miles ahead of schedule....
Today was not an easy day.*

Bob Kronyak of Haskell, New Jersey, joined Dick and Ray to help crew me on this day. All three of these gentlemen were veteran ultrarunners and all were over fifty years of age. Who says you have to be young to run long distances!?!

Harriman State Park was different from any place I had been thus far. It was very quiet and peaceful, sporting many beautiful rock formations. The trail in this park was constantly up, down, and around. The Lemon Squeezer was a group of boulders that looked like a cave with the A.T. blazed right through the middle. It was not easy for me to get through. I can't imagine how anyone with a backpack would make it! Immediately on the other side was a vertical ascent up a rock face. There were two sets of blazes; one up this rock face and another around the rock with an arrow and sign pointing to the "easy way." I went straight up. It was fun and not all that hard. Had I been wearing a backpack, it might have been a different story!

New York marked my ninth state with only five more to go. In fact, this section of the trail was the first to be finished, officially opening on Sunday, October 7, 1923.

After finishing for the day, I made a phone call to Steve Feller of Mahopac, New York, asking him to pick me up at Tiorati Circle. He would be helping for the next two days. I felt lonely because I had just gotten used to Ray, Dick, and Bob, but would now be changing to some city slicker whom I had never met. Steve was a VP of a chain of drug stores in NYC. I was from the hills of northern Arkansas. What a contrast! However, my fears were unfounded, and by the time we got to Steve's house, I knew things would work out well. Steve was interested in what I was doing and asked tons of questions. His wife, Mary Ellen, and two kids welcomed me into their home, and we became fast friends. The Ben and Jerry's™ brownie bars also did much to get our friendship off to a great start.

As I sat waiting for Steve to rendezvous with me, I opened a box of supplies that my wife, Nancy, had sent me. At the bottom was a letter from her, perhaps the sweetest but saddest letter ever written. She told me that although I talked to her nearly every day on the phone, we never really expressed any of our feelings. It was always just business and logistics. She said how lonely it was and how she missed me. "You're not going to believe this, but sometimes I just start crying just because I'm lonely without you. I like being married and sharing a life with you, but don't you ever do something like this again!" I could only read part of the letter before my eyes would well up with tears, blurring my vision. I felt so sad and homesick. It was my loneliest time since the early days of trouble in North Carolina and Tennessee.

DAY 35 - JUNE 12 - 38.9 MILES - 10:35 - CUM. MILES 1401.0

Arden Valley to Tac State Parkway. First 18-19 miles were tough and steep...rocky uphills and downhills.... The terrain got a little better after that.... The first two registers I signed into today Maineak had been the previous person to sign on June 11. The last two registers today, Maineak had also been there today. I thought I might catch him today but I didn't.... I think I'll see him tomorrow.... Saw my first bear.... Blazes went through Bear Mountain Zoo. I had to climb the fence to follow the blazes, and I saw the bear — in the zoo.... No help during the day. Went about two hours with no water and bonked a little. Spirits were a little low in the morning but better in the afternoon.... Left shin a tad sore.... Bottom of right foot is a little sore — has been since PA.... Stopped taking anti-inflammatories yesterday. Stomach had been hurting for a few days.... I think I'll finish in 18-19 days from now... 53 or 54 days if all goes well.

Because Steve had a meeting that he simply could not miss, I had to go it alone. Steve did drive me out to Arden Valley for the start. On the way, we stopped at Bear Mountain Bridge to hide a half-gallon of Conquest™, Skor™ candy bars, and a sandwich. While I was hiding the stuff in the bushes, Steve tried to explain to the bridge attendant what I was doing. I think the guy thought we were nuts or were trying to pull a fast one on him. Steve dropped off more supplies on his way back to town, 18.5 miles from the bridge. I would count on these supplies to make the distance.

Progress was very slow during the first half of the day, as there were many tough climbs and descents. The A.T. actually passes through the zoo, but the gate was locked. I had no choice but to scale the fence and continue following blazes. The elevation through the zoo is 124 feet, the lowest on the A.T.

The distance between drop bags proved to be too great. I ran out of Conquest™, and I was getting tired and light-headed. However, I had no choice but to keep moving, finally arriving at the second drop bag after what seemed to be an eternity. I downed the half-gallon of Conquest™ and was revived after fifteen to twenty minutes. Conquest™ works. I am living proof!

I had asked Mary Ellen to pick me up at Taconic State Parkway at 3:30 p.m. I got there at 3:22 p.m. amidst thunder, lightning, and heavy wind. Mary Ellen pulled up at 3:27 p.m. and a violent storm hit at 3:30 p.m. God was watching out for me. Although it rained on me several days during the trip, I was never subjected to a driving rainstorm.

▲

From the mailbox:
    Don't let the time, the day, the distance, the pace, the weather, the hunger, the pain, the sleeplessness, the hills, the rocks, or the effort cloud your vision of the pure pleasure you will recall when it is all done.

~Suzi T.

▼

CHAPTER 7

Week 6 on the A.T.

As your belief about limits change, the limits themselves change.

- Terry Orlick

DAY 36 - JUNE 13 - 48.4 MILES - 12:11 - CUM. MILES 1449.4

Taconic State Parkway to Conn 4 (Cornwall). "God made a spectacular masterpiece when He made today."... Could see your breath in the morning.... Nice and windy all day long... low humidity and temperatures in the 70-75 degree range.... Made good progress except for two tough sections.... Steve Feller helped me, and Nancy Hamilton helped at the end of the day.... Started in a new pair of shoes.... I felt I could have easily run another 20-30 miles.... Maineak signed the register after US 22 for 6/13.... At Silver Hill shelter he signed it 6/14 and someone after him signed it 6/14 also — but today is 6/13. A lady at the post office in Cornwall Bridge said she saw him in the P.O. late yesterday afternoon which was 6/12.... I can't believe he is deliberately deceiving me.... 74 miles ahead of schedule.

This was one of those days that you dream about encountering on the Appalachian Trail. Everything was perfect: temperature, humidity, terrain, spirits, crew. I had planned to go only forty miles, but I just kept on running since the circumstances allowed, and even encouraged, the extra effort. The landscape in Connecticut, my tenth state, was very pretty. There were neat little cottages and spacious houses that you could tell were very expensive. Steve seemed to get a real kick out of what we were doing, as he had never attempted anything like this before. He had fun claiming I was a celebrity since he had heard an interview I did for radio on a NYC station.

I was wrong about this being the day to catch Maineak. However, I knew that we had to be getting really close to that anticipated first encounter.

Nancy Hamilton and I were very fortunate to stay at the home
of Bert Meyer in Cornwall, Connecticut. Homes always gave a
very necessary respite from the trail. However, Bert and his room-
mate had two large dogs and a cat. My sleep was interrupted on
several occasions when the animals decided they also wanted to
sleep in my bed. But, at least it wasn't a bear in the wilderness
wanting to share my sleeping space!

DAY 37 - JUNE 14 - 43.3 MILES - 12:25 - CUM. MILES 1492.7

*Cornwall Bridge to Holmes Road. Very nice day, but not quite
as cool or windy as yesterday. Tough day. Terrain was very rocky
in stretches.... Got lost in Falls Village. Very poorly marked in
town. Got lost before Highway 7 in Sheffield and couldn't find
trail to go to Holmes Road. Tough section from CONN 41 to Jug
End Road (16.2 miles).... Took 5 hours.... No access and very rocky
and steep.... Bonked in that area until Nancy met me at Mt.
Everett. Nancy saw Maineak at Jug End Road at 12:10 p.m.
Maineak ate five pieces of pizza and a sandwich. She told him I
was close. Maineak said he had been playing games with me the
last couple of days. He told Nancy he only did 30 miles yesterday.
I figure I'm about 15-20 miles behind him. Should take 2-3 days
to catch him.... Today was hard and tough.... 76 miles ahead of
schedule.... Stayed in Sheffield, MA.*

Considering the entire A.T., the places where it was hardest
to follow the trail were in and around towns. Nancy and I had
quite a time finding our way in Falls Village and again once the

trail left Sheffield. We read and reread the guidebooks and maps, but to no avail. Thankfully, someone came along who pointed out the turn that we had missed. In all, I probably ended up running one or two miles further than necessary.

Regardless of our temporary dislocation from the trail, IT finally happened. Nancy had seen Maineak! She had last given me supplies at CT 41 near Salisbury, Connecticut. The next place she could get to a road crossing was at Jug End Road. She drove there after leaving me, and that is where she saw Maineak. I was actually quite disappointed that I wasn't the first one to see him. I had dreamed of quietly coming up from behind, tapping him on the shoulder and saying, "Guess who?" After all, it was I who had been chasing a dream and a Maineak all this time!

That section to Jug End Road had been very tough on both of us. I had run out of food and was bonking before Nancy came running to meet me. Bear Mountain and Mt. Everett were two very high peaks for that part of the country (2316' and 2602'), providing for some great views. Posh homes could be viewed throughout the countryside.

As I left Connecticut and entered my eleventh state, Massachusetts, I was pleased to have come so far. And Maineak was getting so close....

DAY 38 - JUNE 15 - 45.4 MILES - 11:54 - CUM. MILES 1538.1

Holmes Road to Gulf Road (Dalton, MA). Nancy Hamilton helped for awhile then Bert Meyer for the rest of the day.... It got hotter and more humid than it had been the last 3 or 4 days.... Bottom of right foot getting better.... Arch of left foot hurt last 12-15 miles.... A little swelling at the end.... Emotions were so-so all day.... Saw two porcupines and had to run one of them off the trail.... Saw a hen turkey and baby turkeys.... Bert saw Maineak when I stopped at 4:05 p.m. He said Maineak was going on 8 - 10 more miles. 82.7 miles ahead of schedule.

Every time I had a good day, a so-so or bad day seemed to follow. I just couldn't get into it. I was not motivated and was extremely pleased to have the day end. I really did not want to run as much as I did, but the last few miles were either downhill or on pavement through town, leaving me no choice.

During the trip I always tried to finish the day with a downhill. That way, I would always start the next morning with an uphill, allowing me to get warmed up by walking before I started any serious running.

DAY 39 - JUNE 16 - 40.7 MILES - 10:54 - CUM. MILES 1578.8

Gulf Road to VT 9. Felt pretty good early.... Trashy trail most of day.... Figured I'd catch Maineak at 2:00 p.m. Caught him and David Blair at 2:20 p.m. at Congdon Camp and walked with them to the end. They walked very well. It was very nice walking with them. I think Maineak was going on 14 more miles.... Day went fast.... Spirits were very good all day.... Caught Maineak after 1574.6 miles.... 88.3 miles ahead of schedule.... Prospect Mountain into North Adams — hardest downhill yet.

This was the big day that I had been waiting for: the day I would catch Maineak. The miles went by very quickly as I thought about that prospect. The adrenaline was pumping!

Bob Dion of Readsboro, Vermont, met me as he came running back on the trail, having started in Cheshire, Massachusetts. Bob ran with me some during the day, and I stayed at his log home that evening.

Early that morning I went over the summit of Mt. Greylock, the highest mountain in Massachusetts (3491'). The summit was the first in the nation to have a pay-for observation tower, built on the spot now occupied with the distinctive War Memorial. This memorial resembled some kind of temple or mosque that you might encounter in the mid-East. The mountain provides extraordinary views of northwest Massachusetts as well as parts of New York and Vermont. The summit is a bird sanctuary with climatic conditions similar to northern Canada. Auto road races are usually held between May 15 and December 7.

Shortly before noon I reached the Massachusetts/Vermont border. Opening the register at the border, I found Maineak's card. On the back of the card, he left the following message:

"Hey Prof. Horton. Let's rock and roll to the Big K." The Big K was Mt. Katahdin, but was he challenging me or just being friendly? Time would tell. But for now, I had to concentrate on what I was doing. At this point the A.T. actually follows the Long Trail for 101.3 miles to Maine Junction. It had been completed in 1911, more than 10 years before the A.T. was even begun. On I pressed.

All day long I had been seeing one large set of footprints and one slightly smaller set. And then suddenly, IT happened at 2:20 p.m., 1574.6 miles from Springer Mountain, Georgia. Maineak and one of his crew, David Blair (Lone Wolf), were stepping out of Congdon Camp, an enclosed cabin with bunks and a wood

▲

The crew's view:

Being on the trail gives a timeless outlook. It could be 1991 or 1691 — it would be hard to tell. Rocks, trees, and dirt: they change but can't be dated. That's probably why it surprised me so much that nearly every hiker had such up-to-date knowledge of what was going on. They knew about mileage and David ("Professor," they would often call him), where they were and when. Near the summit of Greylock the word was out that Maineak left there in the morning. He was about four hours ahead of David. "I'll catch him in Vermont," David said matter-of-factly.

David had reached Route 9 and caught Maineak, but Maineak continued on past Route 9 after David stopped. David was much faster and was averaging about 42 miles a day. But Maineak was on the trail for more hours each day, averaging about thirty-six miles per day. They would probably pass each other several more times before the end. At the house I reminded David that Maineak had started two days sooner.

"Two days, six hours and fifty-three minutes, but who cares?" He grinned and then added, "I do."

~ Bob Dion

▼

stove. The camp is ten miles north of the Massachusetts/Vermont border on the A.T.

It is difficult to explain my emotions at that moment in time. I had never seen Maineak in person, only pictures. I had thought about him daily for fifteen hundred plus miles. I could easily recognize his handwriting from the registers. But I had never seen him face to face. He told me before the trip that he was six-feet, one-inch and 220 pounds. He didn't look more than 190 pounds, if that. He looked like a fit athlete.

A lot of joking went on between the two of us at that time. We left camp after a brief exchange and headed to VT 9 (near Bennington, Vermont) which was my day's destination. I decided to walk the remaining 4.2 miles with them. I ended up sandwiched between the two of them on our trek. Our conversation was brisk, as was our pace, and I soon felt as though I had known Maineak for years. It also amazed me how fast he could walk and talk. There was not a single moment of silence in those 4.2 miles. One of the three of us was talking the entire time. I don't have any memories of what that section was actually like. A sudden downpour prompted me to "suggest" that we stop; one shouldn't hike in the rain! He just laughed! I think both of us felt like brothers and compatriots in that we had been together, yet separate, chasing the same dream — fifty-six days on the A.T.

My day ended at VT 9, and Bob again took me to his home for the night. Maineak continued up the

First meeting of Maineak (Scott Grierson) and David on the trail in Vermont.

trail. I could hardly wait for the next sunrise to begin the chase anew.

DAY 40 - JUNE 17 - 43.9 MILES - 11:57 - CUM. MILES 1622.7

VT 9 to Mad Tom Notch. First section was very trashy, wet, rocky, full of roots, and slow.... No roads until mile 22.... Spirits were low in the morning but picked up in the afternoon.... Caught Maineak at 4:20 p.m. on top of Bromley Mountain.... Maineak had an 18.7 mile lead on me at the start of the day.... Bob Dion helped me.... We stayed in Manchester, a nice ski town.... 84.4 miles ahead of schedule.

Bob really got some training on this particular day. Because there were only two road crossings in nearly forty-four miles, Bob would drive ahead and run back toward me, carrying necessary supplies. I was so envious of him. Though he had to come miles and miles to meet me and then about-face and travel the same route with me, he ran effortlessly and quickly. It was a little like the tortoise and the hare — and Bob was the hare!

The A.T. took us over two large mountains: Stratton (3936') and Bromley (3260'). It is said that Benton McKaye looked out at these north-south ridges and first envisioned the possibility of the A.T.

Since I had caught Maineak at 2:20 p.m. yesterday, I assumed I would catch him earlier today. I was wrong. I was just reaching the summit of Bromley when I looked up and saw Maineak and Sweet Magnolia (the other part of Maineak's crew). I walked with them for the remaining steps to the summit. I chose to take the time to climb the observation tower and take in the 360-degree view. And what a splendid view it was, one of the best along the entire trail. But I also got to see which way Maineak headed off the mountain. With no marking leading down, I still wasn't sure I had the correct trail until I caught up again with the two hikers.

Fred Pilon (co-editor of *Ultrarunning* magazine) was waiting at Mad Tom Notch to help me for the next few days. Fred, Bob, and I drove back into Manchester for lodging and our evening meal. The town reminded me a lot of the exclusive town of Aspen, Colorado. However, I certainly did not fit the stereotype of a socialite: shoes off, legs up, shins being iced, all the while eating in an expensive Italian restaurant. While no one actually said anything, the stares and whispers were bountiful.

DAY 41 - JUNE 18 - 45.4 MILES - 12:27 - CUM. MILES 1668.1

Mad Tom Notch to Kent Pond. Baker Peak was spectacular. Little Rock pond was beautiful. Killington Peak was a disappointment.... Nice running in the morning.... Slow on Killington.... Passed Maineak at 11:30 a.m. at VT 103. Two tough hills to follow.... Fred Pilon helped all day, and Peter Gargarin helped in the afternoon.

The views in Vermont continued to be spectacular, with Baker Peak taking top honors. Little Rock Pond actually reminded me of my former residence, Little Rock, Arkansas. Had I been vacationing, it would have been a great place to camp for awhile.

Fred and I caught Maineak and Lone Wolf at the Mill Suspension Bridge 0.1 miles from VT 103. There was a deep gorge flowing with a torrent of water under the bridge. Maineak said it was a great place to take a swim. If I was the suspicious type, I may have wondered if he was setting me up to be swept away and out of sight! It probably would have happened, since my swimming ability is, shall we say, lacking. Nonetheless, I offered him some of my Conquest™, which he took and liked. He reciprocated by offering some of his electrolyte drink, ERG™. It tasted like it sounded!

I had really been looking forward to climbing Killington Peak. So much had been said about the ski area and the mountain. Unfortunately, someone forgot to tell me that the trail never actually got to the summit, it simply skirted it. There were to be no outstanding views.

Peter Gargarin of Sunderland, Massachusetts, joined us in the afternoon. Peter is an exceptional orienteer, having won the national US championship five times. He is also a tremendous ultrarunner and former co-editor of *Ultrarunning* magazine.

Kent Pond to RT 120 in Hanover, NH. Caught Maineak at 6:52 a.m.... He ran and walked with me for awhile.... We were going due east from Killington to Hanover, and the mountains ran north and south.... Tough ups and downs but through 20 miles by 10:00 a.m.... I couldn't believe it.... Fred and Peter helped me.... It was real neat going into Hanover (Dartmouth College).... Very hot in town.... Pleased with the progress today.... I should finish June 29 or 30....105.5 miles ahead of schedule.

Ever since the trail went into Connecticut it had been going almost due north. However, where the A.T. leaves the Long Trail in Vermont, it heads almost due east. Maineak had told me early that morning when I caught him that I would really like this section of trail. Based on what we had traversed, I questioned his opinion. The terrain was much harder than indicated by the maps and elevation profiles. As it turned out, much of this section was indeed new, so even Maineak was somewhat surprised by the trail's offering.

Late in the afternoon I entered New Hampshire, passing through the most sophisticated town along the trail, Hanover. This is the epitome of the Ivy League and upscale college towns. I enjoyed the diversity of the town. I was feeling pretty upbeat, wanting to yell out and tell people what I was doing. However, it was as if I was invisible to the town's people. No one paid me a bit of attention. Perhaps I was a bit too "down scale" by their standards.

CHAPTER 8

Week 7 on the A. T.

You must believe, with every fiber of your being not only that you can achieve it, and must achieve it, but that you will achieve it.

- Terry Orlick

DAY 43 - JUNE 20 - 45.1 MILES - 12:30 - CUM. MILES 1757.7

Highway 120 in Hanover to base of Mt. Moosilauke. Earliest start so far at 4:40 a.m.... Warmer today — up to 85-90 degrees.... Smart Mt. and Mt. Cube sections were tough. Bonked a little.... Maineak caught me early. Ran up on me and scared me.... Maineak went 3.8 miles past Highway 120 yesterday.... Saw a beaver and he slapped his tail four times on the water.... View of Mt. Moosilauke was very imposing.... Tomorrow will be an interesting day. 111.3 miles ahead of schedule.

One hiker stated in *The Thru-Hikers Handbook* that when you get to Hanover, New Hampshire, you have completed 80 percent of the miles, but you still have 50 percent of the work. I'm glad I did not read that until my trip was complete! That statement is 100 percent true!

About one mile after Trescott Road (near Hanover), I got the scare of my life. I was walking up a hill, alone with my thoughts, when my quiet little world was rudely interrupted by a deafening war whoop from Maineak as he slipped up behind me. It tickled him that he had scared me so. After I regained my composure, we continued up the hill together. It was at the top when it was time to run that he decided that he would also run. We stayed together until we reached Etna-Hanover Center Road, where we met our crews. After talking for a few minutes, I bid Maineak farewell until tomorrow. I ran and he walked on.

I again miscalculated. We had been playing leapfrog for the last five days over a span of 143 miles. I had figured that I would indeed see him the next day. I didn't. As it turned out, I put enough distance between us that our paths would not again intersect that summer. The logical place to finish out the day would have been at NH 25. After looking at the map, Peter and Fred said that I should continue for 1.6 miles more to the base of Mt. Moosilauke. Feeling good and trusting their outdoor skills, I consented, forging ahead. Maineak ended up stopping at NH 25, continuing his journey at 5:25 a.m. the next morning. I got a jump on him by starting out thirty-five minutes earlier. I was now permanently ahead of him.

This was my first full day in New Hampshire. I climbed three big peaks: Moosilauke, Smarts, and Cube. These were very tough climbs but would pale in comparison to what was coming up. I looked up at Mt. Moosilauke (4802') towering above me and contemplated how tough the climb would be the next day. This mountain was the first that ascended above tree line. But I was confident. I had averaged only 38.3 miles the first part of my trip. Now, since Harper's Ferry, I was averaging 44.4 miles per day. I didn't look tired, my spirits were good, my weight was holding, and I was on cruise control. The Whites would be tough but I was in shape and tougher than those mountains. Right? Wrong!

DAY 44 - JUNE 21 - 35.6 MILES - 12:57 - CUM. MILES 1793.3

Foot of Mt. Moosilauke to Galehead Hut. Mt. Moosilauke was the first mountain over tree line.... Other side of mountain was the toughest downhill section yet.... Kinsmans were very tough.... Went across Franconia Range.... Beautiful above tree line.... Winds 50 mph. Stayed at Galehead Hut.... Washed dishes for free stay.... Saw two fresh moose tracks.... Very tough day. Very rough terrain. Toughest yet. So rocky there was very little running. Peter, Fred, and Glenn helped me.

The White Mountains must be some of the most spectacular scenery in the world. Fred went with me to the top of Mt. Moosilauke. At first, the grade of the trail wasn't too bad and the footing was fair, but as we got closer to the top, things began to change. We climbed over 3300 feet to the summit in a little over four miles. We passed tree line at 4000 feet. Once on top, we regretted the fact that we had failed to bring along any jackets, as it was very cold and windy. Matters were made more difficult with old, faded, and infrequent blazes leading off the mountain. We became all the more confused because that section was not actually called the "A.T." Rather, it had been given the name of an older trail. In fact, we would discover that throughout the Whites, the Trail was often given a regional name, with many of the trails predating the A.T.

When we found a trail on which to descend, it led us through sagebrush with only a gradual decline. However, suddenly it was as though the bottom dropped out. We lost 2600 vertical feet in just over two miles. It was so steep in several places that they had to put steps in the side of a bluff to allow you to pass. Going down was just as slow as going up. The only way it would be faster is if you took a large step. In that case, you would go a long way in a very short time! Welcome to the Whites!

The next seven miles to Eliza Brook Shelter were rocky, rough, and full of roots. It wasn't really the elevation change that made this section challenging; it was the surface that made it difficult for running. Peter went most of the way with me before turning around and heading back to his car. I appreciated that time with him, as the conversation took my mind off the difficulty of the task at hand.

Before the trip began, Bill Foote had told me that the Kinsman Mountain (North and South peaks) were the most difficult on the entire trail. The climb was a hand-over-hand scramble up a vertical slope. The trail was washed out, severely eroded and devoid of switchbacks. While standing, I could reach out in front of me and touch ground. Climbing these peaks was very, very fatiguing. Time after time I thought I could see the summit, my hopes being dashed when I realized that I had reached yet another false summit. Then, the only thing to do was to continue climbing.

Glenn Streeter met me on the summit of South Kinsman Mountain. Glenn is from southern New Hampshire and was at that time a student at Liberty University. He would be helping me through to Mt. Katahdin. Glenn and I ran together to US 3 at Franconia Notch, as the terrain continued to be unforgiving. After grabbing a bite to eat from Fred and Peter's car, I was off again on my way to Galehead Shelter.

The Appalachian Mountain Club (AMC) operates the huts in the White Mountains. They are normally staffed by college students and are large buildings with bunk beds for guests. Along with lodging, an evening and breakfast meal is supplied to the guests for $50 per person. The fee seems to be a little stiff, but all the supplies have to be carried in by backpack. However, as a service to thru-hikers, the fee is waived in exchange for helping to clean up and wash dishes for the other guests. Since my finances were running short, I called the AMC headquarters the previous night to inquire about that service. Thankfully, they were eager to help, even though I would not be around long enough in the morning to help with breakfast. Logistically, I needed to stay at the Hut due to the long distances between road crossings. Otherwise, I would have had to put in fifty miles to the next road, almost impossible in this type of country.

Still pressing on to Galehead, I came face to face with another vertical climb to Franconia Ridge Trail. This time it was 2500 feet in 2.5 miles. These climbs were taking a tremendous physical toll. All around me in every direction were mountains that climbed to over 5200 feet in elevation. In the distance, Mt. Washington, in the Presidential range, loomed menacingly. The sight was almost frightening, but certainly humbling.

I had heard horror stories of how hard the wind blew and how cold it was on top of these treeless summits. Ninety-nine percent of the time I wore only running shorts and a short-sleeved Capilene™ or Polar Guard™ top. However, on this day I took along a long-sleeved polypropylene top as well. It was a good thing. Above the tree line, the wind blew ferociously with gusts of forty to fifty miles per hour. I began wishing I had brought even more clothes with me, especially when I jealously eyed several hikers in Gortex™ jackets and pants. I know they were thinking I was crazy and that I would surely freeze to death.

As I was descending back to tree line, I saw someone rise up out of the bushes next to the trail. Lo and behold, it was Lone Wolf with a large backpack. As he gave me some water, he told me that Maineak was really dragging. They were planning on staying the night at Garfield Ridge Campsite, 1.7 miles short of the Galehead Hut where I would be staying.

After a very long day (12:57), I finally reached the Hut at 5:45 p.m. The meal was being served at 6:00 p.m. Glenn was there, having hiked up the mountain to bring me the next morning's breakfast and more Conquest™. He had talked the management into allowing him to stay free in exchange for helping clean up and wash dishes. The catch was that we had to wait for all paying guests to finish, clean up after them, and then eat IF there was anything left. They wouldn't even allow me one chocolate chip cookie while I was doing the dishes. There was very little food left (and all the cookies went fast), but the crew did find us some other food to eat, preventing us from hitting the sack with empty bellies. After that, the management had everyone come out to watch the setting of the sun, which was usually spectacular. I was the only one to pass. Bed was calling me, for I would need all the strength I could muster for the upcoming days.

In the early part of the trip, I would try to get in twenty-seven to thirty miles before noon. From here on in, it would be a start time before 5:00 a.m. and only nineteen to twenty-one miles before noon. Yesterday I did over forty-five miles in 12:30. Now, foreshadowing the upcoming difficulty of the trail, I could manage only thirty-five miles in almost thirteen hours.

DAY 45 - JUNE 22 - 39.4 MILES - 14:13 - CUM. MILES 1832.7

Galehead Hut to Pinkham Notch. Start at 4:24 a.m. Earliest yet.... Toughest day yet.... Very little running except from Zealand Hut to 302.... Clear and cool day.... Spectacular in the Presidentials. Prettiest place I've seen yet.... Lots of people around Mt. Washington.... Terrain was horrible after Mt. Washington.... Downhill after Mt. Madison was the worst one yet.... Toughest and longest day time-wise.... 109.6 miles ahead of schedule.... 311.3 miles to go.

The beginning of the day gave me an indication of how the rest of the day would be. The trail from the hut led up an immediate vertical ascent. I gained 1200 feet in a half mile of trail that was basically a boulder field. My efforts to make it to the top were rewarded by an awesome pre-sunrise. Multiple shades of fall colors were painted by the glow of the rising sun. I thanked the Lord for allowing me to behold His beautiful handiwork.

The A.T. continued to be full of rocks for the next four miles. Then came a nearly vertical descent off the mountain to the Zealand Falls Hut. Located beside a cascading, pure stream, I refilled my water bottles and braced myself for the next unforgiving climb. However, I was surprised, pleasantly, that I had five miles of relatively flat, smooth trail before the next climb. At times, I wondered if I had gotten on the wrong trail. But I was not alone on this trail. I saw sound evidence of many moose, although I did not actually see any on the trail leading me to my planned rendezvous with Glenn at Rt. 302.

Glenn had convinced the crew at Galehead to allow him to leave his duties at the hut a little earlier than usual so that he could meet me at 302. When I arrived at the spot, Glenn was nowhere in sight. After a few minutes, I left my sign that I had been there (a circle drawn on the ground with an "X" through it) and headed off into the woods. Just then, I heard a car. Glenn had arrived just in the nick of time.

The twenty-five-mile section between Crawford Notch (RT 302) and Pinkham Notch (NH 16) is called the Presidential Range. To say that it is spectacular is an understatement. Most of this section is above tree line, thus offering unobstructed views of the surrounding mountains and valleys. The temperature was around sixty degrees, low humidity, and crystal clear. I was running well. The 1277-foot climb in the three miles up to Mt. Webster's summit was the biggest of the section. At the top I could see the 6288-foot Mt. Washington in the distance. This peak is the highest north of the Carolinas and east of the Mississippi. I would get there by following a ridgeline up from Mt. Webster.

In those nine miles to Washington's summit, I probably saw four hundred day hikers. Some were bundled up in heavy clothing, and some were dressed as skimpy as I was. But most just stared at me as I went by. Feeling like a tourist, I didn't seem to mind the difficult footing. I got to see the coal-fired Mt. Washington Cog Railroad Steam train inch its way up the 37.4-percent grade. The route was 3.5 miles in length, delivering the riders to the summit when the weather allowed. A sign at the base of Mt. Washington read, "Behind this sign lies the worst weather in America. Many have died due to exposure, even in the summer. Please turn back if the weather is bad." This warning seemed rather imposing and out of place on such a beautiful day.

As I reached the Lake of the Clouds Hut, I looked up and saw the summit. It looked like it was just a short distance, but was really 1200 feet of gain in 1.5 mile. This hut is the largest and busiest of the A.T. huts, situated on a crystal clear and cold lake. As I continued past the hut and proceeded to the summit, I don't believe my feet hit soil once. The trail was nothing but rocks.

The summit has a house, weather observatory and transmitters, snack shop, post office, museum, radio and television station, and is the end of the line for the auto toll road. The first path to the top was cut in 1819. Standing well above tree line, the mountain and surrounding twenty-mile ridge form an "Arctic Island" of permafrost and flora similar to those found at the North Pole. The severe weather is caused by high winds and frequent temperature changes influenced by air masses flowing from the south, west, and the St. Lawrence River Valley in the north. In 1934, the observatory measured a wind velocity of 231 miles per hour, the strongest ever recorded in the world. P.T. Barnum declared the view from Mt. Washington as "the second greatest show on earth."

The summit was crowded when I arrived, due to the time trials for the famous auto race up the mountain. In 1903, the first winning auto arrived after one hour and forty-five minutes. In 1904, a runner covered the 4600-foot gain in one hour, forty-two minutes. Today, the auto record has dropped to seven minutes, forty-five seconds while the runners' standard is fifty-nine minutes, seventeen seconds.

As I left Mt. Washington, the rocks were omnipresent. I was unable to run more than a few steps at a time. However, perhaps the most difficult descent that I have encountered was the 3000-

The wife's view:

The last few weeks were also a very draining time emotionally for me. I was tired of being mom and dad and having the day-to-day problems constantly on my shoulders. When David would call he would spit out the information and tell me about his day, but he wouldn't take the time to ask me about mine. How was I doing? How were the kids? He was always in a hurry, or he was so totally exhausted or depressed that he didn't feel like talking. Well, I needed to blow off steam as well. But before I could get anything out, he was already tuned out and ready to hang up. So much for a little comfort, dear!

So, I bottled up my own feelings. I knew he didn't want to hear about them, so I had to cope in my own way. I thank the Lord that I had caring friends and family that I could talk to. Even though I didn't express a lot of my deepest feelings, I got rid of a few of them here and there. I just really needed David, and he wasn't there for me. I think this added a lot to my frustrations.

~Nancy Horton

foot drop in two miles off Mt. Madison to Pinkham Notch. It is extremely dangerous and any slip would be disastrous. Those thirteen miles between Washington and Pinkham took me 4.5 hours to complete and turned me into a whipped puppy. These two days in the Whites, with one more to go, had taken their toll.

DAY 46 - JUNE 23 - 37.2 MILES - 13:41 - CUM. MILES 1869.9

Pinkham Notch to Carlo Col Shelter. Very tough day in the Whites.... Super steep ups and downs and very rocky.... Bonked the last 17 miles...had to drag myself in. Got into Maine at 6:18 p.m., praise the Lord.... Spirits low.... Hard work and slow progress.

I was still pretty tired from the previous two days in the Whites and grateful that the first mile was level and fairly smooth. However, the trail then climbed for two thousand feet in 1.6 miles up to Wildcat Peak. These climbs were really starting to get old and were gradually destroying me. I kept wishing that whoever had laid out this part of trail had been familiar with the term "switchback." I sensed that the trailblazers were really quite sadistic.

The next several miles led to Wildcat Mt. (4422') and afforded me views of the valley and mountains where I had traveled yesterday. Again, the scenery was spectacular. But even the view could not take the edge off descents such as the one thousand-foot descent in 0.7 miles from Wildcat to Carter Notch. When would it ever end? The answer would be "not soon." Gaining a fleeting sense of calm and beauty at Carter Notch hut situated above two mountain lakes, the trail again turned heavenward toward Carter Dome, 1.2 miles and fourteen hundred feet of climbing later.

Glenn Streeter was waiting for me at US Route 2. The last three or four miles coming in had actually been runnable. I was hoping these conditions would continue. Glenn gave me some noodles that he had cooked on his camp stove and also provided a sandwich for me. Then, I was off for the last seventeen miles of the day, leaving the road crossing at 12:30 p.m. I told Glenn to meet me at Carlo Col Shelter at 6:30 p.m. He was to hike our camping and food supplies to this shelter, because the next road crossing was another thirteen miles from there.

The Thru-Hikers Handbook said that the stretch from Gorham, New Hampshire to Stratton, Maine (107 miles) is the toughest section on the A.T. The book said that if it rained, your progress would be even slower due to bogs, wet roots, and slippery rocks. Just what I needed. Fortunately, it rained only one day from here to the end, but my progress was slow nonetheless.

During the last two to three hours I found myself in a very serious situation. I had run out of food and Conquest™, and my blood sugar dropped very low. All I could do was stagger on down the trail, hoping that Glenn would come back to meet me. Unfortunately, because of the time it took him to drive and then hike, he met me only in my last mile, as I entered the state of

Maine. Food and drink made a huge difference in a short time. We were close to the shelter, but had to go a third of a mile off the trail and down a mountain to get to the three-sided structure. Glenn cooked a substantial evening meal, but the night was spent in restless sleep. Three hard days in a row, and Maineak said all of this was only a warm-up for Maine. What did he mean by that? I would soon find out.

DAY 47 - JUNE 24 - 33.6 MILES - 13:09 - CUM. MILES 1903.5

Carlo Col to South Arm Road. Finished at 5:48 p.m. Another very tough day.... Tough ups and downs.... Mentally very low.... Thought about stopping at 14 and at 24.... Bonked last 7 miles.... Crawled up the last vertical hill.... Can't wait to get in better terrain.... 99 miles ahead of schedule.... 240.5 miles to go = 6 days.

Each morning I was awakened by an alarm on my wristwatch. This particular morning was the only morning I overslept during the entire trip. I had set my alarm for 3:50 a.m., wanting to get an early start. When I did awake, it was 4:06 a.m. It was a lost sixteen minutes in my estimation. With the terrain as it was, I really had to make every minute count. Even though it sounds extremely slow, my average pace for the trip thus far was 3.54 miles per hour. However, in the last three days the pace had slowed to 2.74, 2.77, and 2.72 miles per hour. The terrain was unrelenting, and a faster pace was simply unattainable. I prayed that the terrain would lighten up since I was now in Maine, but it was not to be. My pace today was even slower than in the Whites — 2.56 miles per hour!

The day started with five miles of rolling ups and downs, complete with rocks and roots, but giving way to a 1000 foot drop in the next mile down to Mahoosuc Notch. The Notch is famous for being a 0.9 mile section of rocks — rocks as large as a house, literally. *The A.T. Guidebook* reads: "Route through notch is difficult and dangerous. Take care to avoid slipping on damp moss. Follow blazes over and under boulders." I could hear water running beneath me through the notch, although I never saw the stream. There was ice in some of the crevices — ice that you can find there regardless of the time of year. As I neared the end of the boulder field, I was presented with yet another 1500-foot climb in 1.5 miles. Would there ever be an end to these climbs? I mused. I did not know how much more my body and my mind could endure.

Remembering that Maineak had told me that "it was all just a warm-up for Maine," the rest of the day took on new meaning. There was a 2300-foot descent in 3.5 miles to Grafton Notch followed by a 2000-foot climb in 3.5 miles to Baldpate Mountain. Then, a 1200-foot descent to Frye Notch, followed by a 1500-foot descent to East B Hill Road, followed by... you get the picture. Way up was followed by way down.

Glenn met me at East B Hill Road (near Andover, Maine) to replenish my food and drink supplies. After looking at maps, we noted that Glenn could meet me again 1.8 miles further north. Therefore, I elected to give him my fanny pack to lighten my load, if only for 1.8 miles. All that I carried with me was a single bottle of Conquest™. When I got there, Glenn was not. Best-laid plans of mice and men.... I left my mark on the road and continued on. A bridge was out which prevented Glenn from getting to that road crossing. When he realized this, he left his vehicle and ran to the trail crossing. Seeing my mark, he pursued me from behind for several miles, but failed to catch me. I was depending on a half bottle of Conquest™ as my only energy source. It would prove to be insufficient.

Within two miles, my blood sugar levels were precariously low. I had access to water, but that doesn't help in this type of situation. I needed calories. It was all I could do not to fall down the next descent of fifteen hundred feet in less than a mile. Surprised to still be in one piece as I crossed Sawyer Brook, I looked up to view the trail. This time it was eleven hundred feet up in less than a mile. I was so weak by this time I did not think it was humanly possible to make it up that mountain. I sat down and cried. I contemplated waiting for Glenn to find me, but I had no idea when and if he would decide to put on the search. So I found myself claiming God's promises: "I can do all things through Christ who strengthens me," (Phil. 4:13) and "But my God shall supply all your needs according to his riches and glory in Christ Jesus" (Phil. 4:19). I believed that God wanted me to do this task. I told the Lord about all the people who were out there praying for me, praying for my strength, endurance, and success. I called them out by name and said, "Lord, I pray that you would answer my prayers, their prayers, and fulfill your promises." He did answer, and I made it ever so slowly over that mountain. However, the Lord didn't let me forget where I was as the trail once again dropped off eleven hundred feet in less than 1.5 miles to the day's ending point at South Arm Road.

That night Glenn and I drove into Andover to seek lodging at the Andover Arms Family-Style Bed and Breakfast. There were no hotels in town, and the only restaurant was closed by the time we arrived. Thus, we went to Mills Market and guzzled sandwiches, french fries, and ice cream. Anything and everything tasted great by this time!

When we arrived back at the bed and breakfast, the manager told us of a phone call on the answering machine. David Blair, a.k.a. "Lone Wolf," Maineak's crew, had called asking if there was room in the inn. Maineak had stopped 9.5 miles short of where I ended, but they wanted to drive into town and sleep in a bed. They arrived at 1:00 a.m. We ate a delicious breakfast at 4:10 a.m. and left as my friend and his crew still slept. At the first trail register I left a note for Maineak reading, "Maineak, I wish we could have eaten breakfast with you, but I understand." He had become a true friend, and I missed seeing him and talking to him these last few days.

DAY 48 - JUNE 25 - 38.8 MILES - 13:45 - CUM. MILES 1942.3

South Arm Road to Orbeton Stream. Finished at 6:39 p.m. Tough day.... Tough mountains but nice view from Saddleback.... Spirits were very low.... Really tired of all this.... Wanted to quit after each section.... Glenn, Doug, and Jack helped me.... Slept on ground on old RR bed.... 202 to go.

Looking at the altitude profile, there were two major mountain ranges on tap for the day: Bemis Range and Saddleback Range. There would be only two major climbs, but the going was still very slow at 2.82 miles per hour. The footing was actually quite difficult because of the many bogs along the trail. I saw more and more moose tracks, but still had not had any close encounters.

Jack McGiffin and Doug Young drove all night from Virginia to meet Glenn and me at the first road crossing for the day (Maine 17). I welcomed them because they were good friends and it had been extremely difficult for Glenn to handle the task solo.

After another thirteen miles of trail, the easiest since Vermont, another difficult decision needed to be made. The next road crossing was 22.3 miles away, but I did not want to stop after only twenty-six miles. After looking at the map, we saw a place that could get the vehicles to within a mile and one half of where the A.T. crosses the Orbeton Stream. Glenn packed in his stove, sleeping bags, and food supplies so that we could set up camp by the stream. As we lay down for the night, we wondered if a great big moose would stomp on us as he meandered down the old railway bed.

DAY 49 - JUNE 26 - 36.5 MILES - 13:40 - CUM. MILES 1978.8

Orbeton Stream to Long Falls Dam Road. Another very tough day.... Saw four moose in the first two hours.... One moose with a gigantic rack, black and big.... Saw one moose in the afternoon.... Three major sections with big mountains in each one.... The Bigelows were particularly tough.... Wanted to quit again after the first section.... Spirits were better after the second section.... Bonked on third section because the streams were dry.... It was fairly hot the last two days — 85-90 degrees.... I look forward to seeing my baby tomorrow. 165.2 to go — then freedom.

This was definitely a big day in terms of moose. The first one I saw in the morning made me freeze in my tracks. Those beasts are huge! The bull moose did not budge an inch when he saw me. But I assure you that I kept on moving up the trail! Actually, I was told later that, on average, eight people are killed annually by moose in Maine. It's not that they charge and kill, because they are not aggressive. Most of the deaths occur when car and moose become one. The moose's legs are so long that a head-on collision will often throw the animal through the windshield, killing the driver or front seat passenger. What a way to go!

The section of trail between Spaulding and Sugarloaf Mountain was completed in 1937, making the A.T. the longest continuously marked trail in the world. A commemorative plaque was placed in this area in honor of those who labored long to clear the trail. There is no doubt that their task was very difficult and demanding, as was mine.

Mentally, it was a very rough day. My spirits were low, I was unmotivated, and I was definitely in a foul mood. I really wanted to stop short and give myself a break, because I knew I would set a new record. But as I approached the first road crossing where Doug and Jack were waiting, those quitting thoughts evaporated.

After replenishing my supplies, Jack and I headed off to climb the peak of North and South Crocker Mountain. Having Jack go with me helped raise my spirits. We talked constantly, taking my mind off pain, deep-to-the-bone tiredness, and self-pity. Passed by a day hiker, he quickly faded from our view. It was then that I realized how slow we were traveling. But if there was any consolation, this was the only time on the trail that I was passed by anyone.

The last section of the day was to take us over the Bigelow Mountains. The altitude map indicated this was going to be a tough section. But I was looking forward to completing it. Bill Foote of Lynchburg had told me the terrain would get easier after the Bigelows. The Lord knew I really was in need of an "easy day," relatively speaking! But first things first.

Glenn accompanied me through this very steep and severe section of trail. Two springs were indicated on the map, and we chose to bypass the first one since it was a distance off the trail. However, we found the second spring dry. With nowhere else to get water, it was decided that Glenn would backtrack to the first spring and I would slowly continue on. Shortly after Glenn left, the trail dropped off suddenly, and I started to bonk. Several times I stopped for a few minutes, giving Glenn a chance to catch up. I even began to wonder if something had happened to him. Finally, he did come up behind me, explaining that the first spring was also bone dry. Fortunately, he had been able to beg some water from another hiker, and we were able to mix up some Conquest™. That supply was quickly downed by two thirsty and needy runner/hikers.

We hoped to meet Jack and Doug at East Flagstaff Road, but they were nowhere in sight when we arrived. Glenn wanted to wait there for them, but I convinced him to go on with me. There were two more road crossings before day's end, and I was sure that we would find them at the next one. Wrong. However, as we continued on from that point, they met us coming back down the trail, armed with much needed Conquest™ and food. What a welcome sight! Better yet, we knew that seeing them signified the day coming to a close. We spent the night at a bed and breakfast in Kingfield, and my spirits were lifted when I found out Nancy Hamilton was bringing my wife and son up to Maine. We would be reunited within twenty-four hours.

CHAPTER 9

Week 8 on the A. T.

Dream. Prepare. Endure. Achieve.

–Bob Hotel

DAY 50 - JUNE 27 - 46.8 MILES - 14:25 - CUM. MILES 2025.6

Long Falls Dam Road to Shirley-Blanchard Road. Start at 4:58 a.m. Finish at 7:23 p.m. Longest time. Only three 1,000-foot climbs. Second climb was a little hard.... Saw a moose and a bear five miles before the Kennebec River. Took about 30 minutes to cross the river. Harder than I thought. Doug and I bonked in the last 18 miles, no access... dragged ourselves in. Stayed in Monson at Shaw's house.

This day was to be special because my wife and son would meet us in Monson in the evening. I also looked forward to the day because all the tough climbs were behind us except for the final big one — Katahdin. The only major obstacle ahead was the Kennebec River near Caratunk.

The terrain was as expected: easier (3.25 miles per hour for the day), with only three major climbs. None of these climbs proved to be terribly difficult, but that doesn't say anything about the condition of the trail. Much of the A.T. in Maine had been re-routed in the last few years. Newer trails are rougher and not worn down as much as established trails. Additionally, the A.T. throughout this section passed many ponds and lakes. This resulted in a very soft, marshy, and boggy trail that slowed travel considerably. Mosquitoes and deer flies lived in abundance. Stopping in one of these areas meant dinner for the insect world. It was not pleasant.

The first road crossing, where there was sure access, was seventeen miles into the run at US 201 at Caratunk. However, there were logging roads that supposedly crisscrossed the A.T. at several places in that first stage. The problem was finding them. Glenn said that he would try to drive this section and find me. I ended up crossing three good dirt roads, but was disappointed each time when no one was there to greet me. To be unsupported in the wilderness is not a good thing.

As a result of the accumulated physical stress and fouled logistics, I really started to break down emotionally. I would start thinking about family, home, or climbing the last mountain and would suddenly break out in tears. Several times that morning I would find myself in that emotional state. It actually felt good to cry. In fact, I would try to make myself cry, because of the cathartic effect it seemed to have. It produced a sense of relief. The last six days had been extremely hard, and although Mt. Katahdin was close, it still seemed so far away.

As I was trudging on in my somewhat altered mental state, I heard the sound of something running in the woods. Was it a moose? No, it was black and it didn't move like a moose. Slowly moving up the trail to get a better view, I realized I was having a close encounter with a bear — a big two-to-three hundred pounder. Finally, a real bear in the woods! He stood like a statue and stared at me from a distance of about twenty yards. I quickly decided that I'd best move along toward the Kennebec River.

I had looked forward to seeing the river and had heard much about it. It is very wide at eighty to ninety yards across and sports a dangerous and swift current. An unfortunate hiker drowned while trying to cross the river in 1985. Since then, a ferry has been in operation from June to October, running from 10:00 a.m. until 12 noon. Earlier I had asked Maineak if he was planning to use the ferry. He said, "I'm not going to hike two thousand miles to cross the river on a sissy ferry!" I figured that if he wasn't going to ferry across, neither would I. However, he did advise me to cross the river before the dam opened upstream, which causes a dangerous and rapid rise in water levels. The release usually occurred at 8:00 a.m.

Unfortunately, I reached the river at 9:30 a.m. Jack was waiting with a jug of Conquest™ and some food. Doug was still on the other side of the river. Jack said, "You're going to have to wait for the ferry. The water is already over your head. Doug tried to cross and could not make it due to the strong current." Call me strong-willed. Call me stubborn. Call me pig-headed. But don't call me chicken. I told him I was crossing on foot.

When trying to cross, *The Thru-Hiker Handbook* says to go upstream about 0.2 of a mile and cross on the gravel bars. That's what I did. I found a pole to balance myself and started across in water that was mid-calf deep. The rocks were very slippery, and progress was slow. The further I went, the deeper and swifter it became. I would take a step and then find my balance with the use of my pole. I kept thinking that I would fall and get swept away — and I don't swim very well. Eventually, through painstakingly small advances, Jack and I both made it across without mishap. Hindsight tells me this was really dumb — a ride on the ferry would have been appropriate and safe!

Once reunited with Doug on the far side, we made a quick stop at the Caratunk post office and store. This would be my last mail drop. I bought some Ben and Jerry's™ ice cream and ate it while reading over my cards and letters. They were motivating and encouraging, but oddly depressing. Several indicated, "I'm sure you can smell the barn," "You've got it made," or "You can just cruise on in, you're so close." I certainly did not feel close, and I was really working hard. Jay Gamble from Lynchburg wrote, "Everyone asks me how you are doing and I tell them you are doing great. Don't let me down." I felt a great deal of pressure from these people — a pressure to do well and succeed.

Glenn was still nowhere to be found. None of us knew where he was. Doug said that Glenn was going to try to meet me at the first road crossing, but I never did see him. We could do nothing for him at the time, since we had no clue where he was. So, we continued on.

The A.T. out of Caratunk was overgrown, making swift progress difficult. The climb up Pleasant Pond Road was a thousand-foot climb in one mile — steep enough to make it interesting, but nothing compared to the tortuous climbs of days gone by. Still no sight of Glenn. I began to worry about him. At this point in the day I had covered 28.7 miles. The next road crossing was 18.1 miles away on Shirley-Blanchard Road. I really did not want to go 46.8 miles for the day, but stopping here would make it difficult to end by Sunday, June 30th. I thought it would be great to start one month and finish before the end of the next month. We pressed on.

Those eighteen miles turned out to be very long and boring —except for Moxie Bald. Moxie Bald is an extremely rough climb, with rock scrambles and spectacular views. It is so bad that even the A.T. has a bypass around it. Doug and I did enjoy the rocks. However, within two hours of starting this section, we found ourselves to be out of Conquest™. There was plenty of water, but all the water sources were flowing out of streams dammed by beavers. Beavers, being notorious for carrying giardia and other diseases, forced our trek to be a waterless shuffle through the woods.

Both of us had "hit the wall" because of low blood sugar. The last eight miles were like a death march. I was whipped, mentally and physically. I was so tired of being tired. Because of my fatigue, I wasn't picking up my feet. My toe would catch on a rock or root and down I would go. My toes were so sore. Two of them were infected, and the big toe on my right foot had turned into raw, open flesh. Two large blisters on the lateral aspects of each foot caused more pain and agony. Moleskin would not stay on because my feet were always getting wet.

Then, there was the other problem that had surfaced over the last several days. I started having blood in my stool and my rectum became very sore. My first thought was that my ulcerative colitis was acting up. However, upon a physical check of myself (who else was going to check?), I discovered that my hemorrhoids were swollen and were external. I tried using Vaseline™ and pushing them back in, but they would not stay put. They felt the size of golf balls, although I'm sure they were actually smaller. It was a very painful situation. I kept this condition to myself, embarrassed by it all, but wondering what I would do if they ruptured.

All of these physical conditions were weighing heavily on me, weakening my mental state as well. I felt as though I was close to a total collapse. The last six miles of this day's journey followed the Piscataquis River. Rounding each bend was a déjà vu experience. It all looked the same. I felt as if I was getting nowhere, and that was so exasperating!

We finally met up with Jack who had a gallon of Conquest™ and some food. We laid into the food like lions devouring their prey. But then it was off again to stumble over the last several miles. I tripped and fell. Lying on the ground I said to myself, I'm quitting. I am not getting up and going another step. My toes are so sore, and I don't have to do this. They'll have to carry me out! Almost surprised at having entertained the thought, I told myself, No. I am not quitting. I won't do it! With added resolve, I jumped up and started running faster than I had all day.

After what seemed a lifetime of running, we finally reached the destination for the day (Shirley-Blanchard Road). It had been the longest time to be on the trail on any one day (fourteen hours and twenty-five minutes) and resulted in my latest finish. I was wasted in every way and realized I had 118.4 miles to go. I really did not know if I could make it.

Jack met us and drove us into the little town of Monson (population five hundred), situated eight miles away. We dragged ourselves into the Appalachian Trail Restaurant, appropriately named with its huge mural depicting the trail and menus with scenes from the A.T. gracing the cover. I enjoyed these small towns and personally felt that the ATC had made a mistake by re-routing the trail from its original route which went right through the middle of town.

As we were about to place our order, I heard someone call, "Hi, Pops. How's it going?" I turned to see my son, Brandon, wife Nancy, and Nancy Hamilton walking in. It was good to see them. I had not seen my family since the end of May when I was on the Trail in Virginia. Brandon kept grinning as he stood beside me with his arm around my waist. I could tell that he was proud of me and glad to be there. That, in and of itself, was so meaningful to me. Nancy was quiet and just seemed to enjoy being next to me, touching me softly.

The waitress asked if I was hiking the trail. I responded affirmatively, with the added goal of setting the speed record. She asked when I was planning to reach the northern terminus, to which I responded, "Sunday afternoon." (Keep in mind that this was Thursday night.) She gave me a look of disbelief, but remained silent.

Her husband, a forest ranger, later questioned me about my goal of Katahdin by Sunday. He began to recount stories of rescues out of the area, given its great difficulty and isolation. To say that he doubted that I would make it would be an understatement.

That night we stayed in Shaw's Boarding House. There were separate rooms for the men and women. I thought about not being able to sleep with Nancy, but I was so tired it really didn't matter. Regardless, we all ended up sleeping poorly because of hot, stale air and no air conditioning. The temperature had reached one hundred degrees, and the evening did not bring the usual relief from the heat.

A message from Glenn Streeter was waiting for us at Shaw's. His car had broken down the previous day when he had tried to meet me. He was staying in Caratunk for the night. I felt relieved that we finally knew his whereabouts. However, he still had all my Conquest™ and iodine tablets with him. Logistically, this added yet another difficulty to the task at hand.

DAY 51 - JUNE 28 - 36.1 MILES - 13:19 - CUM. MILES 2061.0

Shirley-Blanchard Road to Logging Road. Started at 4:29 a.m. First 6.3 miles was new and trashy.... Mentally very depressed.... Very little sleep at Shaw's in Monson. Nancy Hamilton ran the 30-mile segment with me. Spirits revived, and we made good progress for awhile. Then the terrain was terrible. Pleased to get through the day. Think I can make it now.

After a restless night, morning came much too quickly. I was still very tired from long days and inadequate rest. I could have really used an easy day or even a complete day of rest. I had Maineak beat, and I had the record. But, if I was to get the record, I wanted to make it as tough as possible for the next person to better my time. So, in the pre-dawn, Jack and I began another day's run.

The terrain of the first 6.3 miles was tough: rocky, rooty, and trashy. Progress was slow. I felt more tired on this morning than any other morning. It was hot, and it seemed to me as though a storm was brewing. Doug, Nancy, Nancy, and Brandon met us at

The wife's view:

David was so excited when I told him we were coming after all. The last two weeks had taken its toll on him. He was a basket case. He said he needed me. I was excited, but a little skeptical of what I would see when I arrived. When I finally did get to see him, all I kept thinking was, "I'm glad his mom can't see him now."

I wasn't totally prepared for what the next few days would be like. I expected the depression and exhaustion. I expected the moodiness. I had heard it in his voice for weeks now. But, I also had it in my mind that he would be so relieved to have us there with him that it would help some. WRONG! The first place we met him on the trail he ran right past us without a word! I said something encouraging to him, or so I thought, and he just went right past me and grabbed some aid. Not a hello, kiss my foot, nothing! Now, would that make you feel good or what?

I just stood where I was, and one of his handlers told me that it had been a really rough six miles and that he was taking a beating. So? I had come hundreds of miles to be with him (at his request, mind you), and he couldn't say two words to me. I know, better than anyone, what David can be like. However, we were there to be supportive and help him. (I don't know how his handlers put up with him.) So, I just ignored him and let him sulk. All of us just stood around quietly. We all knew it was better to leave him alone.

Nancy Hamilton was prepared to run with him for awhile and hopefully she could get him out of his "mood." Good luck! There was no way any one of us could know what his mind and body had been through for these many weeks. We accepted, but didn't necessarily appreciate it!

In a way, I felt like it was a waste of time for me to be there. This was not my idea of a "fun" time. I am not a runner. I could not physically help him on the trail. It hurt to see him like this, and it hurt not to be able to do something for him. Yet, I truly knew he was glad I was there.

-Nancy Horton

a road crossing. They broke the news that the next two road crossings were thirty miles away and then in another fourteen miles. Worse yet, it was unclear whether they could even get to the second rendezvous point, as it was on a rough, logging road. I suddenly broke down in tears and cried, "You've got to meet me in thirty miles! I cannot go fifty miles today!" I was mentally worn out, and my outburst had proven the point. Those around me did not know how to react. We just looked at each other in the heavy morning air. Then, embarrassed by my actions, I apologized for my attitude. My wife later said, "No big deal. You were having a rough day." As I thought about it later, I hoped that Brandon would see that although adversity sometimes seems overwhelming, it is possible to continue on.

Filling my water bottles and grabbing my supplies, I took off after pleading with them once again to meet me in thirty miles. A sign read, "Caution: There are no places to obtain supplies or help until you reach Abol Bridge — 90 miles north. You should not attempt this section unless you carry a minimum of ten days supplies. Do not underestimate the difficulty of this section. Good Hiking!" Nancy Hamilton scurried to catch me and keep me company in this wilderness.

Nancy did her best to console me through this section. At first I resisted, because I found solace in feeling sorry for myself. I remember thinking that I could now relate to desperate people on the brink of hopelessness. But then I turned to the Lord and prayed a different kind of prayer: "Lord, I know you're going to think this request is rather dumb, but please lift my spirits and make me brain dead today. Help the miles to fly by and let me not really sense what is happening." I had prayed this prayer before, and God once again answered.

The weather became threatening, with lightning and booming thunder all around. The bottom fell out of the skies, and we were inundated with rain. We found ourselves standing in a stream, filling our bottles. Between the thunder Nancy said, "What are you going to do if lightning strikes and kills me?" "Leave you here!" was my response. "If you're dead, I can't help you!" We both laughed at the absurdity of our circumstances, and the cloud of depression in my soul began to lift as the rain continued to come down.

As we continued on our way, Nancy and I had a special time together as we talked of our families and how God had blessed us with the opportunity to run the A.T. It's a good thing we had lots to talk about since the terrain was dull and the trail devoid of other human life.

Carefully dividing our food supplies, we managed to make them last for about four hours. After that, we just hoped and prayed that our crew would be able to find us. Within thirty minutes of downing the last of the supplies, there came our crew, bearing supplies fit for a king. Was I ever glad not to have to continue on. With 82.3 miles remaining, I planned to go longer on the following day, leaving the miles of the last day not so burdensome.

Nancy, my wife, also gave me good reason to finish two days hence. Before leaving home, she had informed friends and supporters they could receive an update as to the conclusion of the adventure by calling our home answering machine. She told them the final day was to be Sunday. So, the lot was cast for all accounts.

Unfortunately, we had to drive one and one half hours to the nearest town, Millinocket, to find lodging. I slept with Nancy for the first time in over a month. (Of course, Brandon and Nancy Hamilton occupied the same room.) But, rather than being pleasant, it was totally uncomfortable. Every time she would roll over, touch me, or place her leg or arm over me, it would send a wave of pain over my annihilated body.

DAY 52 - JUNE 29 - 48.3 MILES - 14:53 - CUM. MILES 2110.0

Logging road to logging road. Start 4:51 a.m.... Longest day yet. First 14 miles very slow...5 hours. Toes are extremely sore. Not real motivated but felt better after Nancy Hamilton started running with me. Saw two spectacular views of Mt. Katahdin, but it didn't faze me that much. Toes got sorer with each step. Nice weather — 70-75 degrees and very low humidity. Looking forward to tomorrow and finishing.

Just so I would not forget I was still on a mountain trail, the first fourteen miles were really difficult. Initially the trail passed through a swampy area, but then crossed over several little mountains, ending with a good climb up to White Cap Mountain. This was the last big mountain before reaching Katahdin, seventy-one miles to the northeast. Catching my toes on trail obstacles, I fell several times. Each toe catch was excruciating. I wanted relief for my feet!

After the first road crossing at fourteen miles, the *A. T. Data Book* indicated the next road crossing to be forty miles away. We were able to find other logging roads that charged a toll of $5 per head, a seemingly ridiculous amount. However, the gates to these roads normally did not open until 6:00 a.m. We had to do some fancy talking to the guards on the way out both Friday and Saturday for them to allow us early entry the next morning.

Nancy Hamilton ran with me for many of the miles in the middle of the day. It was during this time that I really sensed that I was going to complete the task — obtain the goal. Katahdin was going to be mine. And, with less than forty miles each of these last two days, I was closer to a return to normal life!

Late in the afternoon, as we were running by Pemadumcook Lake, I commented to Nancy that I thought we should be able to soon view the final mountain, still forty-six miles away. Within one minute of my statement, we came upon a sign that displayed these words with a pointing arrow: "Mt. Katahdin View." You would think that with all my suffering, Nancy would have let me have the first look. But no. Not Nancy. Off she went, bolting up the trail to take in the view. There it was. Across the lake and in the background stood the majestic Mt. Katahdin. Nancy was so excited! It was beautiful, even spectacular. But I just could not muster the same enthusiasm. There were still miles to run.

Brandon was my companion as we ran the last eight miles of the day. He said, "I didn't think we were ever going to get to run together — just you and me." His exclamation made me feel great. I was sharing a very special time with my son. Then, as another awesome view of the mountain presented itself to us, his proclamation was, "Isn't that beautiful?! I'm glad to be here with you, Dad."

David and son, Brandon, share some quality time together on the trail.

So was I. I've never felt closer to my son and more proud of him than during those miles. I pray for more times like that in the future.

DAY 53 - JUNE 30 - 34.0 MILES - 12:03 - CUM. MILES 2144.0

The FINISH — Start 4:32 a.m. Felt horrible first 20 miles to Abol Bridge. Took six Tylenol #3™ today. Could hardly run...toes were so sore and blistered and sides of heels were bad.... Felt real good going up to Baxter Park. Perfect weather in the 70s. Light wind and low humidity. Fell four times. Real fun climbing Mt. Katahdin rocks. No emotion really, just relieved. Tough going off mountain.

FREE. The big day had finally arrived. I got to climb the mountain that I had dreamed of for so long. But the first twenty miles were very difficult. We had not been able to get to bed until 10:30 p.m. and had to get up at 2:50 a.m. to accommodate the one-and-one-half-hour drive back to our starting point. This tiredness along with the pain of my raw toes made for a three "Tylenol #3™ morning." I fell several times from my toes catching on rocks and roots. It was so hard to pick up my feet. During this stretch, Katahdin still seemed so far away, so unattainable. I knew mentally I should have been sky-high on this last leg of the journey, but I wasn't. As Jack McGiffin and I covered this first section, he tried his best to cheer me up, but to no avail. I just wanted it to end — to be over — FOREVER!

We finally reached Abol Bridge (14.5 miles from the summit) and the end of the wilderness section. Brandon, Glenn, and Doug joined me at this point. I also had to down three more Tylenol #3™ in an attempt to dull the pain. I felt bad for Doug because every time he accompanied me, I was "down." I didn't want him to take it personally.

As we were running along a river with about eight miles to go, I fell for the final time. I ripped a six-inch gash in my arm and a smaller wound on my thigh. I'm not really sure what happened. But the fact remained that blood was running down my arm and leg. Doug wanted me to stop and clean it up, but I responded with, "I'm so tired of tripping and falling and hurting my toes!" The frustration and pain must have given me an endorphin rush because I took off running. I actually started feeling better.

We reached the Katahdin Stream campground at 2:00 p.m. We had only 5.2 miles to go; however, I was told that the rangers would not allow anyone to start an ascent after 1:00 p.m. Luckily for us, there wasn't a ranger to be found. So, picking up our supplies and with Nancy Hamilton joining us, we continued on our journey. My wife, who had broken her toe, drove the van around to the other side of the mountain where we would come down.

Mt. Katahdin is the highest mountain in Maine, rising to 5267 feet with a thirteen-foot rock cairn on the summit. This pile of rocks made it an even mile above sea level. The way to the summit is on the Hunt Trail that sports a climb of four thousand feet. It is the greatest single climb along the entire A.T.

I had hoped and prayed for a clear day for the ascent. Temperatures at the base were seventy to seventy-five degrees. A perfect day for the long climb.

The first two miles were fairly steep through a wooded forest. After this, the trail becomes much steeper, especially above the tree line at 3500 feet. The A.T. is so steep in this region that it requires technical rock climbing. There are pitons in the rock at various places for hand and foot holds. This rock scramble was actually a lot of fun, and having my crew with me made it even better. They deserved this moment of achievement as well.

We passed many people coming down as we made our way closer to the summit. When asked, they said it had taken them anywhere from four to six hours for the ascent. One man said that he had left at 7:45 a.m. and never did make it to the top. He tried to discourage us from going any further. In fact, he told us that we were "crazy" for trying to make it so late in the day. But nothing could stop us now. We were going for it!

THE LAST MILE

The last mile was more gradual, and as we neared the summit we could see others gathered at the rock cairn. I thought the final moment would never arrive, but it did! I touched the sign that indicated the northern terminus of the Appalachian Trail at 4:35

The crew's view:
The climb was tough but it felt easy because we were all fulfilling a dream — not only David's dream but a dream for ourselves. When we reached the top, I hugged David, with tears in my eyes. He had worked so hard for so many miles. I knew it would take months for him to realize what he had done. He had reached out and touched his "farthest star."

-Nancy Hamilton

Those who joined David to climb Mt. Katahdin's summit:
(top) Jack McGiffin, (2nd row, l-r) Nancy Hamilton, David,
Brandon Horton, Glenn Streeter, (front) Doug Young.

p.m. EST on June 30, 1991 — fifty-two days, nine hours and forty-one minutes after leaving Springer Mountain, Georgia, on May 9. There were no tears during the climb or upon reaching the summit, only a feeling of relief. I felt the words of Martin Luther King with my whole being: "Free, free, I'm free at last." I had heard that the end of the journey is not the reward, but the reward is the journey itself. I'm not sure. At that point, the end of the journey seemed the reward to me.

▲

A mother's view:

I don't know if you remember, but when you were four years old, you had an infection between your hipbone and one leg and couldn't walk for almost two weeks. You would ask me when I would be carrying you, "Will I ever walk again?" You did not only walk, but you ran for fifty-two days, nine hours, and forty-one minutes. There were tears of joy for what you had done, and it brought joy to our hearts.

‑Lois Horton, David's mother

▼

CHAPTER 10

From Maine to Mundane

What goes up must come down.

- Law of the Universe

With the journey over, it would have been nice to get in a vehicle and just drive away. However, as if the trail wasn't through with me quite yet, the final challenge proved to be getting off the mountain. There were no roads to the top. It was 5.2 miles up and 5.2 miles down. We did take a ranger's suggestion to take the "easier and shorter" route along the Cathedral and Chimney Ponds Trails down, but his opinion of "easy" was skewed. Parts of this descent were very steep, made more difficult by loose rocks. It seemed to go on forever. It took 2:25 to climb to the top and 2:30 to get down! But finally the campground and our van came into view. I climbed in with my wife. It was finally over! Now my life could return to normal.

▲

The wife's view:

I was never so glad to see Sunday, June 30th. When I saw him coming off Mt. Katahdin, I was just so relieved that it was over! I expected to see a little lift in his step, a big smile on his face. Nothing! The excitement and jubilation that I had expected was not there. I think he was just so relieved that he didn't have to run another step. We could go home and get our lives back to normal, or so I thought!

-Nancy Horton

▼

Recovery was slower than expected. When asked how long it would take me to recover, I would always say, "Two or three weeks — or maybe a year." I know now that it certainly was not in two to three weeks. The first week I was home was especially difficult. Nancy threatened to send me back on the trail. I had nightmares

The wife's view:

Normal did not come back in a rush! David was so physically and mentally exhausted that I was about ready to put him out in the shed in the back yard. He couldn't sleep. When he did, he tossed and turned. He talked in his sleep. He would get up several times a night thinking that he was still on the trail. He had very little energy. He wasn't a fun person to be with. And the phone calls! I thought our phone would never stop ringing for several weeks after he finished. I heard the story over and over again. I could have quoted him word for word.

There were good times throughout this endeavor, and there were certainly bad times. I don't know which outweighed which. He accomplished what he set out to do. I'm truly proud of him. Doubts? No, I don't think I ever doubted he could do it, only whether he could do it in the time limit he had set for himself. I'm glad he proved me wrong. He's an amazing person. But the best part — IT'S OVER!

What's up next? I know he's got something else on his mind. There's no doubt. I can feel it. Something bigger, something better....

Myself? It was a very hard and lonely two months for me. It may be a long time (if ever) that I would be agreeable to another such adventure; I didn't get married to live alone!

-Nancy Horton

every night, all night, about the trail. I kept dreaming that I had to go more miles, and it was always uphill. Several times I would partially awaken and panic when I realized I was in a bed. My thought was that I had overslept and missed my start time on the trail. I also was disoriented and confused by the fact that my wife was in the bed.

Four days after I got home, I ran two miles and it felt like a hundred miles. How did I ever average forty miles per day for fifty-three days? I was so tired I couldn't do anything. I even hated to walk down the stairs to our family room, because I knew I would eventually have to come back up.

Each passing day since the adventure made it seem more dream-like and surreal. It is inconceivable how I ever did it. The accomplishment means a lot to me. Time will tell how strong my time was. In a selfish way, I hope my record stands forever. But I know records are made to be broken and mine will probably fall someday.

I would be remiss if I did not acknowledge what Scott Grierson (Maineak) accomplished. Maineak reached Katahdin's summit fifty-five days, twenty hours, and thirty-three minutes after leaving Springer Mountain. Scott did achieve his goal of a sub-56 day A.T. trip. We became very good friends, and I truly respect him for what he did. He is an outstanding athlete with great integrity. He averaged a time of 16:10 per day, compared to my 11:25. I don't understand how he did it on so little sleep. Additionally, he also served as my rabbit to chase for thirty-nine days, which definitely contributed to my success. There is now an unbreakable bond between us.

So, what did I learn from this experience of triumphing over the trail? The following serves as my list of observations and those things that impressed me:

1. The power of prayer — mine and others.
2. The unlimited capabilities of the human body.
3. The importance of maintaining a good attitude even when "bad" things happen.
4. How much my wife loves me.
5. How much my crew and friends mean to me.
6. The beauty of God's creation — man, earth, and creature.
7. How quickly friendships develop with people you have never previously met: the Fellers, Haysletts, Hearns, and the Cimeras.
8. How other people who helped me can share in the joy and excitement of achieving a goal.
9. How quickly the body can recover in spite of long hours, many miles, and apparent injuries.

10. The power, strength, and focus of a goal that is meaningful to you.
11. How important it is to appreciate all the volunteer effort put into the maintenance of the A.T.
12. How well Conquest™ works.
13. The difficulty of the White Mountains and Maine.
14. How much I now appreciate switchbacks.
15. How neat it is to know that I have covered the A.T. faster than anyone else in the world.
16. How far it really is from Georgia to Maine!

▲

From a friend:
There is no doubt that it was a once-in-a-lifetime event, managed at a time when most of us simply don't seem to find the time for once-in-a-lifetime events. My reaction is one of admiration and awe, but it is definitely not one of surprise. I know the man involved too well for that. Furthermore, I know that he is now thinking about the next challenge....

-Robert Gaunt

▼

1991 APPALACHIAN TRAIL STATISTICS

DAVID HORTON: 52 DAYS, 9 HOURS, 41 MINUTES

State	Day	Start	Finish	Time	Mileage	Total Mileage
Georgia		(a.m.)	(p.m.)			
	1	6:54	3:38	8:44	37.1	37.1
	2	6:05	6:00	11:55	45.3	82.4
North Carolina/Tennessee						
	3	6:30	3:25	8:55	38.9	121.3
	4	6:37	5:08	10:31	41.5	162.8
	5	6:04	4:05	10:01	37.8	200.6
	6	6:45	2:00	7:15	30.8	231.4
	7	6:33	3:09	8:36	35.4	266.8
	8	6:35	6:29	11:54	34.8	301.6
	9	6:02	5:24	11:22	38.9	340.5
	10	6:16	5:27	11:11	36.4	376.9
	11	6:13	4:14	10:01	33.2	410.1
	12	5:51	3:48	9:57	37.1	447.2
Virginia						
	13	5:43	5:07	11:24	41.1	488.3
	14	6:08	3:17	9:09	35.4	523.7
	15	5:59	3:35	9:56	38.2	561.7
	16	5:39	3:35	9:52	38.5	600.2
	17	5:20	4:50	11:30	41.8	642.0
	18	5:23	4:27	11:04	39.5	681.5
	19	5:38	4:19	10:41	39.6	721.1
	20	5:44	3:43	9:59	37.9	759.0
	21	5:37	4:36	10:59	39.3	798.3
	22	5:32	5:30	11:58	40.2	838.5
	23	5:45	3:40	9:55	36.9	875.4
	24	5:05	5:12	12:07	43.0	918.4
	25	5:30	4:11	10:41	41.0	958.5
	26	5:37	5:11	11:36	43.5	1002.0
West Virginia/Maryland						
	27	5:09	4:56	11:47	43.0	1045.0

Pennsylvania					
28	5:02	5:19	12:17	52.8	1097.8
29	5:09	5:49	12:40	51.6	1149.1
30	4:51	2:58	10:07	41.3	1190.7
31	5:14	3:31	10:17	41.6	1232.3
32	5:13	3:54	10:41	41.1	1273.4
33	5:04	4:38	11:34	45.9	1319.3
New Jersey					
34	4:49	4:25	11:36	42.8	1362.1
New York					
35	4:47	3:22	10:35	38.9	1401.0
36	4:41	4:52	12:11	48.4	1449.4
Connecticut					
37	4:43	5:08	12:25	43.3	1492.7
38	4:45	4:39	11:54	45.4	1538.1
Massachusetts				Caught Maineak at	1574.6
39	4:41	3:35	10:54	40.7	1578.8
Vermont					
40	4:59	4:56	11:57	43.9	1622.7
41	4:45	5:12	12:27	45.4	1668.1
42	4:43	4:10	11:27	44.5	1712.6
New Hampshire					
43	4:40	4:53	12:13	45.1	1757.7
44	4:48	5:45	12:57	35.6	1793.3
45	4:24	6:37	14:13	39.4	1832.7
46	4:44	6:25	13:41	37.2	1869.9
Maine					
47	4:39	5:48	13:09	33.6	1903.5
48	4:54	6:39	13:45	38.8	1942.3
49	4:33	6:13	13:40	36.5	1978.8
50	4:58	7:23	14:25	46.8	2025.6
51	4:29	5:48	13:19	36.1	2061.7
52	4:51	7:44	14:53	48.3	2110.0
53	4:32	4:35	12:03	34.0	2144.0

PART II

FROM SEA TO SHINING SEA

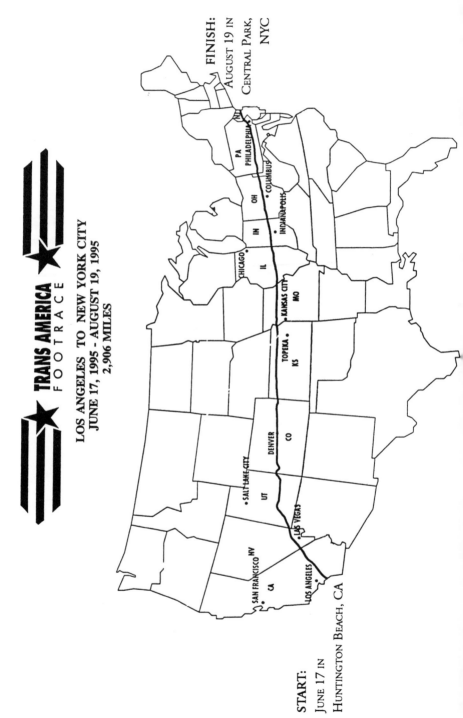

TRANS AMERICA
FOOTRACE

LOS ANGELES TO NEW YORK CITY
JUNE 17, 1995 - AUGUST 19, 1995
2,906 MILES

START:
JUNE 17 IN
HUNTINGTON BEACH, CA

FINISH:
AUGUST 19 IN
CENTRAL PARK,
NYC

PHILADELPHIA
PA
COLUMBUS
OH
INDIANAPOLIS
IN
CHICAGO
IL
KANSAS CITY
MO
TOPEKA
KS
DENVER
CO
SALT LAKE CITY
UT
LAS VEGAS
SAN FRANCISCO NV
CA
LOS ANGELES

CHAPTER 11

Preparing For the Great Race

The greater the sacrifice and price paid,
the greater the reward and satisfaction.

- Author unknown

When I decided to enter the 1995 version of the Trans-Am, I
did so making huge personal and financial commitments. Quite
frankly, my wife, Nancy, was not exactly crazy about the idea. She
had been the one to handle all the logistics for the A.T. in 1991.
She was the one who had to make sure that my support people
showed up at the proper time and place. She was the one to handle
the financing of the endeavor. She was the one who wrote the newsletters to all of my supporters and interested parties. She was the
one who had to hold down the fort at home. She was the one who
had to listen to me cry. She was the one who had to watch me
suffer. She was the one who certainly did not want to go through
that again! So my decision to do the race did cause tension.

A part of that tension resulted from the fact the entry fee alone
stood at $1,200. Additionally, another $1,000 was required as a
deposit for race-provided meals and expenses that would accrue
should the runner require the race organization to supply crew. An
estimate of other expenses — including airfare, ice, food, running
clothes, some crew expenses, etc. — amounted to another $6,000.
(In the end, the race effort cost about $10,000.) Financially, I did
not have the personal resources to pull off my dream without accu-
mulating a great deal of debt. After some discussion, my friend
Gary Trittipoe suggested we capitalize on my many friendships and
acquaintances over the years in an effort to raise the necessary funds.
The result was a letter from Gary and Rebekah Trittipoe to approximately three hundred people who knew me. They simply explained what it was I sought to accomplish, how much it would
cost, and offered them the opportunity to act as my supporting
cast. I was overwhelmed at the tremendous response from so many
people. Daily, words of encouragement and monetary gifts arrived

From the mailbox:

We believe God will not only use this race to help you fulfill your dream, but also for the purpose of bringing honor and glory to Himself. Therefore, every opportunity you have, tell someone about our Lord Jesus Christ. Remember, if you can touch one person with the message that God loves him or her, it will be worth it all.... "I press toward the mark for the prize of the high calling of God in Jesus Christ. (Phil. 3:14)

                                        ~Colson and Madelyn Richey

by mail, averaging about $25 per contribution, to support the longest race of my life. I wanted to be sure all of these generous contributors were made aware of my progress, so they could feel that they, too, had a stake in the race. The method we used to achieve this goal was for the Trittipoes to write a day-by-day accounting of each stage, based on the many phone calls I would place to their home. Every week, a newsletter was mailed to each of my 168 supporters.

The chapters that follow are the body of those newsletters, sometimes edited for brevity. Also included are excerpts from the transcripts of the tapes I made most days, barring the last nine. Although it was impossible to include the entirety of my conversations with the tape recorder, those portions that best reflect my personal thoughts are included.

4/2/95 — Seventy-six days until the race — My training program started on Friday. The morning workout (10 miles) felt like nothing, and the afternoon workout (19 miles) was easy.... I could have run a lot further.... I felt pretty good on Saturday. I ran the whole way (35 miles). Pleased with the back-to-back days.... Mentally I look forward to the training and the challenge of the race. Right now I can't fathom how difficult it will be. But I think I am suited for that type of running (stage running).

(Note: Stage running is the type of race where all the competitors start at the same place and time, running a prescribed course to the finish line. In the case of the Trans-Am, a stage was held on sixty-four consecutive days. Times for each day's stage were recorded for each competitor, and the one with the least cumulative time was declared the winner.)

Once I made it known to people that I was going to run the Trans-Am race, I was frequently asked, "How do you train for a race like that?" My standard response was, "I don't know." And I didn't know. It was difficult to comprehend running 317 miles, on average, for the nine weeks of the race. I was very fortunate to be able to talk with a few of the men who had previously run the Trans-Am. Dante Ciolfe told me that he trained up to 360 miles per week but then later dropped back to 180 miles per week. Istvan Siptos (winner of the 1994 race) trained up to 180 miles per week. However, when I spoke to Ray Bell (winner of the 1993 race), he told me that he really didn't alter his normal training at all! Taking the comments of these three graduates of the race into consideration, I figured that I would have a weekly mileage goal of 180 miles — tops. But I also questioned how difficult so many road miles would be when I was used to long runs on trails. How would I adapt — mentally and physically — to the pounding and monotony of the road?

4/16/95 — Sunday night — I feel very calm and relaxed. My short run today on Apple Orchard Mountain was great. The weather was beautiful. It was very relaxing sitting on the rock at the top and praying…. But one of the depressing things about Sunday night is that you always have "0" miles for the week when you wake up Monday morning and start a new week. I guess life and racing are similar that way. Each day you have to start over, and nothing you did before really counts. This next week will be interesting, as I plan to run more than the 163 miles that I ran last week. That's the most I've trained in one week. I really don't feel any worse than when I normally run 80-100 miles in a week. Mentally, I don't feel tired either, and that's very important.

My first three weeks of training tallied 156, 163, and 174 miles. Some runs went well, and some were not so great. There was one fifty-three-mile run that I was unable to complete. I had big problems with nausea and diarrhea and had difficulty drinking anything. The result was a thirty-four-miler that left me feeling like a whipped puppy. However, I got in the car and drove to the site of the Bull Run fifty-mile trail race that was being held the next day. I approached the start line after having already completed 124 miles that week. I ran remarkably well, running seven hours, forty-six minutes, and placing third. I felt pleased with my progress and training. The accumulated 174 miles for the week set a new standard for me.

4/24/95 — I was very pleased with both workouts today (20 miles each) considering that I ran 174 miles last week.... I am really getting in shape and recovering quickly.... I received the Trans-Am information packet today. I am very excited about it.

I was able to add 137 miles to my logbook the following week. At one point during a run the thought occurred to me that I was a "running machine" — smooth and efficient. I mentally made a note to remember that feeling when I felt tired during the race. But I was also wondering if my approach to the monster of a race was correct. Is a 170-mile week better than 130? Would three or four really big mileage weeks help or hurt? When should I back off? Was I training too hard or not hard enough? I really didn't know the answers, but with six weeks left until the start, I felt confident.

I attempted to find answers to my questions by running a 170-mile week followed by a new high of 190.5 miles. Sometimes I would run big mileage in a single workout and sometimes I would break a forty-five-mile day into three workouts. I was feeling fit, but I was getting tired — not sore — just tired. I started going to bed as early as 9:00 p.m. I did back down the next week to 125 miles, during which the reality of the impending race broke through.

5/18/95 — Yesterday's two 20-milers really took it out of me. I knew that last night, but I really felt it this morning. I was extremely tired this morning. Any effort was work. I ran four miles and didn't want to run at all. I even walked three or four times because I was so tired. I watched the 1994 Trans-Am tape last night and then again this afternoon. I also read the transcript. I broke down in tears. I MUST finish!

Pre-race thoughts written to the Trittipoes:

I am proud of my son and what he has done with his life, but he knows that I am very much against him doing this. He knows how I feel about him leaving his wife and children for this length of time and what effect it has on us as his parents at our age. But we do want to know where he is…. We hope he will change his mind. We wish him well.

-Lois Horton, David's Mom

That next week turned out to be my last "big" week in terms of mileage (135 miles). Then, all of a sudden it was the last day of May. That meant I would be leaving in a scant two and a half weeks for Los Angeles. Nancy and I had some serious discussions as the tension of the fast-approaching race and separation mounted. Though we had been married for twenty-four years, I wasn't sure if our union could withstand the test of this race. It was a difficult time for both of us.

My training dropped back to sixty-three and then forty-nine miles in those first two weeks of June. This left me with more time to contemplate life, love, and running. I wondered what I would feel like when I flew away on June fourteenth. I wondered how Nancy would be. I wondered how I would feel at the start of the first stage. I wondered how I would respond the first time I felt really low. I wondered how I would respond if another runner was running a faster pace than I wanted to run. I wondered if my body would hold up. I wondered if I had trained properly. I wondered about how the other runners might have prepared. I just wondered…

June 13th — It is almost here. I can't believe it. It used to seem so far away. I'm very excited and not that anxious and nervous — but some. Last night's going away party was nice. I thought it might be emotional but it wasn't. I'm sure it will be when I get on the plane tomorrow. I look forward to a great experience. Romans 12:15 — "Rejoice with those who rejoice, and weep with those who weep."

June 14th — As I write this I am 28,000 feet above some desolate looking countryside.... I feel very small and insignificant. Off and on I've felt lonely.... I thought that leaving the airport this morning would be very emotional, but it wasn't. With Mike Lowry, Chuck Burch, and Muffy there, it couldn't be somber and sad! What lies ahead seems unimaginable.... I hope I don't get too homesick.... Being with Nancy last night was great. I really enjoyed sleeping with her. She said I was up against her all night long. I feel sorry for her right now — so alone. I could tell she was hurting this morning and that she was going to miss me. I know she loves me and I love her, but I sense she feels that I have deserted her. Right now, that is the way I feel also.... I just shed my first tear since I left. I'm sure there will be many more. Right now I understand a little bit more about Nancy when she said, "If you love me, how could you leave me for so long?"... Leaving home to do the Trans-Am doesn't feel very comforting right now.... In less than one hour I'll be there.

CHAPTER 12

Week 1 of the Trans-Am

The journey of three thousand miles begins with a single step.
- Written on a T-shirt and given to David
by the Kansas Ultrarunning Society

Rebekah writes: The week prior to the start of the race was busy for everyone. We had a nice "bon voyage" party for him on Monday, the twelfth. About twenty-five friends came to wish David Godspeed, and it gave him a chance to express some of his thoughts about his upcoming endeavor. While he had lots to say (that shouldn't surprise anyone!), he answered the question about what was his biggest fear in one word: "loneliness." We all need to remember to pray for him daily as well as make sure he gets lots of mail along the way.

Despite possessing the organizational skills of an orangutan, David managed to con Nancy into helping him get all his stuff into two duffel bags and two small carry-on bags. After an early morning live interview on Spirit FM 90.3 radio, a small group of friends saw him fly away from Lynchburg on a very small plane. He did manage to make his connections at Dulles and Chicago and met up with Roger and Janet Soule in California. The Soules were host to David for a couple of days as well as to Regis and Diana Shivers, the Horton crew for the first three weeks. Last minute items were acquired, race check-ins completed, and news conferences and photo ops accomplished. Everything was set for 5:00 a.m. on Saturday morning.

6/15/95 - 10:07 p.m.
Just finished the pre-race briefing this afternoon. Fourteen runners registered, including one woman. It's sort of been mixed emotions since I've been here. It was really mixed emotions when I left on Wednesday, watching Nancy, Gary, Rebekah, Chuck, and everyone else there. I really had no feelings, in a way.... It was sort

111

of funny, but getting on the plane I ripped the back of my leg on something and it bled a lot. What a way to start out.

The flight took off okay, landed in Dulles, and gave me a little time there waiting for the flight to Chicago. On the way to Chicago I started writing in my logbook, writing about leaving Nancy and how it was to be with her the previous night. I wrote how she felt this morning, saying how I laid close by her all night long. I really felt sorry for her. I think it was hurting her a lot because I was going away for so long. As I was writing, it was real emotional for me. I sort of realized why she hated me going away... because she had always said she didn't want me to go. And when I asked her why, she would say, "Because I don't want you to be gone for so long." I never could understand that. However, as I wrote more, I began to understand.

Flying from Chicago to Orange County Airport, it was amazing crossing the Rockies and seeing all the snow. And then the desert: how desolate it looked, all brown and dead. Very few roads and no greenery whatsoever. You could see only a few houses. This country is so big!

As I drove up to the motel where we were to start, you could look out and see the ocean. It was cool, very cool. Probably 70 degrees. I felt a little nervous. Then I went over and met the race directors, Jesse Riley and Michael Kenney. It was interesting to meet both of them. Jesse is very friendly but seems too young to be directing such a big race.

We had a meeting today from 1-4 p.m. Sounds like it's going to be a great adventure. I'm looking forward to it. I hope I'm man enough to make it across the country. I hope the Lord will give me the strength that I need. I claim His verses in Philippians 4:13 and 4:19.

I was very impressed with the runner from Slovenia. Dusan looks tough, very, very tough. He reminded me of the big, tough Russian in Rocky III or IV. Ray Bell and Patrick Farmer, veterans of this race, look tough as well. It's going to be a hard race.

6/16/95 - 6:50 p.m.

In ten hours I start the longest race of my life. I'm not quite sure how I feel. We had our press conference today. It was primarily a

1995 Trans-America runners: (Top row, l-r) David Horton, Michiyoshi Kaiho, Eiko Endo, Kiyoto Nagata, Masao Nakaza, Nobuaki Koyago, Ray Bell. (Bottom row, l-r) Don Winkley, Patrick Farmer, Jun Onoki, Ed Kelley, Manfred Leismann, Dusan Mravlje, Mike Sandlin.

photo op. Everyone came forward and received their numbers. The number I received was #1. Basically, they gave everyone their number as they entered the race, and I was the first one to enter.

Right now I have a little knot in my stomach... a little tight... a little nervous. Not quite sure what lies ahead, although I know that it will be a real test. I'll need the Lord's help and I'll claim his promises. I'm sure I'll ask for strength, endurance, and patience.

It's hard to imagine that it will be more than two months before this race is over. Flying out here was very humbling. I felt very weak and insufficient. I still feel that way. Tomorrow night, maybe I'll have a different feeling. I trained very hard for this race. In fact, this was the hardest I have ever trained for anything. Training has gone well. I've studied. I've read. I've talked to people. I've done all I know that I think I should do.... But is it enough? I don't know. If it's not, I'm not sure what more I could have done or how I could have done it differently.

It's hard to believe that tomorrow I'll start something I've wanted to do since the early 80's... to run across the country. Ever since I read the story of Flanigan's Run, *I've wanted to make the trek. Now it's here. Now it's almost time to start. It's hard to believe that it's about to happen.*

6/17/95 4:10 a.m.

Here it is. Supposed to start in 50 minutes. I ran into Jesse Riley last night, and he said that more than likely we would be starting late. I really hate that. I asked him how late. He said, "Probably 6:00 or 6:30 a.m." That means we will be running in the heat an hour or hour and a half longer. I wish we were starting on time...

Slept real, real good last night. In fact, I can't believe how good. I dreamed some but don't remember what the dreams were about. Looking forward to a great challenge. I heard the alarm at 4:00 a.m., bright-eyed and bushy-tailed. I hope to wake up like that sixty-three more times.

David with Regis and Diana Shivers, his crew for the first three weeks.

DAY 1 - JUNE 17 - HUNTINGTON BEACH, CA TO RANCHO CUCAMONGA, CA - 52.8 MILES

The day started off unseasonably cool, but warmed up quickly as the sun rose across the sky. With a gradual but steady climb from sea level to a thirteen hundred-foot elevation, David began the race with the pack of fourteen runners. (Two registered runners never even made it to the starting line.) The going seemed to be slow, and Dusan Mravlje, Ed Kelley, Patrick Farmer, and Ray Bell pulled away from the group. However, with time, David caught up with these runners and vied for the second and third positions the rest of the day. David reports that the last twelve or thirteen miles were straight as an arrow, flat, and therefore a bit difficult mentally. But with just three miles to go, he slipped past Ed Kelley to come in second for the day at (7:41:41), just fifteen minutes behind the leader Dusan Mravlje (7:26:36). Ed Kelley clocked 7:45:01, with Patrick Farmer in at 8:19:38. The 1993 Trans-Am winner, Ray Bell, was fifth in 8:46:24. Not bad for the first day!

David's big question throughout the day was wondering whether he was running too fast, too slow, or just right. These nearly fifty-three miles were uneventful and undertaken with little difficulty. He hopes the next week or two will teach him something about pace for the remainder of the race. Perhaps the most significant comment for the day was from Steve Harvey, the race publicist, who said, "Just remember you only have one continent to go!" Run, David, Run!

Day one completed. I'm not sure if it was harder than I expected or easier. Things don't always turn out the way you think they will.... So, I'm into it now. Haven't gotten in shape yet. That's going to take awhile. But I'm looking forward to it. "I can do all things through Christ who strengthens me." Phil. 4:13.

DAY 2 - JUNE 18 - RANCHO CUCAMONGA, CA TO VICTORVILLE, CA - 44.6 MILES

The second day of racing gave the runners a taste for both the upcoming mountains and the desert. David reported the first ten miles were okay, but the next seventeen turned into work. He just didn't feel good or strong. However, he started to feel better when the first big climb of the day started. Any of you who know David know that he can walk uphill faster than most can run (and the four runners in front of him did run the whole way). David steadily moved from fifth place into third place by the top of the mountain. By forty miles and heading into town, David caught the next runner, Ed Kelley to take second place. The terrain turned into wide and open space with sand and sagebrush. (Sounds like desert to me!) Nevertheless, even a quick but necessary pit stop in a Red Lobster Restaurant did not prevent David from again finishing the day in second place (6:56:39) with Dusan Mravlje taking the top spot in 6:39:10. Ed came in at 6:59:55 and Manfred Leismann of Germany was in at 7:02:10.

David is icing his feet and shins after each stage in hopes that "prevention is the best medicine." He did get a blood blister on one of his toes yesterday, but injecting zinc oxide under the skin seemed to clear it up overnight. He is also taking advantage of his crew by getting a nightly massage, especially for his quads and hamstrings. He says he can hardly wait until he reaches the next level of fitness, probably in another two or three weeks.

His accommodations tonight will be the Victorville Recreation Center floor. As the race rules state, all the runners are required to stay in the same place at night. However, if a runner chooses, he or she can sleep outside the building. David took a tent with him. Since the place is a little on the small side, he is actually planning to set up his tent inside the Center for a respite from the crowd.

It doesn't feel like Sunday with not going to church this morning or tonight. The way I feel right now is "disjointed."... I don't feel really lonely. I don't feel sad. I don't feel happy, excited or glad. I'm just thankful to be here right now, and I hope and pray I have a good night's sleep and another good day tomorrow.

DAY 3 - JUNE 19 - VICTORVILLE, CA TO BARSTOW, CA - 36.9 MILES

Day three started out like the first two, with a 5:00 a.m. start but with a considerably shorter distance to cover. With relatively cool weather in the morning and temperatures "only" rising into the eighties, the relatively flat terrain brought the top five runners in under six hours. After playing cat and mouse with Dusan all day, David again came in second with a time of 5:06:49, just five minutes behind Dusan, who crossed the finish line in 5:01:22. The top five was rounded out by Manfred Leismann (5:12:27), Patrick Farmer (5:48:44), and Ed Kelley (5:50:25). David stated yesterday that he felt "disjointed," meaning that he felt no real emotion. Not sad, not glad, not good, not bad. However, after today's run, he feels good. And his wonderful crew, Regis and Diana Shivers, say they are seeing a fight in David's eyes. Dusan is undoubtedly a fantastic runner, but if I were him, I'd be getting a little worried!

The overall standings for the top five are as follows: Dusan Mravlje 19:07:07, David Horton +38:00, Ed Kelley +1:28:12, Manfred Leismann +2:27:27, Patrick Farmer +3:26:13, and Ray Bell +4:33:38. The only woman, Eiko Endo, is in eighth place.

(Note: The overall results are listed so that the leader's cumulative time is shown. The position of the other runners is indicated by the amount of time they are behind the leader. For example, Dusan's time is nineteen hours, seven minutes, and seven seconds. David is thirty-eight minutes behind Dusan and Ed Kelley is one hour, twenty-eight minutes, twelve seconds behind Dusan.)

One runner dropped out yesterday and another was taken to the hospital today after completing the stage. This runner, however, remains in the race.

The stay in Barstow should be comfortable, with this being one of the twenty nights when the runners will stay in motels, albeit without air-conditioning. The runners are certainly enjoying this, because in the morning they face nearly fifty-two miles of the Mojave Desert.

David now seems to be establishing a routine. The afternoons are taken up with icing shins and ankles, eating, sleeping, and taking care of communications back home. Regis and Diana are doing a superb job crewing and being there for David during the afternoons and evenings. They are continuing with the massages that David was used to getting in his pre-race training. In other words, they are doing a great job pampering him! David is also enjoying getting to know some of the other runners, and he has reported that most of the foreign runners speak some English. (Pity them because they now have to listen to all those Horton "stories.")

Dusan, a sports trainer in Slovenia (a part of the former Yugoslavia) has won all three stages. He is an excellent runner — very good, very tough mentally, and very tough physically. Before today I thought he was invincible. Today I think there's a possibility of catching him. He is a faster runner than me, with more leg speed. Who knows? It's a long way to NYC and maybe neither one of us will win, but I think it may be one of us. I just hope I make it for sure. Anything else would be gravy. I know today was the first day I felt like I was getting somewhere. I felt like I was making progress and getting in shape a little bit. I think there is hope now.

DAY 4 - JUNE 20 -BARSTOW, CA TO LUDLOW, CA - 52.9 MILES

With the temperature hovering around one hundred degrees and not a cloud in the sky, it made for a warm run. David reports that his wrap-around sunglasses, desert rat hat, and lots of Bullfrog™ sunscreen are real lifesavers. One of the runners had not been as careful and has some serious sun blistering.

At one point, out in the middle of the run at an abandoned shack, the runners were greeted by the locals, including two teenage "beauty queens" who were graciously providing refreshments. Other than that, the run was straight and flat with nothing but sand and sagebrush.

Dusan and Patrick won this stage in 7:17:26. David was next in with a time of 7:22:39. Overall, the standings are as follows for the first five runners: Dusan Mravlje 26:34:25, David Horton +43:13, Manfred Leismann +2:58:21, Patrick Farmer +3:26:13, Ed Kelley +4:08:06.

Real desert... unbelievably long stretches (probably 12-15 miles long) with absolutely no curves and extremely flat. No shade.... I checked my time at the fifty-mile mark and it was 6:58:01. This pace was entirely too fast. Toward the end I started getting tired. Dusan and Patrick pulled away. I thought they were going to blow me away, but in the end they didn't. There was only a five-minute difference.

From the mailbox:
> Sometimes you must feel like Moses in the desert —
> just you and God. Of course, God led Moses into the desert
> for a specific purpose. And perhaps He has led you into this
> race so He can have some time with you apart from the
> distractions of the world. Sometimes God wants our com-
> plete attention so He can freely communicate with us and
> teach us valuable lessons. What better place for that than
> where you are now.
>
> ~Colson and Madelyn Richey

DAY 5 - JUNE 21 - LUDLOW, CA TO AMBOY, CA - 28.5 MILES

Today's stage was significant for a number of reasons. First, this was the first full day of desert running. In fact, temperatures in Ludlow have traditionally been the hottest on the entire course. Starting at 5:00 a.m., however, allowed the front runners to be finished before 9:00 a.m. when the temperature was a cool ninety-five degrees. The temperature throughout the day was projected to be in the 110-degree range. Secondly, each stage so far has been run in record time — and today was no exception. Ray Bell, the 1993 Trans-Am winner, won this stage with the record pace of 7:26 per mile. Some of the middle miles were run at close to a six-minute pace. Keep in mind that this is after 188 miles in the previous four days! His finishing time was 3:33:03. Dusan Mravlje and Patrick Farmer tied with 3:36:49 and David Horton was fourth, clocking a 3:44:18.

Overall standings are as follows: Mravlje 30:01:24, Horton +50:42, Farmer +3:26:13, Leismann +4:09:38, Kelley +5:09:42, and Bell +5:34:25.

Incidentally, Amboy is a town with no running water (it has to be brought in by train), with a population of twenty. It has a post office, but no store. There is an elementary school that services six students from the surrounding fifty miles. The sole teacher has a sixty-five-mile one-way commute just to get to Amboy. (High school kids get bussed seventy-five miles one way to school). The

119

runners are staying in one of two classrooms in the school, which do have air-conditioning. David reports that he is not quite sure why anyone would want to live in Amboy, but all the racers and crews are very appreciative for this small respite from the hot desert sun.

Competition is unbelievable. Patrick moved into 3rd place overall. Right now I think it's a four-man race: Dusan, Patrick, Ray, and myself. If Dusan doesn't get hurt, I'm sure he'll win. He is the most talented runner here, without a doubt. However, the most talented runner doesn't always win.

DAY 6 - JUNE 22 - AMBOY, CA TO KELSO, CA - 39.5 MILES

When we talked to David, his first statement was really a question: "How hard are rocks?" After the appropriate "huh?!?" from our end, he said that some rocks are harder than others, but all are hard. (Profound, isn't it?) His point was that all these miles are hard, but some are harder than others. Today's temperature was in the 100-105 degree range, and after the first five miles there was a steady climb for the next twenty miles. He said that mentally he had a pretty tough time going up. It was particularly disheartening when Dusan and Patrick pulled away from David and Ray, and then Ray subsequently left David on the climb. But he kept on plugging and eventually got to the top. The last fifteen miles were basically downhill, and Horton was able to pick up a minute to tighten the gap. However, even the downhill was tough, because the finish line could be seen from about twelve miles away, and it seemed like you were never going to get there. The stage ended with Dusan and Patrick crossing together in 5:33:09, Ray in at 5:40:00 and David ending with 5:50:02. David does remain in a strong second place overall. Dusan set a sixth straight stage record and told the race director that for $1 per stage, he would set records in all the remaining stages as well! David says he is a superbly talented athlete!

The finish of the race was in Kelso, but since there is nothing but a closed train station and about fifteen residents, the runners had to be bussed into Baker, California, for lodging. However, the operative word here is "lodging." Real lodging with beds, air conditioning, and showers. The only down side is that it will be an earlier-than-normal morning in order to get back to the start in Kelso. But I'll bet traffic won't be a concern!

After tomorrow, I have one week in with eight more to go.... Saw two crows and one lizard today. Real barren desert.

I had a phone interview this morning on Spirit FM.... Barry asked me what the highlight of the trip was so far, but I couldn't answer him. There haven't been lots of outstanding moments yet — not anything earth-shattering. It has sort of just been a run.... I'm sure I'll have great days, and I know I'll have days that will be much harder. I'll just have to be thankful for both the good and bad. The Lord is in them all.

DAY 7 - JUNE 23, KELSO, CA TO STATE LINE, CA - 49.5 MILES

Today was another "hard rock" day. The temperature was high (106 degrees at the finish), with not a cloud in the sky. The route actually had to be changed at the last minute because permission to run across a dry lake bed was denied for ecological reasons. The runners were not particularly happy to be running the resultant extra two or three miles, but what can you do? The first twenty-two miles were a steady, gradual climb (like yesterday), but with a headwind to make things a little more challenging. Dusan, Patrick, Ray and David started out running together, dropping Ray at about five miles. It was David, Patrick, and Dusan until about twenty-four miles when David's hamstrings started getting a little

Mojave Desert.

tight. However, with the next twelve downhill miles, David got within sight of the leaders. Unfortunately, the leaders caught sight of David and took off, finishing together in 6:59:49. David was only 4:54 minutes behind, clocking in at 7:04:43, and Ray was fourth in 7:51:14. Overall, Dusan is first at 42:34:22, David is second at +1:12:29, and Patrick is third at +3:26:13.

David is pleased that they have now covered 305.15 miles and passed through one entire state. He feels that he is finally getting somewhere. The tendonitis in his right shin has been treated very aggressively with icing and massage and is now barely noticeable. His hamstrings are getting sore, but hopefully the massage will take care of this problem as well.

Just finished one week and one state. We now have 305.1 miles under our belts.... An article came out today in the Wall Street Journal *about the Trans-Am. It was a very good article. I'm very pleased with the publicity.*

This thing I do is hard! I'm now a little over ten percent finished. The Lord willing, I'll make it.

For four days in a row, Patrick has gained a little bit on me. Hope he doesn't gain much more... but he may.

From the mailbox:

"From the moment you begin until the moment you finish you are committed to an indivisible problem whose only solution is constant and unrelenting effort." (Source unknown.)

But, your commitment is only one day, one mile, one step at a time.

~Rebekah Trittipoe

CHAPTER 13

Week 2 of the Trans-Am

Nothing in the world can take the place of persistence.
Talent will not; nothing is more common than unsuccessful men
with talent.... Persistence and determination alone are omnipotent.
- Calvin Coolidge

DAY 8 - JUNE 24 - STATELINE, NV TO LAS VEGAS, NV - 35.5 MILES
Today's stage was overshadowed by some bad news. The state
police came to find Regis and Diana to tell them there was an emergency at home. Unfortunately, Diana learned that her father died
yesterday of a heart attack. They have decided that Diana will fly
home while Regis stays with the race. She will rejoin David and
Regis sometime at the end of next week in Utah. Please pray that
the family will feel God's grace in this very difficult time.

The stage today was again very hot, with the first twenty miles
being uphill and into a headwind. (The runners were actually running on interstate with the trucks for the first third of the stage.)
This time, a pack of five, including Mravlje, Horton, Farmer, Bell,
and Koyago, ran together early on. The group dissolved, however,
as time went on. On the way up (gradual enough to force Horton
to run and not walk at all for the second day in a row), everyone but
Horton decided to pick up the pace. David said that while it was
difficult not to go along, he feels he is running the kind of pace that
will allow him to continue to get stronger rather than breaking him
down. Nevertheless, David did catch and pass Koyago and continued to make up ground on the front runners. According to Regis,
Dusan and Patrick had passed Ray and were running a steady pace.
But, when they looked back and saw David within two minutes of
them, they took off and virtually sprinted the last 1.5 miles to the
finish. David said he could have caught them, but he felt the price
he would have had to pay was too high. So, Dusan and Patrick
finished in 4:45:55, Ray in 4:47:04, and David in 4:50:40. Overall, Mravlje (Slovenia) remains the leader at 47:20:17 with Horton
firmly in second at +1:17:14. Farmer (Australia) maintains the third

124

position (+3:26:13) with Bell (USA) in fourth (+6:34:31). Kelley (USA), Leismann (GER), and Koyago (JAP) follow for fifth through seventh place.

We asked David if he has had a chance to talk with Dusan about his training. Although this information came second-hand, it is reported that Dusan has been training for the Trans-Am for the last two years, basically running twenty-five miles a day. I guess this would explain his strong showing so far in the race!

Somewhere around thirty-two miles I noticed that Ray Bell's wife was crewing for me, as was Denise Jones. I thought it was strange that Diana wasn't helping. When I crossed the finish line, Ben Jones told me that Diana's father had a heart attack yesterday morning at 9:30 a.m. This news put a pale cast over all we were doing in terms of the significance of the race and the significance of life.

Overall, today was an easy day. I ran the whole way. The bad thing was that I didn't urinate at all. Not at all. Yesterday, I didn't much, but today — nothing. I drank quite a bit, but I guess it wasn't enough. I'll have to force fluids tomorrow.

DAY 9 - JUNE 25 - LAS VEGAS, NV TO MOAPA, NV - 55.05 MILES

Talking with David last night, he said the mood at the nightly race briefing was very somber. The death of Diana's father saddened everyone, and the race directors emphasized the difficulty of today's stage. They told the racers that although the first day is tough mentally, the hardest day of the entire race is day nine. Fifty-five miles through desert, running in the heat of the day, and having the last twenty-six miles on interstate were all contributing factors for their comments. David called before he began this morning to say, "Please pray. I'm scared." Well, people did pray, and David ran very well. He stated that while fifty-five miles are never easy, this day was actually the easiest day for him yet! Prayers were answered!

Like the last several days, the first twenty-two miles were uphill and into a headwind. In general, David, Dusan, Patrick, and Ray were together early on, with Ray taking off after several miles. However, the other three caught Ray at about sixteen to eighteen miles, and the foursome ran together the rest of the way, having good

125

discussions between themselves. The rest of the miles were long, five- to six-mile rolling hills. The interstate had just been repaved, and the blacktop was very hot and sticky. Apparently Ray and Patrick did not feel very strong, and it was difficult to assess how Dusan really felt. But David felt strong and was tickled when Dusan stated at about fifty miles: "David, how about we not race today? We will all just run in together." David was happy to agree to the plan, but felt that he could have raced it in if he had to. Now that the day is over, David is feeling relieved and physically, very good.

The lodging for tonight was a very small recreation hall, and supper was to be prepared by the Moose Lodge members in the town. There actually is a restaurant in town that has a phone in every booth. (David thought that was pretty neat!) Anyway, David was thankful that he could sit and talk while he was drinking milkshakes. What a life!

David's time — 8:44.

I was scared to death about this stage. I called Nancy this morning and broke down. I was really, really concerned and apprehensive. I wanted to make sure the Sunday School class was praying for me.

This is the first time I've won part of a stage. All four of us finished together. I'm pleased with the time. I felt I could have run faster — and several times thought about it — but I didn't want to race. No one did. Basically, all we were thinking about was survival, but I think tomorrow will be different.

DAY 10 - JUNE 26 - MOAPA, NV TO MESQUITE, NV - 36.5 MILES (CUMULATIVE MILES - 432.2)

In David's own words, "This is a race. This is not fun! Every day is hard!" The stage started with twenty-two miles of interstate on Route 15. The first four miles included one thousand feet of climb, and although David was running eight-minute miles, Dusan, Patrick, and Ray took off and left him. So what's a runner to do?! Keep on running! (He walked a grand total of about thirty yards today.) By mile twenty-six he closed within 3.5 minutes of the leaders but then fell into a physical and mental slump. Understandably, this was not the first time and it won't be the last. But as scripture states, "And it came to pass..." - and it did. With 3.5 miles to go, David picked up the pace and brought the stage to a strong finish. Keep praying for David! It is really an encouragement for him to mentally recall all those who said they would pray for him and to actually feel their prayers being answered. Dusan and Patrick were in at 4:55:51, Ray at 4:58:34, David at 5:05:09 and Ed at 6:10:55.

The scenery today was desert, interrupted only by one house and one hawk. The temperature was ninety-five degrees at the end but rose to 110 degrees by early afternoon. David says he has yet to feel hot. The heat is very dry, and with all the sponging, drinking, ice in the hat, and water poured over him, he has not been terribly uncomfortable during the run. He wears plenty of Bullfrog™ SPF35 and has not been bothered by sunburn. (However, his tan does continue to deepen! What a sun stud!) Daylight hit early this morning because they are very near the end of Pacific Time. In fact, during the run tomorrow, they cross time zones, but they will go by Pacific Time all day tomorrow so that no one gets confused. All the runners are looking forward to the next day when they will be on Mountain Time and therefore have more of the stage shrouded in darkness.

The following is a list of the thirteen runners, cumulative times, and time deficit to the leader.

RUNNER	COUNTRY	TIME	DEFICIT
1. Dusan Mravlje	Slovenia	61:00:15	———
2. David Horton	USA	62:29:47	+1:29:32
3. Pat Farmer	Australia	64:26:28	+3:26:13
4. Ray Bell	USA	67:37:37	+6:37:22
5. Nobuaki Koyago	Japan	70:44:39	+13:44:24
6. Manfred Leismann	Germany	74:56:19	+13:56:04
7. Ed Kelley	USA	78:28:09	+17:27:54
8. Eiko Endo (woman)	Japan	86:55:55	+25:55:40
9. Mike Sandlin	USA	87:00:33	+26:18:00
10. Jun Onoki	Japan	91:29:32	+30:29:17
11. Michiyoshi Kaiho	Japan	94:40:06	+33:39:51
12. Kiyoto Nagata	Japan	96:23:13	+35:22:58
13. Don Winkley	USA	110:20:36	+49:20:21

(Note — On day two, one runner dropped out.)

Yesterday we didn't race, and I figured today would be different. It was.

Ray Bell was walking around tonight looking like he was limping. I heard Patrick's crew guy say that Patrick has blister problems. Those are signs of struggling. My right ankle is swollen up to a pretty good size. My right knee is also hurting a little. I'm concerned about both. My right shin is now in real good shape, and my hamstrings seem to be getting better. Tomorrow will be 47.9 miles followed by three successive days of fifty miles. It will be a tough four days.

DAY 11 - JUNE 27 - MESQUITE, NV TO ST. GEORGE, UT - 47.8 MILES

David has always told me there are good days and there are bad days. When he left, I reminded him of his own words. Today when he called he said, "Remember when you told me there would be good days and bad days? Well..." I responded, "How bad?" "Pretty bad," was the reply. There was a steady climb for the first nineteen miles and a BIG climb from nineteen to twenty-six miles. Six runners actually stayed together through nineteen miles, but the front runners started widening the gap up the steep mountain, leaving behind David and Manfred. David, having a hard time and not feeling well today, needed to walk some of the distance. A hamstring that was bothering him made this a tough stage physically and mentally. In fact "a real struggle" was his description of the day. However, if there was a bright side to the stage, it was the spectacular scenery once the summit was reached and the descent began. There were rolling hills, some grass, an inhabited town (as opposed to the few ghost towns in the desert), and some houses and people who actually live in them. Dusan finished in 6:51:30, Patrick in 6:52:58, Ray in 7:02:23, Manfred in 7:08:04, and David in 7:18:44.

Please pray for David. He was quite discouraged today with the way he felt and was very distraught with finishing in fifth place. He is also concerned that Patrick is closing the gap between second and third place. Your encouragement in prayer and letters to him is essential!

I knew there would be days like this.... My right ankle was hurting a little, my foot was hurting, my Achilles was hurting... but what was of most concern was my left hamstring. Shooting pains would go through it. I wasn't running well. It was very hard. Afterwards I was emotionally distraught when I called Nancy and Rebekah. Very down. I'm concerned about both my physical and emotional problems.

I guess I'll have to back off tomorrow. I pray that the Lord will direct me with respect to my problems — to help me know what I should do or shouldn't do in terms of pacing, drinking and eating, and injuries. If the Lord doesn't give me the strength and direction, I won't be able to make it. I know there are a lot of people praying for me. I appreciate that. I just hope they keep on praying.... I have to make it. I don't know how I would live with myself if I don't. I have to make it. This may just be the beginning of the struggle. I don't know.

DAY 12 - JUNE 28 - ST. GEORGE, UT TO CEDAR CITY, UT - 51.5 MILES

When David called, I was relieved when he said he was pleased with his overall performance. But that being said, he did have a really tough mental battle for the first thirty miles. Part of the reason for this is that they started off at an elevation of 2700 feet and ended at 5800 feet! This climb was on interstate, about seven miles in length, and into an extremely forceful headwind. David thought it was in his best interest to walk this big climb, although Dusan surged on as if he didn't even notice the "little hill." That can be pretty demoralizing. However, at the top of the pass David was treated to spectacular scenery that included a big lake off to the left and a wide-open green valley. Quite a switch from the desert doldrums! The runners were also treated to a significant flour message on the road: "500 miles." That's five hundred down, nearly 2500 to go. The temperature at stage end was a very pleasant eighty-five degrees, with little or no humidity. To cap off the day, David, the scavenger that he is, added a box of 22-caliber gun shells, his third knife of the race, a quarter, and several pennies to his Trans-Am treasure chest. (He finally admitted he didn't want to waste any time on the pennies so he left those for someone else.)

Today's results are as follows: Dusan 7:40:00, Patrick 8:06:13, Ray 8:06:13, and David 8:32:42. Overall, Dusan has tallied 75:31:45, with David at +2:47:29, Patrick at +3:53:48, and Ray at +7:09:54.

Mentally, the first 20-30 miles I felt really, really low until I got to the top of the mountain. One of the negative thoughts was that I didn't want to hurt like this for the rest of the summer. Then I found out that Patrick was really fried, and Dusan had run off and left him.

It was really encouraging to me that Nancy watched all of the tape that Diana and Regis had made and sent home, and she seemed to be really interested in it. I liked that. It meant a lot to me.... Looking forward to tomorrow because it's another mail drop day.

DAY 13 - JUNE 29 - CEDAR CITY, UT TO BEAVER, UT - 54.5 MILES (586.2 CUM. MILES)

The Trans-Am runners could definitely tell they had come through the desert this morning: it was a chilly fifty-three degrees at the start and only seventy-five degrees at the finish. Although the elevation was 5800 feet at the beginning, the course was basically flat with some rolling hills as they ran across the valley. There were no big climbs or descents. They were treated to views of mountains, green pastureland, grazing sheep, and irrigated farm fields. Sound idyllic? It probably would be if you didn't have to run close to fifty-five miles!

Keep in mind that David has broken the previous course record for thirteen of thirteen stages! Quite a feat. He ran faster today (8:26:26) than he did yesterday (8:32:42), even though it was three miles further. The running surface was blacktop at the beginning, some gravel road, six miles of interstate, and ten more miles of dirt road. He had Dusan, Patrick, and Ray all in sight until about twenty miles. David fell into a mental low for the middle part of the day as the front runners began to open the distance. He did, however, pick himself up later on to finish the stage in a great time. He ended up in fourth place for the stage, behind Patrick, Dusan (7:53:11), and Ray (7:59:14).

Encouraged by the absence of the physical aches and pains of the last week or so, David has a brighter outlook on the coming stages. He has even conceded that the hamstring and Achilles tendon stretching he has started to do may even be helping! His feet have also gone back to normal, so he is again wearing size twelve shoes instead of the thirteens he was in across the desert. However, he reports that as hard as he tries, he feels emotionally disjointed. He cannot remember what it feels like to be a "normal" person going about a "normal" day. (I could say something, but that would be too easy!) Keep him in your prayers, that he would have the patience to relax, run his race, and not be adversely effected by the intense daily pressure of racing such outstanding runners from around the world.

Ran real well... kept the three guys in sight until 30-32 miles. Then I started to struggle a little, but had a long downhill into Beaver, finishing at the high school. I took a cold shower due to the lack of hot water. I'm sleeping in a hallway next to the coach's office.

Patrick will probably catch me tomorrow or the next day. The 60 Minute crew from Australia is coming in tomorrow, and I'm sure he'll want to do his best.

DAY 14 - JUNE 30 - BEAVER, UT TO MONROE, UT - 50.7 MILES

Four years ago today, David Horton finished his record-breaking 2144-mile Appalachian Trail Run in fifty-two days, nine hours, forty-one minutes. Today, David ran nearly fifty-one more miles in his quest to cross America on foot. His quotable quote for the day is, "This is not as much fun as I thought it would be, and it's a whole lot harder than I thought it would be." He explained that if it was just dealing with the miles it would be okay, but the racing (and the ego) adds another dimension to the task. Except for the one fifty-five-mile day (that was touted as being the most difficult of the entire race), David says there is at least one section every day that is extremely difficult and seemingly never-ending. Is he whining? No. He is just being truthful.

Today's temperatures were conducive to running: below fifty degrees at the start, with only seventy degrees as the high. The sun stayed hidden for the entire day. The course was diversified in terms of running surfaces with dirt and gravel roads, paved secondary roads, and interstate. The beauty of the area was spectacular, particularly several miles from the end. The runners were treated to the sight of a village nestled at the foot of huge snow-capped mountains. However, there was one point in the stage that the beauty wasn't appreciated as much because of the two thousand-foot climb in less than eight miles. (Elevation was 7000 feet at the top.) The extremely hard effort and the altitude are probably the reasons why Patrick became a bit sick today.

Dusan finished in 7:20:43, Patrick in 7:52:47, David in 8:28:25, and Manfred in 8:32:54. Dusan strengthened his lead overall, while Patrick slipped into second place over David by a mere four minutes and twenty-nine seconds. The outcome of the remaining fifty stages will really be interesting! Don't be distressed by this change of position. David is running with some restraint so that he will not pay the price of total fatigue later if he races too hard now.

David was tickled today when a car with a guy and a girl pulled up beside him as he was running. He was asked if he was running the Trans-Am. When David replied affirmatively, they simply said, "We read about you last week in *Ultrarunning*. Good luck." Then they sped off down the road.

Although he says he is really tired of forcing himself to eat so many calories and drink so much fluid (and pee and pee, naturally), and ice himself down, he is in high spirits tonight. He has a good attitude about the remaining stages and is beginning to regain the confidence of finishing.

Two weeks finished and seven more to go. Seems like an eternity ago that I started. Seems like I've been doing this all of my life. Even as little as three days ago I wasn't sure if I could make it. Now, with the Lord's help, I think I can make it. I can envision spending time out here... before I couldn't. But again, it's with the Lord's help.

Today I lost second place to Patrick. There is no way to catch Dusan unless something happens to him. I know that. I think it's starting to sink into Patrick. But tomorrow he will probably go out like gangbusters.

I do feel lonely. I miss the family life. Basically, we are living like nomads out here. We go from one place to another, sleeping in a different place every night.

A mother's "wish list" sent to her son:
1. To finish the race
2. Do good (Satisfied with any place - Of course, first would be good)
3. To be in good condition — I know there will be some effects on it
4. To make it safely home
5. To never do this again
6. Get some rest
Hope this isn't asking too much.

~Lois Horton

CHAPTER 14

Week 3 of the Trans-Am

Keep making forward progress.

- David Horton

DAY 15 - JULY 1 - MONROE, UT TO SALINA, UT - 28.55 MILES
So much for the high spirits of last night. For the first time in this year's Trans-Am, no one, including Dusan, broke the stage record today. David stated that of all the stages yet, he "hated" this one the most. The course was straight as an arrow, flat, and boring. He admitted that if he had been in a better mood, he might have noticed and appreciated the green farm country that surrounded him all the way through the valley. The constant running and pounding seemingly took its toll on all the runners. Although David was running with Dusan and Patrick at first, he took a little longer than usual at one of the aid stations and they got away. Actually, David was a little relieved for two reasons. First, he wanted to use today's shorter run to recuperate a little. Then, the *60 Minute* Australian film crew was filming all day, driving a truck right in front of Dusan and Patrick, complete with big, bright lights that were constantly focused on the runners. He really was content to stay out of the limelight for the time being.

Incidentally, one hundred yards from the finish, Dusan and Patrick were running step for step. Dusan queried Patrick with, "War or Peace?" Patrick boldly said, "War!" and they both took off in an all-out sprint. Dusan won by one second. Must have looked pretty good on camera, although Dusan later told David that he didn't like sprinting like that. He just accepted the challenge.

Today's results: Dusan 3:59:01, Patrick 3:59:02, Ray 4:00:44, Koyago 4:14:03, and David 4:17:32.

Overall standings are as follows: Dusan 94:44:40, Patrick +4:25:53, David +4:48:54, Ray +9:43:20.

Without the Lord's help, I can't do this. Mentally and physically, I need to get into this — I need to get my body together. I don't feel like I'm getting stronger now. In fact, I'm just holding on. This has been a very tough thing. I haven't been in good spirits or a good mood for several days. I feel sorry for Diana and Regis. They keep trying to cheer me up. It's hard to be cheered up when I'm out there and I'm hurting and in pain all the time.

I do miss home. Nancy says she misses me and would like me to be there. I told her I would like to be there. I know that things will probably get worse before they get better.

DAY 16 - JULY 2 - SALINA TO I-70/MEADOW GULCH REST AREA - 32.9 MILES - 698 CUMULATIVE MILES

David really suffered today. Although the stage was "only" 32.9 miles, miles three to thirty included a climb from 5200 feet to 8000 feet. For much of the distance David walked. He experienced intense stomach pain that virtually rendered him unable to run, regardless of the terrain. Additionally, his right ankle and foot are swollen and sore for some unknown reason. It is our hope that icing and keeping the foot elevated will cause some rapid improvement. Needless to say, David is really down. Any of us who know him realize that he is intensely competitive, and the fact that he seems to be moving backward in the standings rather than forward is a great concern to him. He feels "humiliated" (his word) by his sixth place performance today. Obviously, none of us look down on him for this rough time that he is going through. But it does emphasize how much we need to uphold him in prayer for both physical healing and strength as well as mental fortitude and encouragement.

Today's results: Patrick 5:01:57, Dusan 5:02:09, Ray 5:24:34, Koyago 5:47:54, Jun 5:58:58, David 6:14:40

Sixteen days down, 48 to go. One-fourth of the way through. Somewhere around mile three, my gut started really hurting. It finally dawned on me what it was. I'm sure it's all the Aleve™ I've been taking. I've been taking 7 a day when the normal dose is 2-4. I felt like my stomach was going to explode. My right foot was swollen. My right shin was swollen. It hurt to run, so I just walked and walked and ran just a little. Finally it got to where I was walking all the time. Mentally very tough.... I cried again after I finished.

Nancy misses me and wishes I were there. To be truthful with you, I wish I were too. I miss her. I miss sleeping with her and being with her. I miss a normal life.

DAY 17 - JULY 3 - MEADOW GULCH REST AREA TO I-70 EAGLE CANYON OVERLOOK - 29.5 MILES

This is the only day of the race that we will not have an opportunity to speak with David. The stage ends in the middle of nowhere (although the view is supposed to be awesome) at a rest area with no facilities or water. This will prove to be a "roughing it" night. I sure hope no one forgot anything, because they won't be able to run down to the corner market!

However, you might be interested that we had a chance to speak with David again last night after the daily report went out. It was a relief to hear him laugh and joke around with us. He had spent the afternoon keeping his ankle iced and elevated and watched golf on TV. A few good meals really seemed to help in the restoration process. So, while he is still hurting, he does not seem nearly as depressed.

A few other things that you might be interested in: Manfred Leismann, the German runner, apparently tore (at least partially) his Achilles' tendon on day fifteen. He is so tough that he walked every step of day sixteen because it was impossible for him to run. All these runners have great physical and mental stamina!

Also, you probably noticed that Patrick won yesterday by twelve seconds. You will also recall that the *60 Minute* film crew from Australia was still taping. After allowing Patrick to finish in front, Dusan joked, "My gift to you, Patrick — for TV. But no more!" Many a truth is said in jest.

We are pleased to announce that Eric Steele and Warren Bushey, of the newly-formed Kansas Ultrarunners' Society, have filled an unexpected hole in the crew schedule for three days in Kansas. They are now covering just about the whole state of Kansas. The guys deserve special thanks for going above and beyond the call of duty.

I hate to say this, but I thought about quitting today. I thought about how I could get back home and what I'd say to everyone. I

just kept asking myself if I wanted to keep hurting like this for the rest of the summer. It was embarrassing, running again so slowly. I finished another position back in 7th. Unless a miracle happens, it may get even worse tomorrow. Mentally, I'm very low. I'm feeling very sorry for myself, very homesick, very lonely.

I did a lot of praying today like I've never prayed before: "Lord, show me exactly what you'd have me to do in terms of the rest of the Trans-Am." I have to have God's direction — I really believe that— whether to stay in, about my running, about my pace, about my attitude. I really need help in that area. It's difficult running when you see these old people running around town, barely shuffling, barely moving. That's the way I look. It's very embarrassing to me. I guess it's a pride thing. Maybe the Lord is trying to teach me something. I have to be patient.

DAY 18 - JULY 4 - I-70 EAGLE CANYON REST AREA, UT TO GREEN RIVER, UT - 44.95 MILES - 772.85 CUMULATIVE MILES

First of all, the report from yesterday was not so good. David experienced lots of pain (stomach, Achilles, hamstrings, tendonitis in his right shin) and came in seventh place. He said he was really struggling all day. Patrick and Dusan were first in 4:09:31, Ray in 4:16:43, Koyago next in 4:25:16, Manfred in 4:34:55, Jun in 4:59:27, and David in 5:24:08.

Today was equally a struggle. He did not rest well last night because they were camping out and he had a really hard time getting comfortable with all his aches and pains. You can imagine how bad you would feel if you were not able to get a shower after a hard run! He said that the campsite was on the rim of a canyon and was really spectacular, although he did not feel up to enjoying its full value. The elevation was 7100 feet and the temperature at the start was a chilly forty-five degrees. The stage was run on interstate except for one and one-half miles at the beginning. There were several good climbs, and the last ten miles presented a drop of three thousand feet. David reports he felt like an old "grandma" trying to run: a "shell of a runner that I once was." He had perhaps his greatest mental struggle yet. But he had prayed that if the Lord wanted him to continue, He would have to make it clear to him in terms of something improving. As an example of the faithfulness and graciousness of God, the intense pain in his stomach almost completely went away and his hamstrings did not hurt quite so much. He now feels he needs to continue on even though he still has some significant injuries to overcome. It is very difficult for him to have other runners that are probably not of the same caliber run stronger. This race is definitely as much of a mental contest as it is a physical contest. We are trying to convince him to hang tough — it can only get better!

Results: Dusan 6:10:59, Patrick 6:11:03, Ray 6:27:53, Manfred 6:40:54, Koyago 7:03:34, Jun 7:37:19, David and Mike Sandlin 7:44:37.

Overall: Dusan 110:07:19, Patrick +4:25:45, David +8:49:42, Ray +10:30:51, Koyago +22:45:26, Manfred +23:36:46.

I struggled early today. Last night I had prayed that the Lord would give me a sign as to what to do: whether to stop or keep going. I did decide to quit, but I planned to go ahead to the finish line. I kept going, and as usual, people kept passing me. Then we got to some big downhills and I thought my Achilles' tendon was going to rip. I kept walking/running, and finally I began to feel a little better...

Talked to my mother today. She said she has confidence in me. My wife says she has confidence in me. Rebekah told me that she would come out here and kick me if I quit. So basically, everyone expects me to go on regardless of how slow I go. I will go on. The Lord willing, I will make it.

Diana and Regis have done a great job. Just three more days and then they'll be leaving me. In their place will be crews that change every couple of days. Hopefully, this is the turning point in the race for me. I think it is.

DAY 19 - JULY 5 - GREEN RIVER, UT TO CISCO, UT - 47.9 MILES

What a relief to talk to David today! He seems to be a different person compared to the last several days. David's mental attitude has definitely improved, and he seems to be his "old self" again. And he ran pretty well! The stage was long and boring as it went through desert-type terrain again. After six miles of inter-state, they turned onto some obscure road and came across a tiny little town at twenty miles. At twenty-six miles, they went through a crossroads where there were just a few houses. Between twenty-six and forty miles there was nothing, absolutely nothing. No people, no houses, no trees — just nothing.

The stage ended at Cisco, a ghost town where each runner was allowed to pick any of the deserted buildings as their own personal abode. David's crew picked a building with a cross on it, perhaps a church of yesteryear. This architectural wonder featured see-through log walls, a "holy" roof (pun intended), rough boards on only one-half of the area that was intended to be floor, and furbished with many evidences of rodent habitation. It was really quite lovely! Apparently, the other buildings were similarly fashioned. But the weird thing was that there was a pygmy one-room post office that was open on "M-W-F from 10-12 a.m." No one could figure out who used the thing since the population of Cisco is "0." Go figure. Anyway, he was at least excited to see two live things: a snake and an antelope.

David's stomach problems seem to be a thing of the past, and his hamstrings are much better. He is a bit concerned, however, with his left Achilles. The first eight to ten miles of each day is pretty painful, but this

Not exactly the greatest shower facilities, but the best that could be found in the ghost town of Cisco, Utah.

pain decreases as he continues. Lots of ice after the run is the treatment of choice at this time. Although he came in sixth, he felt pretty good about the way he ran. I have a feeling things will be turning around in the near future.

Today's results: Dusan 6:54:18, Patrick 6:54:19, Koyago 7:01:11, Ray 7:03:04, Manfred 7:17:29, and David 7:58:36.

Incidentally, all the runners were treated to massages from professional massage therapists. Two ultrarunners from Salt Lake City read about the Trans-Am in *Ultrarunning* and decided to make their way to Cisco to give free massages. You better believe it was much appreciated.

My attitude was good today. I thank the Lord for that. Again, last night, I asked the Lord for a sign. That's when the Lord took over, and I thank him for that. I could feel all the prayers from the people who have daily prayed for me. The Lord does answer prayer!

Today was a mail drop day. I received 14 letters. That was very humbling. I especially enjoyed a letter from Madelyn and Colson. I really enjoy getting mail. It means a whole lot to me.

From the mailbox:

Words can't express how proud we are of you. We know the race has been very trying and challenging. But you are a dreamer. Not only a dreamer, but a person who is willing to pursue his dream until it becomes a reality. Every worthwhile accomplishment begins with a dream: whether it be the building of a nation, becoming a godly husband and father, or the running of a race. Thomas Carlyle once said, "Conviction is worthless unless it is translated into conduct." And so, you must keep dreaming. There are many kinds of races in this life and each begins with a dream. With God's help we will finish our races. Remember, carry the dream!

"But my God shall supply all your needs according to his riches in glory by Christ Jesus." Phil. 4:19

~Colson and Madelyn Richey

DAY 20 - JULY 6 - CISCO, UT TO FRUITA, CO - 44.15 MILES (864.9 CUM.)

Today's stage started in never-never land and ended in a little town in a green valley in a different state. The course covered about five miles of desert, thirteen miles on I-70, and about twenty-five miles on old Route 6. They saw a total of two cars on this whole stretch. The temperature at the start was cool (in the fifties) but reached a fairly humid ninety-six degrees by stage end. But the runners were looking forward to dinnertime. The town of Fruita is sponsoring an old-fashioned town barbecue this evening in honor of the Trans-Am runners. This will be the first of this type event for the runners.

You'll be interested to know that David has been adding to his collection of treasures over the last several days. He gained possession of another seventeen pennies, pliers, a socket, an electronic poker game (that Diana might not give back), and a hard hat. Can you picture David running down the road in a hard hat? Well, maybe that would not surprise you who know him!?!

Dusan and Patrick played the "war or peace" game again today. This time Patrick's response was, "You know I can't come in holding your hand every day. I've got to race. I've got to make an effort." He did. He lost by less than a second.

David stated he was "mentally fine" and it's now a matter of his body holding together. I think he was really excited to be back in the top four even though he still has some physical healing to go!

Today's results: Dusan 6:45:19, Patrick 6:45:19, Ray 6:45:20, David 7:14:51, Koyago 7:29:54

Overall: Dusan 123:46:56, Patrick +4:25:46, David +10:26:32, Ray +10:39:38, Koyago +23:36:54.

Day 20. Forty-four to go. Crossed another state.

DAY 21 - JULY 7 - FRUITA, CO TO PARACHUTE, CO - 56.35 MILES

The Trans-Am runners started out today as they do everyday: a light breakfast provided by the race organizers (continental) and a few, very few, sleepy "good-mornings." No one was looking forward to this extremely long and difficult stage. But with the sound of the buzzer, they started out for the first six miles on secondary roads. Then, it was fifteen straight miles through the heart of Grand Junction, Colorado. The runners were supposed to stay on the sidewalk at all times. This became increasingly aggravating, because at every block there was a step down onto the road and then back up onto the sidewalk. Can you imagine how many of these little up-downs there are in fifteen miles? And then throw in all the dips in the sidewalk for driveways and parking lots. Now, we aren't suggesting that David ever grew weary of this routine, but there is a slim possibility that he may have run a few paces on the road. Then, once out of town it was eighteen miles through DeBeque Canyon on I-70, complete with very narrow shoulders and very fast cars. The runners were all glad to have a reprieve from all of that by running the last miles on a less-traveled paved road. The day proved to be the hottest day yet for the area, with the stage-end temperature hovering around ninety-eight degrees.

Except for the beginning of the stage when David's Achilles hadn't yet loosened up, David reports that physically he feels okay. This is not to say that the Achilles, knee, and shin tendonitis are all gone, but he was able to run at a decent pace. The last three days he has been running a little faster than ten-minute miles. Now, that may seem slow, but consider that he has basically run an average of two marathons per day for the last three weeks! A tiny sombrero, two dimes, two quarters, and a fourth knife were all added to the "Adventureland coffers." Although he ended the stage in fourth place today (his highest in awhile), he is feeling lonely and homesick. However, the spaghetti dinner given in the runners' honor by the local United Methodist Church helped take off the edge just a little bit.

Today's results: Dusan 8:10:42, Ray 8:26:32, Koyago 8:55:01, David 9:16:04.

Overall: Dusan 131:57:38, Patrick 136:23:24, Ray 142:53:06, David 143:29:32, and Koyago 156:18:51. (Note: David slipped from third to fourth place overall.)

Day 21. Forty-three to go. That's all I've got to say.

CHAPTER 15

Week 4 of the Trans-Am

*The fishermen have always known that
the sea is dangerous and the storm is terrible.
But they never considered those sufficient reasons to remain ashore.*

- Vincent VanGogh

DAY 22 - JULY 8 - PARACHUTE, CO TO GLENWOOD SPRINGS, CO - 40.3 MILES

As of late, the stages usually start out with Dusan, Patrick, Ray, and Koyago running as the lead pack. However, at four miles everyone was surprised to see Koyago take off. The group responded, but it wasn't too long before Patrick dropped off from the pace, followed by Ray. Therefore, it was Dusan and Koyago until about thirty-two miles when Dusan apparently felt the need to take it to the line in solo fashion. And he did.

The stage was relatively flat, gaining only seven hundred feet over the entire distance. The course scenery was very bland for the first thirty miles, following along the Colorado River. Miles thirty-two to thirty-five were much better, with beautiful canyons to view. But the bubble burst when the run concluded with five more miles on I-70. But at least another stage ended.

Personally, David reports that his tendonitis and Achilles problems remain about the same. He says he really hobbles along early on because it takes so long for things to loosen up. However, after about eight to ten miles, his running form is normal and smooth. It is only after the stage that things look swollen and tight once again. Of course, David continues to ice anything and everything that he can get in a bucket!

They say that parting is such sweet sorrow. David isn't so sure it's all that sweet. Regis and Diana left today after spending three weeks tending to all of David's needs. They video taped him at about twelve miles as he crossed the fifteen hundred km mark. David said the emotions were really hard to control as he ran past, knowing that they would not be there at the finish again. There is no one who appreciated all their hard work, patience, and love more than David. They saw him through thick and thin and were ever ready (yes, like the batteries) to make things as comfortable as they could for him. Their organization and efficiency were superb. Thanks so much for a job well done!

But never fear, David is not without a crew. Alan Thomason, an ex-Lynchburger transplanted to Colorado, was with David today and will be staying through tomorrow. David says he has picked up on things and is doing a great job.

David is pleased with his run today. He reports the usual middle-of-the stage "I feel like a jogger" slump but otherwise was happy with how he felt. He seems to be learning to be content (to some degree!) with running according to how his body feels. Gary and I both sense that he is seeing the light at the end of the tunnel, believing himself to be on the mend and running stronger. (Hopefully, the light in the tunnel isn't a train!) He knows he did not run poorly for his sixth place finish; the other five runners just ran faster.

Today's results: Dusan 5:30:46, Koyago 5:41:28, Patrick 5:46:17, Ray 6:02:33, Manfred 6:16:08, and David 6:28:44.

Seems like I've been here forever.... I just pray that the Lord will give me the strength to hold my mind and body together. There are some good experiences here, and I'm sure I will appreciate them later. But right now, it's difficult.... I will be glad when this is all over. I feel sorry for Nancy being home alone. I miss her ... I miss a normal life.

DAY 23 - JULY 9 - GLENWOOD SPRINGS, CO TO AVON, CO - RE-ROUTED MILES - 36.9 MILES (998.25 CUM)

What an interesting day! The route was to use seventeen miles of bike path, a welcome relief from pounding the pavement of interstate. However, record snows this year (including eight inches last weekend) contributed to the entire path being under water. The authorities obviously disallowed the race to enter the area, but they also denied access to the closest section of interstate that would join with the rest of the stage. Therefore, the runners were actually transported seventeen miles down the road to begin where they would have exited the bike path. The run was thus cut from fifty-four miles to 36.9 miles. The elevation was six thousand feet at the start and 7400 feet at the end. The scenery was better today, with fifteen miles along the Eagle River and the rest winding through a canyon. Fifty degrees was the starting temperature, with the mercury hitting seventy-five degrees at the end.

As usual, Dusan, Patrick, Ray, and Koyago took off together at the start. David was surprised to see and pass Patrick at three miles, the latter obviously having trouble. David went on by and ran pretty well except for that nagging low midpoint. He said he actually enjoyed the last half of the run. His knee even stopped hurting from mile twenty to mile twenty-eight!

It was a relief to hear him actually say that he is "excited now — things are coming around." His spirits are so much better than before! He was again content with his time of 5:42:17 for a fifth place finish. Dusan ran a 7:59 pace today, but David is simply not healed enough yet to push the issue. And as it turns out, Patrick may not be pushing much of anything for awhile. It is believed that Patrick's foot or ankle may have a stress fracture. He is in tremendous pain. Obviously, no one wants this to happen to any of the runners. David is sure he will show up at the start, but it is unclear whether he will be able to continue and make the cutoffs each day. This is the worst time it could have happened, given that the next two days involve tremendous climbs taking them over ten thousand and eleven thousand feet. We would ask for you to pray especially for Patrick. What a tremendous disappointment if he were not able to continue.

Two massage therapists from Vail provided massages for the runners today. David's crew also changed to Cliff Moore and Howard Scott, both runners from Colorado. They will be with him tonight and tomorrow. Thanks, guys!

Today's results: Dusan 4:54:33, Ray 5:09:45, Koyago 5:17:30, Manfred 5:26:37, David 5:42:17. (Patrick - 11th place - 8:13:31!)

Mentally, I'm up right now. Physically, I think I'm recovering. Ran very well today. Pleased with my effort.... Patrick may have a stress fracture. I hope that's not the case. I'd like to beat him, but I'd hate for this to happen to him or anyone else.

The crew's view:

Why? The constant question to these lacerated and limping roadsters was, "Why?" Why do it? Why try this impossible test? Why come up with over $1000.00 as an entry fee, plus several thousand of support and sustenance costs? A big prize? No. The winner gets a plaque. Second place earns a plaque. For that matter, every finisher gets a plaque. Not for reward. Not for fame. The 64 days are not televised. No camera truck leads the runner, no commentators gab for a watching bevy of couch potatoes. No crowds line the long, tortured miles where runners pound along, alone with implacable pain. Deep, debilitating doubts, eversorer muscles, screaming knees, labored breathing, and sunscorched eyes in pursuit of an impossible dream…. Home comfort, friends are far away; every fiber and cell calls for stopping, but a supreme and centered will says, "Move on." And so Dave and his fellow runners found the will to move on, painful step by grinding step. Each ascending stride more painful than the one before, moving the depleted body up the exacting grade, moving the wracked body a bit closer to the day's goal and to the distant, unreachable finish line.

~Howard Scott

DAY 24 - JULY 10 - AVON, CO TO FRISCO, CO - 37.9 MILES

In David's words, "Today was a great day!" What a difference a week can make! The day started with a chilly and windy forty-five degrees. He reports that it only took one and one-half miles to get loosened up and begin running smoothly. The stage had them running on I-70 for four to five miles until they hopped on a paved bike path that led the runners through spectacular country. The elevation at the beginning was 7100 feet, but the bike path passed through Vail Pass at 10,466 feet. The majestic peaks, with snow on the highest mountaintops, were quite an impressive sight. (Let me point out that this is the first day in many that David has even noticed the scenery. His attitude and outlook is

180 degrees from what it was last week. Thank goodness! It was getting pretty depressing!) Anyway, the descent went right through the Cooper Mountain ski area and followed the path of a rushing stream. David said there were at least a hundred bikers on the path, but no runners. I suggested that perhaps this is why they call it a "bike path"! (Duh!) The stage ended in Frisco with a temperature of seventy degrees, no humidity, and gorgeous surroundings. David was very pleased with the way he ran, since the pace was quicker today (even with a huge climb) than in the last week and a half. He added three pennies, three dimes, and a wire stripper to his collection on this very significant day as he passed the one thousand-mile mark!

Anne Huntzicker (from Breckenridge) is to be thanked for arranging an hour and twenty minute professional massage for David. No wonder he feels good! Additionally, she gave him a gift certificate to a restaurant and some great cookies and bagels. He also reports that he received at least twenty pieces of mail and some wonderful boxes of Power™ bars, cookies, candies, nuts, and Skor™ bars. This really means a lot, so keep the mail flowing!

And for an update on Patrick: It is still unclear whether his foot is actually fractured. He is really suffering! In today's stage that took Dusan 5:43 to complete, it took Patrick 9:50:12. But what a gentleman! Don Winkley, who is soundly in last place, told Patrick that if he happened to be with him as they passed the one thousand-mile mark, it would be a huge honor to have their picture taken together. Patrick said this would be fine, but unfortunately the camera crews were not ready when they crossed over that marking. About a third of a mile later they looked back to see the crews arrive. As hard as it was for Patrick to walk, he told Don that they should turn around and go back so he could get the picture. That is true sportsmanship, and Don got his coveted snapshot! Continue to ask for patience and rapid healing for Patrick in your prayers.

Today's results: Dusan 5:43:38, Manfred 5:54:31, Ray 5:58:47, David 6:18:58, Koyago 6:53:21.

Spectacular scenery. I've enjoyed this stage more than any other so far.... Snow-capped mountains.... Could smell the firs.... Patrick

From the mailbox:

Personally, I think you should focus now on the metaphysical aspects of your effort. You are accomplishing something grand and epic. I know from the inside the event does not seem romantic — just long, painful, and tedious — but it is these characteristics that enable you to transcend any mundanity. Instead of dissociating, focus on the pain and discomfort; revel in it. The suffering you endure determines the quality of the life experience and your character. You enter the gauntlet of your own choosing and you will emerge, for better or worse, a changed man. Life is to be lived and you are on the starting line every day. Do not be content to be a spectator.

~Eric Clifton

finished last today. I'm really concerned. Ray took over second place. If Patrick continues to do poorly, I should take over third place tomorrow. I really feel for him. I will be praying for him to recover. I think he raced too hard there for awhile…. Emotionally and physically I feel like I'm coming along…. Just have to be careful.

Day 25 - July 11 - Frisco, CO to Georgetown, CO - 34.9 miles

Today was another beautiful day — in more ways than one. The thirteen runners began the stage in the cool (forty-five degrees) and clear early morning. Half of the perimeter of Lake Dillon served as the eight-mile warm-up for the rest of the day. At an elevation of 7900 feet for those first scenic miles, they began a gradual climb past Keystone ski area for the next two miles. Then things became interesting as they climbed from mile ten to mile nineteen. They passed by the Arapahoe Basin, where it snowed only last week, providing great skiing for the July Fourth holiday! The summit of the climb brought them to 11,990 feet, the Continental Divide. (It probably won't surprise you that David climbed a big snow bank just to say he was at 12,000 feet. What a Kodak

David climbs to stand atop the Continental Divide.

moment!) Ray and Dusan, animals that they are, ran the whole climb, while David used the more civilized mode of locomotion — walking. Manfred Leismann passed him running up the mountain, encouraged by David's hearty, "Go get 'em!" But after a few miles David managed to pass a walking — and very tired — Manfred. The six-mile descent down Route 6 and past the Loveland ski area was very steep and pounding. Once on I-70, the route continued downhill into Georgetown. The temperature at the end was a warm and sunny eighty degrees. David had a good day, finishing third to Dusan and Ray.

It wasn't such a good day for others. Patrick continued to struggle, finishing in eight hours and forty-two minutes. Mike Sandlin of Texas decided to throw in the towel at the base of the big climb. He said that he just could not deal with the pain in his ankle any longer. (Later x-rays revealed a stress fracture in his foot.) Ed Kelley finished the stage just five minutes over the cut-off time. Unfortunately, this now disqualifies him from the race. All the runners are very saddened by these two drops. So much time and energy was put into these past twenty-five days, not to mention all the preparation for the race in the first place. So the race now continues with just eleven runners heading east toward New York.

Today's results: Dusan 5:10:23, Ray 5:22:37, David 5:55:16, Koyago 5:59:41, Manfred 6:06:00.

I moved into third place today. Patrick finished 11th. Mike Sandlin dropped out at 10.25 miles. The reason he dropped was that he got tired of the severe ankle pain over the last couple of weeks. I was sad to hear that. He will speak to us tonight.... It was a very emotional meeting tonight. Ed Kelley missed the cut-off by five minutes.... It was very tough.

DAY 26 - JULY 12 - GEORGETOWN, CO TO DENVER, CO - 34.7 MILES - 1105 CUM. MILES

The eleven runners laced up their shoes and left Georgetown in fifty-degree temperatures and at an elevation of about eight thousand feet. Throughout the course of the day, the stage would take them along I-70 through Golden, Colorado, up and down a bunch of "hills," and into Denver, along with lots and lots of traffic. The last five or six miles were run on sidewalks right down Colfax Avenue in Denver. (Final elevation was about 5600 feet, and temperatures were heading for the record-breaking hundred-degree mark!) David said all those little steps on and off the sidewalk were uncomfortable and annoying. But just like every other day, the finish line did become a reality and it marked the beginning of the "icing and eating" post-race routine. They are again staying in a hotel tonight, so recovering is a little easier.

Crewing David today and tomorrow are Phil and Delores Rogers from Grand Junction, Colorado. They were originally supposed to do just one day; however, they agreed to stay on for an extra day when extenuating circumstances prevented the original crew person from being there. David reports they are doing a great job, and he is really enjoying getting to know new friends.

A big thank-you to the Brooks Shoe Company which sent him two more pairs of Adrenaline™ shoes. He has already gone through about four or five pairs of shoes and now wears a size thirteen rather than a size twelve. We put in a call to Vicki Hempelmann at Brooks on Monday, and she made sure he had them today.

Mr. Okada, president of Moonbat, returned to the race and spoke at the racers' briefing tonight. Following Ed Kelley's farewell speech, nearly everyone was deeply touched by the emotion of the moment. Both Ed and Mr. Okada urged the runners to keep on going, no matter how slow. Stay focused. Make it to New York. It will be worth it all! He then presented each runner with a special Japanese sponge cake and a silk scarf.

Two pieces of trivia: First, Jesse uses ten bags of flour per day to mark the course. Second, David picked up a cup of "water" to chug down a couple of Advils™. This isn't so special, except that it was the cup of peroxide in which he had been soaking his big toe. I guess it was quite the surprise. I'm astonished that he admitted doing something this stupid, but at least he lived to tell it!

Today's results: Dusan 4:37:31, Koyago 4:46:16, Ray 4:49:20, Manfred 5:02:06, David 5:11:29.

Four weeks ago today I left Lynchburg, Virginia. At the time, I did not realize that I was embarking on the most difficult journey of my life. I'm thanking the Lord for things coming around physically and mentally. That doesn't mean I'm out of the woods or pain free, but things are getting better. We had a very sad but inspirational meeting tonight. Ed Kelley spoke to us again and told us how important it was to make it to New York.... I am very motivated now to finish, no matter what position. I hope I can keep this in perspective, especially by not hurting myself or doing anything dumb.... Patrick finished last, but he's in it for the long haul. I think he will finish. I admire and respect his courage.... I was also able to get some medicine for my stomach today — thanks to Rebekah and Dr. David Frantz, a cardiac surgeon in Lynchburg. He called a medical doctor friend of his here in Denver, Grant Peoples, and he was able to call in a prescription for me to get some Cytotec™. Now I should be able to continue taking antiinflammatories without it tearing up my stomach.

DAY 27 - JULY 13 - DENVER, CO TO BYERS, CO - 46.2 MILES

When I first spoke with David today, I commented that he sounded tired. He said, "I should be. I ran fast." In fact, you know he ran fast if he didn't stop to pick up money so he could stay with the trio of Dusan, Ray, and Koyago! The stage began on the west side of Denver and had them run fifteen straight miles on Colfax Avenue. The runners were again supposed to stay on the sidewalk, but.... Anyway, on they went, past the Denver Bronco stadium, the penny mint, and the state capital. Then it was up and down long rolling hills that eventually led them into Byers, a small town of three hundred to four hundred people. The route of choice was again I-70, but tomorrow they will leave Byers on Route 36 and stay on it for one thousand miles!

David stayed in sight of the threesome until about twenty-six miles when he began to feel a little tired. As it turned out, Dusan started to pull away and ended up winning the stage outright with Koyago in second. When David asked him if the other guys got tired or if he picked up the pace, he coyly smiled and said, "Maybe the little Japanese went too fast today." You get the idea he's just playing with the other runners. David came in just twenty minutes behind Dusan and was very pleased with his time. Although his knee is still bothering him, the Achilles and shin problems are better. His spirits are good and his outlook positive. Hopefully, things will continue to improve with time.

One incident that occurred involved two little boys, perhaps nine or ten years old. They asked, "Are you going to New York?" "Yes," was the reply. "Are you going to get a gold medal?" "No," responded David, "But maybe a plaque." The boys weren't real impressed with that, but ran at least a hundred yards with David until they were too tired to continue. Cute, huh?

Today's results: Dusan 6:35:19, Koyago 6:40:56, Ray 6:42:11, David 6:55:45, (Patrick - 8th in 8:13:02).

Staying in Byers. The Moonbat people fixed our meal tonight. This is the second day Phil and Delores crewed for me. They left tonight, so this will be the first time I won't have a crew. I'm going to put my stuff in the Penske truck with Frank (Dusan's crew), and Jesse (one of the race directors) will crew for me tomorrow.

DAY 28 - JULY 14 - BYERS, CO TO ANTON, CO - 53.5 MILES (1205.5 MILES)

This day was marked by a beautiful sunrise. According to David, the sky was aglow in a magnificent orange color. The course, straight down Route 36, treated the runners to the sight of a herd of buffalo at mile ten, a crop duster flying thirty to forty feet off the ground, huge fields of wheat as far as the eye could see, "humongous" tractors and plows, two dead snakes, and a dead fox. Additionally, David earned a single quarter for his efforts as he found it laying on the road. Except for a low point from mile twenty to mile thirty, this long mileage stage passed by pretty quickly. But I guess that's what happens when you run fast. David covered the first thirty miles in just four hours and thirty minutes and the entire 53.5 distance in 8:06:42. His fifth place finish was actually only fifteen minutes behind the leader's time. The top five runners really challenged the pace by running the long rolling hills at a seven-minute pace near the end. Pretty incredible. Although David felt he could have kept up with the front runners, he has again showed restraint (still amazing!), knowing that he must give his body sufficient time to heal more completely. (Speaking of which, his shin splints on his right leg were hurting a little more today and his Achilles remained about the same.)

Patrick seems to have made a miraculous recovery. His physical problem appears not to have been a stress fracture, but rather very bad shin splints. He must have a magic formula for healing, because he ran like the wind today! (I told David he needs to find out his secret!)

The stopover tonight is in tiny Anton. The runners are treated to staying in Elva's garage just beyond the silo. (Elva is a farmer.) Yes, you read it correctly. A garage. Just like the place in which you park your car. There is only room for the runners, so crews may have to stay under the stars. The garage does have electricity, however, so David is able to blow around the hot air with his fan. The shower is outside under a five-gallon solar water bag hanging from a nail. The only toilet facilities are inside the one restaurant in town. But, the people are friendly. Count your blessings, it could be worse!

A special thanks goes to race director Jesse Riley who crewed for David today. The prearranged crew person was still not able to get to the race, but Jesse did a great job for David in addition to his RD responsibilities. (Jesse always marks the course, but since there were zero turns, his marking duties were fairly easy.)

Today's results: Dusan and Koyago 7:51:09, Patrick 7:52:18, Ray 7:52:24, David 8:06:42.

Overall standings: Dusan 172:24:57, Ray +12:09:30, David +15:43:41, Patrick +21:10:25, Koyago +27:04:15.

Tomorrow is just 31 miles. I am sure it will be a blistering pace. I just hope to run a good time and not hurt myself. Sort of hate it now. My cassette player is all torn up and I can't use it.... My crew person for tomorrow still hasn't shown up — it's 7:40 p.m. — so I'm not sure what will happen tomorrow.... Little bit lonely but not too bad. Looking forward to seeing friendly faces.... Praise the Lord for continuing to help me and heal my body.

CHAPTER 16

Week 5 of the Trans-Am

As your belief about limits change, the limits themselves change.

- Terry Orlick

DAY 29 - JULY 15 - ANTON, CO TO JOES, CO - 31.0 MILES

Today marked the last full day in Colorado. Due to pouring rain all last night, the air was thick with humidity — and mosquitoes! A can of Off™ has now been added to David's equipment list. As normal, David took the early lead for the first quarter of a mile or so. In fact, running out of the parking lot, he laughingly asked Jesse Riley for a guess on how long he could keep "the boys" running slow. There was no need to wait for an answer. Dusan, Ray, and Patrick took off flying and never slowed down. Koyago caught David at sixteen miles, but David was able to catch up and come in only two minutes behind Koyago. Dusan and Patrick tied with Ray less than two minutes behind them.

The course was as flat as a pancake in every direction. David walked only fifty to sixty yards through the aid stations. He saw only dead deer along the way and didn't find any money today. The town of Joes, the end point of the stage, was so named because there were several guys named Joe who first established this little town of sixty to seventy people. There is one cafe and hotel, both being owned by the same family. The hotel has only six rooms, each furnished with an air conditioner that doesn't work, a fan, and an old twenty-five-inch console TV that gets only two fuzzy channels. Since there are about fifty people in the Trans-Am entourage, everyone but the runners will be sleeping out in the elements. Our thanks to Rick Trujillo, David's friend and runner from Colorado, for serving as the crew today.

Today's results: Dusan and Patrick 4:01:52, Ray 4:03:41, Koyago 4:16:28, and David 4:18:59.

Saturday night. Doesn't seem like Saturday night. Doesn't feel like any particular night. That's sort of how things are around here…. Eric Steele and Warren Bushey arrived to be my crew beginning tomorrow. They gave me a shirt and a hat from the Kansas UltraRunner Society…. Talked to Nancy tonight. I know she misses me a lot. I miss her…. I want to thank the Lord for getting me through these trials and tribulations…. I am sure I will have fond memories when this is all over. The afternoons and the evening meetings are nice. What is not nice is the morning when we start and when we run — that's tough.

DAY 30 - JULY 16 - JOES, CO TO ST. FRANCIS, KS - 51.1 MILES

In the words of race director Jesse Riley, "I have never seen anything like this!" What he is referring to is the blistering pace, the degree of competitiveness, and the jockeying each day for position at the front. David set the pace for the first quarter mile when Ray, Patrick, and Dusan caught up. By four miles, the trio was ahead of David by half a mile. Then at six miles Koyago caught David while making the comment that the guys up front are crazy for running so fast. However, no sooner was that statement out of his mouth than he took off to catch them. Sure enough, taking advantage of a faster aid station stop, Koyago jumped out to a forty-yard lead. The threesome didn't really want to give chase, but did. David could see this story unfold in front of him and reports that at forty-two miles he saw someone take off. This break again turned out to be Koyago. Dusan is the only one who followed, and at forty-six miles Dusan asked Koyago if he wanted to finish together in a time of seven hours. Without a word, but with a sideward glance, Koyago answered by sprinting off and eventually finishing four minutes in front of Dusan. David, in fifth for the day, finished a scant ten minutes back from Dusan. After 1287.6 miles, these guys are really booking it down the yellow brick road!

The course itself was flat in Colorado, but gave way to rolling hills, better scenery, and a better road surface in Kansas. The significant mark of "2000 km" was marked on the road today with the halfway point (day wise) coming up later on this week. The temperature at the beginning was sixty degrees, but rose to a not-too-humid ninety-one degrees at the end. David stated that although "everyday is a race — everyday is hard," he enjoyed the

last fourteen miles of the race. He is also appreciating the camaraderie and fellowship with the other runners, crews, race organizers and supporters.

Today's results: Koyago 6:58:17, Mravlje 7:02:24, Bell 7:05:54,
Farmer 7:05:58, Horton 7:12:19.

*It really seems like we are getting somewhere now. We have
gone 1286 miles total to date.... The town's people fixed part of
the meal for us tonight. It was a very pleasant evening. It was also
nice talking to Mike Lowry and Tim Crance tonight when I called
Rebekah with the day's results. Nancy and those other families
were all at the Trittipoe's celebrating Seth's fourth birthday. I was
envious of them, but again thankful of where I am. I am becoming good friends with a lot of the runners. We are family now —
except for when we are racing. I really enjoy it. Before, I didn't.
Early on, it was just hard work, but now there is some enjoyment.... Thirty down and 34 more days to go.... "Thank you
Lord for allowing me to do this, and I thank you for not allowing
me to quit."*

DAY 31 - JULY 17 - ST. FRANCIS, KS TO ATWOOD, KS - 41.45

I don't know about the rest of you, but here in Virginia it is a
sweltering ninety-five degrees with a heat index of 105 degrees!
David called this afternoon just as I had returned from a run,
dripping with enough sweat to fill a swimming pool. (Lovely, huh?)
The Trans-Am runners are a bunch of weenies because they only
had to run forty-plus miles in sixty-to-seventy-degree weather over
gradual rolling hills surrounded by beautiful, lush farm fields.
According to David, he only got hot once when the sun poked
out for a couple of minutes. But he did add that the stage was
particularly tough because they had to dodge fleets of road-hog-
ging, giant threshing machines. We feel so sorry for them!

Seriously, today was a hard day just like all the rest, because
the guys at the front were racing. David said that if they were just
running and not racing, the distance he would be capable of covering might be lots more than the three thousand miles of the
Trans-Am. But this is a race, and that is exactly what they did

today. Patrick and David took the early lead with Dusan catching up and drafting off David's heels to guard himself against the headwind. But at twelve miles, Horton figured that turn-about was fair play as he fell in behind Dusan. Entering an aid station further down the road, Dusan barely slowed down as he gained a ten, then twenty, then fifty yard lead. Saving himself for the sixty-one-mile day tomorrow, David was content to watch Patrick, Ray, and Koyago take off to catch Dusan. This certainly quickened the leader's pace and pulled the foursome further away from David. However, with time, David caught up to Patrick, and their brief verbal exchange was something like, "Those guys are crazy for running so fast!" David went on past and finished behind Koyago, Dusan, and Ray. Interestingly enough, it was Dusan who told Koyago to just go on ahead at mile thirty-six. Patrick ended up finishing in eighth place, ninety-nine minutes behind the leader.

David's Achilles and shin splint problems are continuing to resolve themselves. However, the right knee is really giving him fits. Today it hurt the whole way. He cannot find a specific place where the pain is localized, but he is sure that it hurts! Maybe he should take after Nagata, who brought along his own personal acupuncturist. Apparently Patrick made use of this form of medicine a week or so ago, which may have contributed to his miraculous comeback.

The troops are staying in the Atwood High School gym, home of the Buffaloes. Since the Pizza Hut in town is open only Thursday through Sunday, the only choice for food is the Buffalo restaurant. The bank in town has a gentleman by the name of Barnabas Horton as its president, who is not related to our very own Horton. (If he was, do you think he would admit it!?!) And no, he did not contribute money to the cause of this so-named runner. The town also lays claim to fame in several areas: 1) home of Mr. Wendelin, creator of Smokey the Bear; 2) home of the oldest road race in Kansas (the twenty-four-year-old Kansas Ten-Miler); and 3) home of two stuffed passenger pigeons, the now extinct birds. (The only other stuffed pigeons are held in the Smithsonian.) So, Atwood isn't such a bad place after all. The Moonbat people will be cooking to provide the evening meal.

Today was mail drop day. David loves it! The race directors say that David's mail is more than everybody else's combined — thirty-two pieces of mail just today. He says to tell you that he cannot adequately express his appreciation for your thoughtfulness, kind words, sincerest wishes, and boxes of edibles. Even though some of the cards really pull at his emotions, he savors every last word on every card and letter. Gary and I want to encourage you to keep up the good work!

Today's results: Koyago 5:31:21, Dusan 5:38:00, Ray 5:40:11, David 5:57:26, Manfred 6:37:26

Mail drop today. Got 32 pieces of mail. I am very, very thankful for the time people take to write to me. It is very meaningful and very humbling. I cried when I read a couple of letters, especially one from Linda Sledge. She said I was her hero and that I was doing great. I am pleased with the way things are going now. I look forward to each day and finishing strong. I hope I can hold onto third position.

▲

From the mailbox:

And now David, I hope that you get this letter and card in Atwood, Kansas. That seems such a long way from California where you started. But you are SO tough and so strong, so talented and so humble, and I hope more than anything that you will win the whole thing. But winning isn't the most important part, but the experience, and even the pain, and what you learn about yourself, and hopefully, what you can teach others as well…. Because in life, as my dear mentor told me long ago, when the student is ready, the teacher will appear. And… when the teacher is ready, the student will appear. So whichever we are, student or teacher, at different times of our lives, should prove interesting. I know I continue to learn and to observe, and that is one of the wonderful things about life, isn't it?

David Horton, you are our HERO!

~Linda and Webb Sledge

▼

DAY 32 - JULY 18 - ATWOOD, KS TO NORTON, KS - 60.6 MILES

You put your ear to the ground. There. Hear it? The sounds of thundering hoofs of a buffalo stampede. Or is it the sound of the stagecoach racing across the plains. Or maybe it's Buffalo Bill Cody, Horace Greely, and Billy the Kid speeding into town to rob the bank. But then again, it could be the pitter-patter of twenty-two little feet as they run the longest stage in the Trans-America footrace — 60.6 miles. Yep. It's the twenty-two feet (maybe not so little) that you hear. From Atwood to Norton, they pass through only one town, experiencing rolling hills, farm fields and overcast skies with temperatures ranging from sixty to seventy-five degrees. The owner of size thirteen feet, our very own David Horton, was also privileged to find a dead pheasant (which he did not drag to the next aid station), wire strippers, and a little red flag that he carried across the finish line. He did have sense enough to leave two porno magazines laying on the road, leaving them to be gathered up by another runner, who shall remain nameless.

The top five runners did an incredible job today. Dusan cranked out a time of 8:08:34 with a fifty-mile split of 6:38. David completed in 9:07:02 with a 7:30 split for fifty and was very pleased, despite having an occasional tough time mentally. That's an 8:03 and 9:02 pace, respectively — after 1389.65 miles! The previous course record was very close to David's time, set by Tom Rogozinski in 1992. But to keep things in perspective, the cut-off time today was 17:19:00.

David's crew is keeping things lively. Eric Steele and Warren Bushey wrote numerous chalk messages on the road, had the Beach Boys cranking from the car, and met him at fifty-six miles wearing Groucho Marx disguises! David says they were successful in taking his mind off the distance and the pain. They had also brought David a shirt that read, "The journey of three thousand miles begins with a single step," on the front and the stages they are crewing on the back. They could also be picked out of a crowd for wearing Horton crew shirts and Kansas Ultrarunners Society hats. Both guys are great massage therapists and are also giving David's roomie, Dusan, an occasional massage. As Tony the Tiger would say, "You're gggreat!"

The town of Norton, population 3500, is known (self-proclaimed) as the Pheasant Capital of the World. Now isn't that special! They are staying in a hotel, and the Moonbat folks are cooking dinner: rice and chicken. David seems to be in good spirits and is really starting to have fun — once the racing is done for the day!

Results: Dusan 8:08:34, Ray and Patrick 8:34:08, Koyago 8:46:42, David 9:07:02.

Longest day of the run. I was very scared and intimidated.... A little tired all day long.... I didn't look at my watch until 50 miles — 7:30 — a nine minute pace exactly.... Glad to have this day behind me...

DAY 33 - JULY 19 - NORTON, KS TO KENSINGTON, KS - 47.4 MILES

The day was hotter (ninety-five degrees), the sky was sunnier, and the run was harder than yesterday. Those sixty-one miles made today's forty-seven a challenge both mentally and physically. Through the first twelve hilly miles, the lead pack consisted of David, Dusan, Ray, and Patrick with Koyago trailing by just fifty yards. However, at the twelve-mile aid station, Koyago made his move, and Patrick, exclaiming, "Here we go again. Welcome to Groundhog Day," took off after him. Ray also answered the challenge of the little Japanese man from New York (5-feet, 5 inches, 108 pounds). Although Dusan was in front of David, at mile twenty-six David passed a very tired, shoulders drooping, head down Dusan. Dusan was not to finish in front of David today. (He was seen icing his inner leg right above the knee last night, something that he had not previously done. Could he be human and not an android after all?!?) David reports the last couple miles were searing, sapping the runners of the much-needed energy to finish out the day. But just think of the slower runners who would be out on the course for many more hours, broiling under the hot sun. In fact, it was so hot David couldn't talk very long to us, because the phone booth was in the sun and it was unbearable.

The town of Kensington (population 600) welcomed the runners with lodging in the high school's un-airconditioned gym and an evening meal of steak and potatoes. But, the best thing about the town was the local drugstore, a throw back to years gone by. Built in 1905, it possessed wooden, squeaky floors, a metal roof, soda fountain counter, and the best chocolate milkshakes in the world. David made himself at home by striking up a conversation with the man who had been working there for thirty-eight years. He found out that the high school "Goldbugs" (different kind of mascot, huh?) were class 1A basketball and eight-man football state champs. (With only eighty students in grades 9-12, eight-man football is the only option.) And the town's most famous son, Full Admiral Kent Gene Carroll, served as the chief of staff in the Bush administration. All the runners really appreciated the hospitality of these mid-America people.

In another conversation, David told us more news about Patrick. His experience includes a 1991 6000-km run across Australia (north to south), a 1993 Trans-Am trek in which he placed second, a 1994 2000-km run in Australia, and then the Trans-Am this year. A very competitive, yet humble man, he commented, "Ultrarunning is money poor but rich in experiences." I believe David concurs.

Today's results: Koyago 6:34:50, Patrick 6:44:30, Ray 6:44:31, Manfred 6:59:46, David 7:01:51, Dusan 7:12:45.

Here it is 7:54 p.m., July the 19th.

DAY 34 - JULY 20 - KENSINGTON, KS TO MANKATO, KS - 43.3 MILES

Today's stage was significant for several reasons. First of all, the runners passed the halfway mark in terms of miles. Secondly, they ran within four miles of the geographic center of the United States. And thirdly, David ran very well, beating Dusan again and coming in only eleven seconds behind Patrick for third place. The race went something like this. Staying together for four miles, Dusan, David, Patrick, and Ray made up the lead pack. Then everyone but David started to pull away a little bit, with Ray picking it up again at six miles and putting distance between himself and Patrick and Dusan. However, at eighteen miles, the three were in David's sight. Then at twenty miles David passed Dusan by working it hard going up a hill. Running hard for those two miles suddenly brought him up on Patrick at mile twenty-six. The boy from down under and David started shooting the breeze, making the miles just fly by. According to David, this made today the easiest day yet. Nonetheless, with 1.2 miles to go, Patrick said that he thought they should race it in and David agreed. Off they went, exchanging the lead several times. But then David's knee, which had been silent all day, started hurting, and he decided that to finish just seconds behind would have to do. From what David says, at least he and Patrick had a very enjoyable day!

They are staying tonight in the town of Mankato, population eight hundred. The elevation here is 2300 feet, which is about five hundred feet lower than yesterday's stopover. There is an old bank that is declared an historical structure and a Pizza Hut that is open five hours a day; a forty-five-minute drive will get you to the closest Wal-Mart. But as bank tellers were relating to David, it is a wonderful place to raise a family, where you don't have to lock doors and your car keys are safe left in the car. Even the motel, The Dreamliner, has a certain pure, simple, and nostalgic ring to it.

Today's results: Ray 5:51:20, Patrick 6:10:51, David 6:11:02, Dusan 6:32:43, Koyago 6:34:47.

I am sitting in a rocking chair here in front of the Dreamliner Motel. Very nice, very cool, very pleased with the day's run. Only took two Advil™ before the stage started this morning but none during the run. It [the knee] hurt less than it has for several days.... Did get some shocking news when I called Rebekah with the day's report. Seems like her foot may have broken — again.... We passed the mileage halfway point today. Thirty-four days down, 30 more to go.... Dusan is hurting, and he received acupuncture tonight. I really enjoyed talking to Patrick this evening. He is a good man, a real good man.... Nancy misses me more every day. She asked me tonight if I wanted her to come to NY for the finish. I said that I did. She is talking about coming with Nancy and Charlie Hesse and "Muff." I hope they come!

163

Do you recall some of those TV commercials that show a couple of old mid-westerners sitting on the porch in the middle of summer wiping their perspiring brows, watching the world go by and drinking an ice-cold Coke™? I think the runners could relate to the perspiring part, only wishing they, too, were on the porch drinking an ice-cold Coke™! With shade not to be found, nondescript landscape, and temperatures in the mid-nineties, the runners ran only because they had to. The pack of David, Dusan, Patrick, and Ray stayed together through four miles, but Patrick and Ray never stopped at the aid station, choosing rather to push on. Dusan commented that they were crazy and that he was going to run with David. The two did stay together, but by twenty miles they had lost sight of the two front runners. Manfred, the German, caught David and Dusan and was going to stay with them until Dusan told him to go on ahead. This is not to imply that they were running poorly (David's average pace for the stage was eight minutes and thirty-two seconds per mile), but that Manfred was having a pretty good day. As it would turn out, David pushed the pace enough to drop Dusan, finishing in fourth place, but only twelve minutes back from Patrick's first place win. The only thing even remotely interesting about the course was that they crossed over the Republican River. Of course, David's question was, "Where's the Democrat River?"

The town of Cuba is only 250 strong and in the middle of nowhere. The school they stay in tonight is on a dirt road outside of town. The town itself has only one paved road, and the "main" street is the old, wide type where cars can park in the middle. Czechoslovakian people settled the town in the late 1800s. Many in the town still speak the language. Down the road are towns of Swedish people and another settlement of French folks. Those Europeans must have really liked Kansas if you consider that they and their descendants have been around for a hundred years. Or, of course, their wagons might have broken down there and they had no choice but to stay. But the town of Cuba is certainly friendly, as the town's people fixed a huge spaghetti dinner tonight.

Here is one piece of odd trivia: David's tan looks weird. I know this might not sound real important, but David thought it was noteworthy. By his description, his legs are very tan as well as his face and neck and part of his arms. The part that looks funny is right by the inside of his elbows. Because of the way he holds his arms when he runs, he says his tan (or lack of it) looks like a really bad paint job. I told him if he wanted the Coppertone™ endorsements to start rolling in, he should hold his arms out straight to even out the sun exposure! But, (pun intended) if that is too difficult, he could always go for the traditional Coppertone™ billboard look?!? Having told you this, I'm sure you will all sleep better tonight!

Today's results: Patrick 5:42:07, Ray 5:42:08, Manfred 5:49:54, David 5:54:18, Dusan 5:56:28, Koyago 6:31:36.

Overall standings: Dusan 216:57:43, Ray +11:18:42, David +16:53:52, Patrick +22:11:38, Koyago +27:49:30, Manfred +39:23:33.

Just finished the 35th stage, so 28 days to hold off Patrick and Koyago. I think that barring a major breakdown, I can hold off Koyago. But, holding off Patrick is another thing — he is highly competitive. I thought I was competitive, but compared to him? As long as I can run consistently, I think I can hold the margin.... It is sort of drudgery out there but you just keep doing it, day after day. This is a tough life. This is not a normal life. I doubt if I will ever do anything like this again. Basically, you put your hand to the plow and keep your head down... I look forward to four weeks from tomorrow — we'll be rolling into NYC.

Chapter 17

Week 6 of the Trans-Am

Accept the day as it comes. Push on. Keep moving.

- Author unknown

DAY 36 - JULY 22 - CUBA, KS TO MARYSVILLE, KS - 43.6 MILES

Hot and humid was the mark of yet another day in paradise. The runners all knew they were in for a hard day when the starting temperature at 5:00 a.m. was a very sticky seventy-five degrees. The course was fairly hilly, with the most hills coming in the last seventeen miles. As usual, the pack of Ray, Patrick, Dusan, and David was together until four miles when Ray and Patrick blasted through the aid station to get a jump on David and Dusan. Dusan eventually pulled away from David, and Koyago and David played cat and mouse from twenty-four to thirty-two miles. By thirty-eight miles, David was very surprised to look up and see a runner not far from him. It turned out to be a failing Patrick. He was really looking tired, but apparently sucked it up enough to hold off both David and Koyago by just a few minutes.

One of the race directors was speaking with David about the pace of this race as compared to other years. The gold standard previously was an average of six miles per hour. Today, five of the runners were running better than seven miles per hour. What an incredible field!

The runners have the privilege of staying in a stuffy school gym tonight. Not even a fan seems to help. It only serves to move the hot air from one place to another. But this town of three thousand people is interesting from the standpoint that it was the first "home station" of the Pony Express. In 1860 and 1861, the Express ran between St. Joseph, Missouri, to Sacramento, California, never losing even one parcel of mail. (That's quality control!) The help wanted ad in the paper of yesteryear read something like this: "Wanted: young, skinny, wiry fellows, expert riders, willing to risk death daily, orphans preferred, wages $25 per week." (*Running the Trans-America Footrace—Trials and Triumphs of Life on the Road*, by Barry Lewis.)

Most of the Trans-Am runners would actually qualify on several accounts except they would be overpaid at $25 per week. After all, it's costing them anywhere from $8000 and up to suffer like this!

The crew guys, Eric and Warren from Kansas, left for home today. They did a wonderful job tending to David this week. Following in their footsteps are Bob and Rosemary Marston from Hannibal, Missouri. Rosemary got right into the swing of things, running the traditional two-mile crew track race this evening. David cannot express enough gratitude for the assistance that so many have given to him!

Today's results: Ray 5:44:25 (7:53 pace), Dusan 5:57:05, Patrick 6:04:22, Koyago 6:05:28, David 6:09:27 (8:27 pace).

We are staying in a gym tonight, and I am lying here on the sideline of the basketball court. I am very sleepy. However, I am pleased with my run today. Even though I was fifth place, my time was only four minutes off the record time for the stage.... Concerned about tomorrow's 59.95 miles. Will need to drink a lot and pace myself in the heat and humidity.

DAY 37 - JULY 23 - MARYSVILLE, KS TO HIAWATHA, KS - 59.9 MILES

Sundays to the Trans-Am runners are definitely NOT days of rest! Last week they had a sixty-one-mile stage, and this week they ended up 59.9 miles. There was that same sense of dread last night and this morning, but once into the run David became more confident. Despite the hot and sticky conditions, he ran well through thirty-one miles. David, Ray, and Dusan all ran together during this distance. However, David says he really got tired around thirty-two miles and knew that he had to save something for later on in the race. So he made the decision to walk some portions of the long, gradual two to three mile hills. That gave him the ability to run consistently through the rest of the stage, although the last three or four miles were really tough. Despite his fatigue, the exit off Route 36 that marked the last bit of the stage was the "Hiawatha-Horton" exit. He later teased Dusan that it was only he and not Dusan with an exit in his honor!

If you are wondering if there was much conversation between Dusan, David, and Ray during those first thirty-one miles, there was not. According to David, sometimes not even one word would be uttered between aid stations. As far as other stage trivia, Dusan acquired his first two blisters of the entire race, Patrick had a terrible case of diarrhea (leading to a time of 12:31 and tenth place finish), and David saw three dead raccoons and a dead skunk all within ten feet of each other. Although he picked up a pen and a very old quarter, he says that he really has lost interest in picking up the coins. It's just too much effort to bend over and stand back up!

Dusan and David run together through farmlands.

The entourage has a very nice air-conditioned hotel tonight. This is a welcome relief from the stuffy gyms and hard floors of the last several nights. Hiawatha is touted as being "The Home of the Beautiful Maples." David said he really had not noticed. And in answer to prayer, the only thing that still hurts on David is his right knee. Sometimes the pain comes in a healthy dose, while other times it is barely noticeable. He is encouraged because it seldom gets worse as he runs, which is a good sign. His Achilles is also back to a normal size and has not hurt in two weeks, and his muscles are not sore at all! That is unbelievable! No wonder his outlook has improved considerably since the desert!

Today's results: Koyago 8:48:05, Dusan 8:49:02, Ray 8:56:05, David 9:09:31 (Patrick - tenth place - 12:31:36).

We just finished a very difficult stage. Not the longest but probably the hardest.... Good day for me but bad day in a big way for Patrick Farmer. He finished 3 hours and 20 minutes behind me. Koyago was 21 minutes ahead of me. I need to keep that spread to no more than that.... Passed three pig farms that really stunk.... The last few nights we have been staying in hot, hot gyms, so I am especially thankful to have a hotel tonight.

DAY 38 - JULY 24 - HIAWATHA, KS TO ELWOOD, KS - 36.5

David reports that today was his worst day since Utah. This is not to imply that he ran poorly (8:41 pace), but he struggled with the oppressive heat and humidity. As usual, David, Dusan, and Ray ran the first eight miles, with Koyago just a tad behind. However, at eight miles Koyago made his move and took off, first pulling along Dusan and then Ray. David made a conscious decision not to go with the boys. In questioning him about this, David explained that he needs to run the pace with which he feels comfortable. So once again David is showing a wise and premeditated restraint. As the stage continued, David hit a wall at about eighteen miles and decided to walk some of those long hills. In fact, he said he probably walked more today than all the other days in Kansas combined. By the last six miles, the terrain became very flat, and he didn't particularly like that either. Had it not been a race, David may have walked the rest of the stage. But after changing his soaking wet socks and shoes at thirty miles, he did persevere and ran the rest of the way in. He was really glad to be finished, but figured the leader probably beat him by at least one hour. Surprisingly to David, the stage winner, Koyago, had arrived a mere twenty-four minutes earlier. So the results were much better than David had anticipated based on how rotten he felt.

The stopover tonight is in Elwood School, a facility complete with AC! Coming into town there was a sign indicating that Elwood, being right on the Missouri River, was "The Survival City" from the great flood of 1993. Bob and Rosemary Marston, David's crew, have a home in nearby St. Joseph and treated David to a nap in a La-Z-Boy® recliner. What a treat! This is the first home that David had been in for six weeks, and he really appreciated this brief, but wonderful, respite from the Trans-Am. Another thing that David did for the first time since Denver was to buy a *USA Today* newspaper. This is his favorite paper, but he had not even seen a *USA Today* paper box until yesterday. Unfortunately, that box was sold out. David did luck out by getting the last paper available today.

Today's results: Koyago 4:52:07, Dusan 4:55:26, Manfred 4:57:43, Ray 5:00:50, David 5:16:43, and Patrick (tenth place) 7:43:31.

Lying here in Elwood's 5th grade classroom.... This was our last day in Kansas. Looking forward to getting into another state. Four days in Missouri and then three in Illinois. I feel like we are starting to make real progress.... Today was one of the hardest days I've had for a long time — probably since Utah. Had to walk a lot. In fact probably more than in all of Kansas. I felt extremely slow. I had no energy and my knee was hurting a lot.... Koyago is ten hours, five minutes behind me. That means I could lose 24 minutes a day to him before getting passed.... Manfred is really excited because his wife arrives tomorrow. I wish Nancy could come.... Lots of encouragement from back home, but they just don't understand how difficult this is.

DAY 39 - JULY 25 - ELWOOD, KS TO HAMILTON, MO - 48.65 MILES

Today was a good day. David even used the word "easy" in describing the stage. I think this has something to do with the fact that he ran well, and hardly anything hurt. On this hot and humid day (like the last several), David, Dusan, Patrick, and Ray led early with Koyago not far behind. At about 6.5 miles, Dusan looked over his shoulder and exclaimed, "Oh, no, it's Koyago! I don't want to race!" Patrick replied, "Yes, but he does!" So when Koyago took off at ten miles, the crowd (except for David) was sure to follow. The surprisingly hilly course went by pretty fast, especially when David caught up to Patrick (who had been taking a break in the bushes). As they had done in the past, the two talked all the way in. David ran every step and felt comfortable despite the heat that was particularly burdensome for the last hour or so. (As an aside, to those of you reading Patrick's diary on *America On Line*, you know that there is no love lost between him and Dusan. However, David gets along great with both of them, and they both seem to like David.) Although Patrick urged David to take it to the finish line first, David decided that running hard for the last hundred yards just to get a few seconds on Patrick really was not necessary. So the two friends crossed together.

Hamilton is the town from whence J.C. Penney hailed. To show you that David is starting to loosen up, he even visited the J.C. Penney museum. (Yes, it was free.) Opening his first store in 1893, Penney felt it was important to put the customer first. Some of the residents must feel the same way, since they contributed the pizza for the evening meal for their "Trans-Am" customers. They are staying in the J.C. Penney High School where the AC is so effective it is almost too cold. (First too hot, then too cold. What a whiner!)

Manfred's wife and son arrived from Germany today and were greeted with great enthusiasm by all — especially Manfred. Actually, the guys are jealous that their wives aren't there to keep them warm in that cold school!

A new crew person started today. David was happy to have Lou Peyton join Rosemary Marston in the task of taking care of all his whims. Seriously though, we can't stress how important the crew people are. Lou is an old friend from Arkansas who will be with David through stage forty-two. David was glad to see her and says she will do a great job for the next couple of days. Also a special thanks to Rosemary and Bob Marston for their work during stages thirty-seven through thirty-nine. All the crew people have done a great job, and much of David's success has to go to their diligent work.

Today was also mail drop day. When Michael Kenney checked the mail, so that he could forward anything mailed to those who had dropped out, the postmaster commented, "I sure hope that Horton fellow is still in the race. I wouldn't want to forward it all!" As it turned out, his mail took up an entire mail bin. He loved it! Some of the items made him cry, some made him laugh, but all made him grateful for such loyal friends and family. So that we can break the all-time record for mail, here are the remaining mail drops. Flood him with stuff!

Today's results: Koyago 6:45:42, Dusan 6:49:05, Ray 6:54:41, David and Patrick 7:10:03.

Ran good, felt good. I am pleased.... We are sleeping in a hallway tonight but at least there is air conditioning.... Received 34 pieces of mail today. Always a joy to get the mail. Had a very special letter from Nancy — very special. She told me how much she loved me and how proud she was of me. She also said she missed me.

DAY 40 - JULY 26 - HAMILTON, MO TO BROOKFIELD, MO - 49.9 MILES

Today was much like the past three days. Hot and humid (ninety-five degrees by the end), rolling hills, some farmland, and a continued run on Route 36. At this point, Route 36 is a four-lane divided highway with eighteen-wheelers so heavy and the shoulders so narrow that the runners are nearly blown over as the trucks blast by. This stage was also similar to previous days in that the front pack included David, Dusan, Patrick, and Ray with Koyago following just a little behind. At three miles, it was again Koyago who broke from the pack, pulling the trio with him. Interestingly enough, David kept running his pace and was rewarded to pass Koyago at thirteen miles and to catch the rest of the pack at sixteen miles. The only thing was that at sixteen, David just happened to catch a glance behind him and saw Koyago within ten yards. What happened at the three-mile mark was repeated at mile seventeen, leaving David to watch the runners slowly pull away. Because of the knee pain and the heat, David is still convinced that it is in his best interest to continue to be "reasonable." If Koyago continues to run as strong as he is now, David will need to use whatever reserves he has to pour it on later. Koyago is making it quite clear that he intends to move up in the standings. Time will tell if he has what it takes for twenty-three more racing days.

The runners are again sleeping in a school in Brookfield, Missouri (population 4888). David was able to get on a scale and discovered that he now weighs in at a bulky 146.5 pounds. Prior to the race he was 154, and two weeks ago he was at 150 pounds. What a way to lose a few pounds! Nevertheless, the Moonbat folks tried to put some meat on those bones by cooking a great meal of ribs and spaghetti. The town's people brought salad and desserts for the group. Additionally, since it was Michael Kenney's birthday, cake and ice cream was also enjoyed by all.

Today's results: Koyago 6:48:54, Dusan 6:51:25, Ray 6:54:53, Patrick 7:03:48, David 7:18:02

I am sitting in the hallway leaning up against locker #53. It's appropriate — many days we run that much.... Heavy tractor trailer traffic today.... No cloud cover... so hot and humid.... Tough race as usual. What it boils down to is waiting to see when Koyago makes his move and then seeing who will go with him. I lost 29 minutes to Koyago today, so I'm a little depressed by that.... When I finished, I called Nancy. That was sort of sad. She was cooking pork chops for my cousin Steven, Muffy, and the Trittipoes — and here I sit.... Nancy said she watched two romantic movies last night and it really made her sad. I can understand that. I am not sure I would want to watch a romantic movie now because it would make me sad, too. This afternoon when I finished, I felt like crying. I went in, put on a certain cassette tape and sure enough — the tears came. Did I feel better? I don't know. I just have to get up and do it again — day after day.

DAY 41 - JULY 27 - BROOKFIELD, MO TO CLARENCE, MO - 45.65 (1805.3 CUMULATIVE MILES)

Does anyone want to venture a guess what the weather was like for the runners? If you guessed sleet and snow, you're wrong. If you guessed humid and ninety-six degrees, you're much closer to the truth! But regardless, the pack of four (Ray, Dusan, David, and Patrick) ran together until Koyago decided to blow by everyone at about 12.5 miles. But this time no one followed. So until about thirty-eight miles, the foursome ran together. The pace picked up and with a "Let's go" exchange between Patrick and Ray, they took off. Dusan followed shortly thereafter. David says he really struggled from mile forty on into the finish. The heat was oppressive, and Route 36 had no shoulders on which to run. It is simply the white line on the side of the road and a drop off from the blacktop down onto uneven and off camber gravel. The trucks came roaring by, almost knocking over the runners. But David did finish in fifth place, incredibly separated from the leader by a mere fourteen minutes! These guys are really pushing it. The previous stage record was 6:50 and David ran a 6:45 for that fifth place!

Lou Peyton, David's crew person, said they went through fifty pounds of ice today with not a cube left to spare. She says this race is "the most intense and exciting thing that I have ever seen." Adding to the difficulty of the racing are the conditions after the race. They are thankful for a motel tonight that at least has beds. The un-thermostated air conditioner doesn't condition much of anything. There is a truck stop in town for lunch (Moonbat cooked the evening meal) and a convenience store to restock all the ice needed for tomorrow. The 7:00 p.m. race meeting produced a very somber attitude among the runners as they were told the next morning's stage would be run entirely on un-shouldered road. Apparently the truckers were annoyed at finding runners on "their" road last year and called the state police to complain. The police failed to find the five Trans-Am runners, but hopefully there won't be that kind of problem this year.

Although his knee still hurts off and on, David's chief complaint now is his lips. Several weeks ago, once out of the desert, he wasn't quite as conscientious about keeping stuff on his lips. They burned, and ever since he has had problems eating because they hurt so much. So you might even want to put David's lips on your prayer list. Not literally, of course — they would probably get stuck! He wants to eat, he needs to eat, and he is tired of eating in pain! He has plenty of pain during the race. He doesn't need more at dinnertime.

Today's results: Koyago 6:31:12, Ray and Dusan 6:39:31, Patrick 6:43:03, David 6:45:35.

We are in the Trail's End Motel and it feels just like that.... We have one more full day in Missouri.... Hotter than the dickens out there.... I was shocked that when Koyago made his move, no one responded.... My 40-mile split was 6:56, and yesterday it was 6:56.... Just 14 minutes behind Koyago today. Very pleased with that. Doing the best I can under difficult circumstances... The mood at the evening meeting was again very somber. Starting tomorrow, 10 of the next 14 days are 50 miles or more. I will be really, really glad when this is over. I don't think I will ever do anything like this again. I can't imagine a normal life. I feel like I am in jail. I hate taking care of myself. I hate icing all the time. I hate these sore lips. I would like to watch TV. I would like to make love to my wife. I

▲

From the crew's view:
Thank you for a really great experience crewing you. This was so demanding, intense, and ten times more rewarding. Thank you for offering me this opportunity. What if I had not done this? I would have missed so much.... I had the most exciting week with you. Thanks — I want more.... I want more and I don't want to wait a long time either. I'm praying for you....

-Lou Peyton

▼

miss parties and get-togethers. I miss going to church. But soon it will be over. "And this too shall pass..."

DAY 42 - JULY 28 - CLARENCE, MO TO HANNIBAL, MO - 49.7 MILES

Good news! It was ninety-two degrees today but not quite as humid! Thank God for small blessings. As usual, the front-running fearsome foursome took off and ran together for the first sixteen miles. Although it was not spoken, the question on everyone's mind was when (not if) a little Japanese runner from New York would catch them and blow by. It was at sixteen miles when Koyago went by, but once again no one responded. The group quietly and efficiently ran single file on the shoulder of the road through twenty miles. By twenty-four miles, David was getting a little tired and backed off the pace just a tad, although he did pass and gain position on Patrick. With Koyago out of sight, David still kept Dusan and Patrick in sight for quite awhile. But with time, these two slowly slipped into the horizon. The last five or six miles were particularly tough, with surprisingly steep hills. David walked some of these hills in order to save a little energy. However, the last hill gave the opportunity for some good running, as it was all downhill with the mighty Mississippi River right in front of them. You could almost hear Mark Twain beckoning the runners on toward the finish line. (Well, okay. Maybe that is just a little bit too much poetic license!)

David reports he is running well although his knee continues to hurt him off and on. He now says it is something he will just have to put up with for a couple more weeks. It is frustrating to be running so well and so consistently and still come in behind three or four other guys. It really does emphasize the nature of this race: incredible pressure every minute to run your guts out! Which reminds me of my four-year-old son's favorite joke: "Why didn't the 'skelkin' (his pronunciation) cross the road? Because he didn't have no guts!" With David down to 145 pounds, he might be mistaken for a skeleton by the time he reaches New York City. But one thing is for sure: These guys (and lady) all have deep down guts, courage, and toughness!

Today was another changing-of-the-crew day. Lou Peyton traveled back to Arkansas, and Reid Lanham, a great friend and running buddy in Lynchburg, took over for the next six days. Muffy (Reid's nickname, but don't ask why) said tonight he was a little surprised by the seriousness of everyone. While he knew this was a race, he said that you really don't understand it until you see it. But things did lighten up a bit when David introduced Muffy at the evening meeting as his fourteenth crew person. Everyone cheered because David is the only runner with such a wide variety of crew support. In fact, David is unique because he has over two hundred individuals who are supporting his effort, thanks to all of you!

Today's results: Koyago 6:43:32, Dusan 6:50:54, Ray 6:54:49, David 7:18:40, Manfred 7:58:10, Patrick 8:35:23.

Overall standings: Dusan 263:50:41, Ray +11:30:58, David +19:09:25, Koyago +27:31:32, Patrick +31:01:26.

I am sitting out in front of the hotel. We have nice rooms, air conditioning, and phones in the rooms. We don't always have phones. I was real pleased with my time until I heard what Koyago ran. But he would still have to beat me by over 24 minutes every day in order to overtake me.... Glad Muffy arrived today.... Heat index is supposed to be 120 degrees tomorrow.... Called Nancy but she wasn't home.

From the mailbox:
    Can't say I wish I was there because it doesn't sound real fun yet.... The card read: "Many new faces" (Dusan) — "great places" (Ghost towns and deserts) — "fun things to do" (get up at 4:00 a.m. every day) — "and days full of good time be waiting for you" (running through deserts and climbing mountains)... "They that wait upon the Lord shall renew their strength. They shall mount up with wings like eagles. They shall run and not be weary. They shall walk and not faint." Isaiah 40:31

                                                    ~Courtney Campbell

CHAPTER 18

Week 7 of the Trans-Am

In God is my salvation and my glory: the rock of my strength,
and my refuge, is in God. Trust in him at all times.
                                              - Psalms 62:7,8

DAY 43 - JULY 29 - HANNIBAL, MO TO PITTSFIELD, IL - 33.2 MILES

Something new happened today. Koyago was warming-up by running up and down the street before the start of the stage. If this was his way to say, "I'm serious about racing today," then he held true to his word. He took the lead early (first fifty yards), hit the bridge crossing the great Mississippi at a quarter of a mile and kept right on going. Over the relatively flat first twelve miles, David ran well and controlled the second position. However, the trio of Dusan, Patrick, and Ray came up on David and passed him. He ran close to them for quite awhile, but after Dusan pulled away, he later lost contact with Ray and Patrick as well. David reports that from fourteen miles through the end of the stage, they encountered another strange phenomenon: shade. The road was graced with overhanging trees and made the otherwise hot and sticky conditions more bearable. The heat index was reported to be 120 degrees at mid-day. But David was not expecting the number of hills — long, tiring hills. He ran an average pace of 8:16 per mile and finished in fifth place for the day. He really is frustrated that he is running well and yet three or four guys are always in front of him. What's a guy to do?!?

The Trans-Am folk have a decent hotel tonight despite what its name might imply — The Green Acres Motel. Pittsfield's claim to fame is that Abe Lincoln would visit the town for extended periods of time. Today, it relies on the hog industry for its livelihood. David, an Arkansas native and die-hard Razorback fan, should feel right at home!

Today's results: Koyago 4:18:52 (a 7:48 pace!), Dusan 4:25:06, Patrick 4:28:22, Ray 4:28:26, David 4:34:45.

Crossed the "Mighty Miss" today.... Koyago has to average 24 minutes ahead of me every day and then he will still be 5 minutes shy. Can he do that? I don't know.... Three weeks from right now we will be finished. Am I thankful for that? You bet I am!... Just finished having a nice talk with Patrick. We get along very well.... Nancy said someone asked her if I was ever going to do this again. She said she didn't know. But I do know this — I don't ever want to be away from her and the family for this long again.

DAY 44 - JULY 30 - PITTSFIELD, IL TO NEW BERLIN, IL - 53.5 MILES

Well, the race took another twist and turn today. David won a stage, Koyago (Mr. Invincible of late) took a decided step backwards to the tune of an hour and a half, and David treated everyone to ice cream tonight. Think he feels pretty good about things? You bet! Want to know what happened? Okay. I'll tell you.

When the call to the start line took place, Koyago came limping. David noted this with interest and went out at the front of the pack the way he always does. He was running at a very comfortable pace and actually enjoyed the scenery of the first twelve miles. Gentle downhills, a light fog followed by a spectacular sunrise, and a path through several towns not yet risen to meet the new day, were what he enjoyed. But what he also enjoyed was the fact that the trio of Dusan, Ray, and Patrick were behind his own little tail. This position was maintained through the two steep hills around twenty miles and on a beautiful and shaded narrow road from twenty to twenty-six miles. Passing through Jacksonville, a good-sized town, he started to feel a little tired with the hazy and hot weather becoming quite noticeable. BUT, the boys were still behind. At forty miles, David had a six-minute advantage. At forty-two and forty-four the difference was seven minutes. Then eight minutes at forty-six, ten minutes at fifty miles, and with David's speed control set on cruise, he finished thirteen minutes ahead of the others. There is no doubt that he was excited to finish first, but he was especially excited to have put almost an hour and a half on Koyago. Muffy (David's crew, not a pet poodle) commented that his attitude has been renewed. David seems to be his old self again, talking and joking about stuff rather than dwelling on the heat and the hardness of the task. He did send Muff to the one store in town to buy five half-gallons of ice cream for the entire group. Everyone really appreciated this and is hoping that he wins more stages if it means more free ice cream.

The host town of Jacksonville is lodging the runners at the local fairgrounds. They are in a building that is air conditioned, although the floor is hard cement. There was one lady from Iowa who tracked David down, saying that she has been following his career for a long time and wanted to meet him. She was also kind enough to deliver a couple of e-mail messages. David liked that almost as much as getting mail.

In talking with David, he mentioned to me a scripture verse that has been written to him many times. Isaiah 40:31 says, "They that wait upon the Lord shall renew their strength; they shall mount up with wings like eagles; they shall run, and not be weary; and they shall walk, and not faint." Although Isaiah probably did not have the Trans-Am in mind, the application is very clear. David has run very patiently, and today he was rewarded with the physical strength to persevere. What the next days bring is yet to be seen, but for today our man Horton is feeling pretty good. He relaxed, ran comfortably, didn't try to win but did, got video of the end, got to tease Dusan about beating him, and ate ice cream. What could be better? (Actually, those eagle's wings would

The loneliness of a Trans-Am Runner.

help, and his knee and burnt lips could feel a lot better, but we won't complain today!)

Today's results: David (#1!!!!!!!!!!) 7:48:23 (8:45 pace), Dusan, Patrick, and Ray 8:01:42, Manfred 8:44:33

Today was a special day in many ways. It is the 44th day. Nineteen days of racing left to go. One day of real enjoyment. I won the stage, and I beat Koyago by over an hour and a half. I had Muffy buy five half-gallons of ice-cream for desert tonight in celebration and every one seemed really tickled about that. They all gave me a good hand when I was introduced as winning the stage. I think it was partly for getting the ice cream and partly because most of them like me. I hope they do anyway. I like them. This was a very special day. We'll see how I run tomorrow.

DAY 45 - JULY 31 - NEW BERLIN, IL TO DECATUR, IL - 55.7 MILES

One thing that Gary and I learned early on was that if David was really "up" one day, we could expect a "down" day pretty soon. Now, don't get too worried. David ran well today, sharing a first place win with Dusan, Patrick, and Ray. But the problem with the day was that they were baked in a giant sauna throughout the day. The heat index was 105-plus degrees and no one escaped its effects.

Patrick, Ray, David, and Dusan all took the lead and ran together for the ten miles that took them to Springfield. At ten miles, Manfred Leismann joined the group as they got the straight-through sight-seeing package of the town. Of course, the street going through town was quite busy and required a bit more concentration than usual. However, the road out of town basically led to nowhere. The only thing that the runners saw were corn and soybean fields on either side of a straight and flat road that seemed to stretch on forever. The day was really heating up, and the five runners' crews all stopped at a store and purchased ice cream for the racers. They were pretty surprised to be handed ice cream treats at twenty-two miles. The video should be pretty good, with the five fierce competitors walking (yes, walking) down the side of the road licking ice cream cones and chatting. Almost sounds like a walk in the park. Well, it wasn't and it sure didn't last long. Manfred wanted to run faster, so with Dusan's encouragement — "Go on ahead, Rooster. You can buy the ice-cream tonight!" — the pack watched him pull away. But at thirty-eight miles, the pack could see a suffering German, and they did catch him and pass by at forty miles. The pack did not enjoy it. They ran from aid station to aid station at a survival-only pace. Some of them commented that the heat was so intense that it must be what hell is like. The content of the sporadic conversation was just to get through the next very difficult stages and make it to the finish line. There was no talk of anyone beating anyone else. The four runners were united by their common focus on the goal: finish alive. That was enough of an incentive for them to run the last several hilly miles into the town of Decatur and get into a good shower once across the finish line. The four crossed the line as one. Today, the collective force of the group was probably what saved them all.

Their stop in Decatur is just three miles short of the two thousand-mile mark, thirteen hundred of those miles being run in July. The runners are staying in the Student Union Building of Miliken University. David was interviewed by Channel 6 TV (out of Decatur) and that went pretty good. Even "The Muffster" was interviewed to get his perspective as a crew person. David seems to be really wiped out emotionally and physically tonight. He is not planning to go anywhere or do anything except eat, drink, and sleep. And even that seems to require too much effort.

Today's results: David, Dusan, Ray, and Patrick 8:44:49, Manfred 9:11:34, Koyago (who could barely walk to the start line) 11:15.

Sleeping tonight in a carpeted and cool room in a recreation center.... Did have one surprise mystery guest today. Colleen Fletcher, Chris Fletcher's sister, [volleyball coach at Liberty University], brought me a couple of boxes, a bunch of suckers, and some balloons. It was really nice, and I appreciated it so much! The Decatur Running Club brought us spaghetti, salad, and ice cream.... I feel on again, off again. Up and down.... Gary

The Boys: (l-r) Dusan, David, Patrick and Ray finish a stage together.

[Trittipoe] told me that he read in Patrick's AOL diary that he doesn't think he can catch me. I just need to maintain this lead.... Look forward to tomorrow because it will be mail drop day.

DAY 46 - AUG 1 - DECATUR, IL TO NEWMAN, IL - 37.9 MILES

David's quote for the day: "We started and then we finished." How profound! He said it in a matter-of-fact tone and with no emotion. Not even the passing of the two thousand-mile mark could elicit a response other than, "So what? Who cares?" Obviously, the stage was fairly nondescript and the runners are now more interested in putting in the miles than in racing. It did help that the day wasn't quite as humid as yesterday, and the quartet of Dusan, David, Patrick, and Ray ran as a group until six miles. David felt as if they wanted to run a little quicker than he did, so he eased up just a bit and let the other three slowly pull away. However, twenty miles down the road David caught the group and they ran the next ten miles together. With just one mile of this very flat and straight course to go, Patrick took off with Ray following after just a moment. As Patrick pulled away, Dusan shook his head and smirked, "Huh, there goes Koyago II." All the effort that Patrick and Ray put into that last mile only earned them about a three-minute advantage. David and Dusan chose to be sane and took it home at the same pace.

The runners have a hotel tonight with really cold air conditioning. In fact, as I was talking with David, he was snuggled under the covers to stay warm. He was impressed that this town produced two actresses: one from the movie *I Love Trouble* (no, it wasn't Julia Roberts, but he can't remember her name) and Jenny Garth of "90210." Can you believe that he actually likes that show? Strange, but true! He has been taking it easy this afternoon and evening, saving up his strength for the next three days of fifty-six, fifty-three, and fifty-five miles. He really enjoyed the twenty-six pieces of mail he received today. Once again, this bundle of mail was far more than anyone else received. He sends his thanks!

Today's results: Patrick 5:36:58, Ray 5:37:05, David and Dusan 5:39:45. (Koyago was over eight hours, suffering from severe shin splints.)

Overall results: Dusan 290:42:04, Ray +11:31:37, David +19:05:45, Patrick +31:01:58, Koyago +33:56:18, Manfred

---

From the mailbox:

I shouldn't have been surprised when I received notification that you intended to run from the west coast to the east coast.... When you are beating your feet on that hot pavement each day I know that there are many times when you would get sensory messages from your joints and muscles — and I'm sure the bottom of your feet — to quit and go home, to think about a cool place that's relaxing, and something cool to drink and a soft place to lie down and relax. However, if it is God's will for you to continue, then you need not worry because He will give you the strength and the courage to do whatever it is that He wants you to do.... I ask that He encourage your family in your absence to understand what you're doing and to be an encouragement to you as well.

~Bill Irwin, Blind A.T. Thru-Hiker

+50:45:33, Jun Onoki +82:15:40, Eiko Endo +102:25:19, Kiyoto Nagata +105:50:57, Michiyoshi Kaiho +116:45:19, Don Winkley +207:18:44.

We passed the 2000-mile mark today.... Patrick feels like you should sprint to the finish, and to a certain degree I agree. I don't think that we should tie every day like we did yesterday. But I am not so sure how hard you should sprint. I think sprinting hard could be counterproductive.... Koyago was way back again. He is out of the running.... Mentally, I feel real good. Things seem to be going pretty well. I haven't been real low in a long time. But my lips are bad and my knee pain comes and goes. I will probably take a lot of Advil™ tomorrow, but Lord willing, I'll make it through.... I really appreciate all the cards and letters that people send to me. It means so much to know that people are praying for me and do really care. And I know that Nancy really misses me a lot, and I feel for her. Look forward to being back with her at home.

DAY 47 - AUGUST 2 - NEWMAN, IL TO ROCKVILLE, IN - 55.9 MILES

David is happy tonight. He ran well and set the pace for the distance today. He likes control, and today he had it. At times Patrick would pass him (the four front-runners were basically all together again), but since he runs an inconsistent pace, it would not take long before David would once again be in front. The temperature at the start was seventy-one degrees with ninety-seven percent humidity. There was cloud cover until about 11:00 a.m. at which time the sun came out blazing, raising the temperature to about ninety-seven degrees. That's enough to make you sweat just thinking about it! For the first twenty-eight miles the road did not have a single bend — just straight as an arrow. The runners passed into Indiana, at which time the surroundings suddenly seemed to take on a completely different character. The road was curvy, the grass green, forests thick, the little towns quaint, and the terrain hilly. David said it was actually very pretty. That's a good thing, given that there wasn't much conversation the first twenty miles of the stage because Dusan and Patrick had on their headphones and Ray doesn't ever say much. Later on, David and Patrick talked about fishing, and David, the good Arkansan that he is, tried to explain what a good catfish tastes like. There was also talk of what it would be like at the finish. After their first Trans-Am races, Patrick could not run for six months and Ray took off sixty-four days, tried to run four miles, couldn't, and added another month of rest. Obviously, the fact that they "couldn't" run was mental, but very real. David is hoping that he will not react like that!

The runners continued on, and they encountered a big, long hill somewhere around fifty miles. David eased up just a tad, but all of the runners got some relief when a big storm cloud opened up. It became dark very quickly and was raining so hard they could hardly see. The crews weren't too happy about being out in the rain, but the runners loved it. I think they were very disappointed when it stopped raining one-half mile from the finish line, the sun once again shining its fury. They took it to the line — Ray, Dusan, and Patrick finishing a mere thirty-eight seconds in front of David.

The runners behind this front pack should not be forgotten. They are out there on the road a lot longer than the leaders and really pay the price in terms of heat and effort. Yesterday, one of the Japanese runners was taken to the hospital for fluid replacement since he became sick, was vomiting, and was not sweating or urinating. He was back out on the course today, although still in a very weakened condition. Every one of the eleven runners is accomplishing great things! It may also help in terms of comparison that the top five runners are all ahead of the record pace for the Trans-Am. That's what you call a tough field!

Today's results: Patrick, Ray, Dusan 8:47:43, David 8:48:21, Manfred 9:18:31.

We finished the 47th day. We are in the — I can't even think of the name of the motel. Hard day.... I went to see a doctor about my lips. He thought it was wind damage. He gave me a prescription for a couple of medicines. Hopefully that will take care of the problem.... Patrick is a little over one hour behind me and Koyago is four hours behind him.... Two weeks from today this will be all over. What a tremendous feeling that will be! I just pray that the Lord will help me make it there. I appreciate all the people who pray for me and appreciate what Gary and Rebekah have done.... Tomorrow's distance is 52.5 miles. But it doesn't really matter. As Patrick said, we just need to take one day at a time.

DAY 48 - AUGUST 3 - ROCKVILLE, IN TO INDIANAPOLIS, IN - 52.5 MILES

In David's words, "Today was relatively easy, if there is any such thing." Even though the temperatures ranged from seventy-two degrees to a sunny and humid ninety-three degrees, the scenery was decent, with rolling hills and beautiful farms to enjoy, providing a point of focus other than the weather. Parts of the run even reminded him of Virginia. As usual, it was Dusan, David, Ray, and Patrick running together as the lead pack, but at ten miles Manfred caught them and went right on by. He pulled away a little bit at a time until he was out of sight. No one really worried about this for two reasons. First, he was no threat to challenging anyone's position. Secondly, even if he did hold the lead, this would be Manfred's first stage win. Since he seems to have earned the Mr. Congeniality award, everyone would truly be excited for him. As it turned out, Manfred did win the stage by about seventeen minutes, bellowing out his now legendary rooster call. The boys were together until one mile to go when Patrick surprisingly encouraged David to take off. However, he refused multiple proddings, because any increase in speed puts more strain on his knee. So, why take a chance for the sake of a few seconds? Eventually Ray, and then Patrick, went ahead by a few steps, and Dusan and David "jogged" it in. (David's words, not mine.) David said that if it were not for his knee, he could really run well, even better than now. He does not feel tired physically, but he is feeling mentally fatigued. David is ready for this race to be over!

Which reminds me, the race did unfortunately end for Kiyoto Nagata today. After being briefly hospitalized two days ago for dehydration, he managed to finish yesterday, but it cost him everything. Today he retired from the course at fourteen miles and was again hospitalized for possible kidney failure. He is expected to be in the hospital for several days. But the amazing thing is that he and his crew are planning to continue along the Trans-Am course in hopes of completing what was started.

Koyago seems to be making a comeback from his serious shin splints and was even seen lifting weights in the rec center that is home for the night. Patrick is very frustrated by the arrival of additional TV crews from Australia, feeling the intense pressure of the winning expectations. In his words to David, he is "totally spent and cannot win." This is a bit different from the defensive and sometimes arrogant-sounding Patrick who daily writes to the cyberspace community on *America-On-Line*. I guess we all say and do things as a matter of pride and self-respect.

Daniel Bellinger from Ohio took over Reid Lanham's position as crew person tonight. Reid did an excellent job of washing David's clothes, getting him food and drink, meeting him every two miles, playing photographer, and knowing when to laugh and when to be serious. Single-man crewing is very difficult, but we are confident that Daniel will do a fine job as well.

Today's results: Manfred 7:52:07, Ray 8:09:57, Patrick 8:10:34, David and Dusan 8:10:34.

DAY 49 - AUGUST 4 - INDIANAPOLIS, IN TO DUBLIN, IN - 56.6 MILES

When David called in tonight, he was full of lots of little fun-facts. So I'll describe the stage first and then get to the other stuff. In his own words, this was the best day for running since they left the Rockies. The temperature ranged from seventy-three to eighty degrees, a light rain fell for several hours, and cloudy skies prevailed for the rest of the day. What a welcome relief from the blistering sun! The boys ran as a pack again, with David taking the lead and setting the pace as usual. Apparently, Dusan loves for David to be in front, Ray doesn't mind, and it depends on how Patrick is feeling whether he fights David for the front. There was no idle chatter except for an occasional, "Hey, watch that car!" as they ran the first seventeen miles through downtown Indy. At mile three, they actually got off Route 36, which had been the route for the last thousand miles, and started on US 40. Route 40 has been around for a long time, running from Maryland to Utah and previously known as the National Highway. At eighteen or twenty miles, Patrick began to fall off the pace and by mile twenty-two was one whole aid station back. So the "Farmerless" group ran together to the end of this very long stage. There was extremely heavy truck traffic and no shoulder to run on. If you stepped off the road to avoid getting hit, you would find nothing but rocks and very uneven surface. (Come on, David! And you call yourself a trail runner!) However, between truck blasts, the conversation did actually pick up between Ray and, you guessed it, David. This is no surprise to those of us who know him. Since there is now no "energy" problem in running these miles, it seems to make the time pass more quickly if he can become involved in a conversation. David really developed a stronger appreciation for Ray after spending that time talking and listening. Dusan chose to be the silent one today. But regardless of whose mouth was moving faster, the group crossed the line together for the win.

Now for the "funfacts," stated in no particular order. Funfact #1: Today's mileage brought the total to 2199.85. That surpasses the mileage of 2144 when D.H. set the speed record for the Appalachian Trail in 1991. Funfact #2: The mileage for the past seven days was 345 miles, the heaviest week of the race. Funfact #3: The top six runners are all ahead of the record pace for the Trans-Am! Funfact #4: Each of those top six runners have won individual stages. This has never happened before. Funfact #5: Eiko Endo is ahead of the women's record pace. Funfact #6: Eiko was chased by a dog, fell, and badly sprained her wrist yesterday. Funfact # 7: David's typical breakfast is a bowl of cereal and one cup of coffee. (Aren't we all better for knowing this?) Funfact #8: They passed a historic marker in Lewisville which stated that this was the home of Marion Pierce. Don't recognize the name? He once held the record for the most points scored in an Indiana high school B-ball game. Funfact #9: To live successfully in Indiana one must (a) be a Republican, (b) be able to intelligently discuss soybeans, corn, and sow bellies, and (c) know and love H.S. B-ball. Funfact # 10:

The runners are staying in the R&R Motel tonight. It could very easily stand for "Rodents and Roaches"! Funfact #11: David has experienced no bed softer than his tonight except for his Grandma's feather bed. Funfact #12: He had to check the sheets to make sure nothing other than he (dead or alive!) was in bed. Funfact #13: David is opting for the floor tonight, if he can get past the stench. Maybe outside in a tent would be better! Funfact # 14: The race directors had to pay $20 for these wonderful rooms. What a bargain!

Today's results: David, Dusan, and Ray 8:44:55, Manfred 9:15:55, Patrick 9:45:10, Koyago 9:47: 07.

Overall standings: Dusan 316:25:16, Ray +11:31:00, David +19:06:23, Patrick +32:01:54, Koyago +36:32:33.

▲

From the mailbox (and on the lighter side):
    Congratulations, and remember, as you run, jog, walk, or crawl down the road of success... don't pick your nose!
                                              ~Greg and Janet Comfort
                                                    Donna McDowell

▼

CHAPTER 19

Week 8 of the Trans-Am

Commit thy way unto the Lord; trust also in him;
and he shall bring it to pass.

- Psalms 37:5

DAY 50 - AUGUST 5 - DUBLIN, IN TO LEWISBURG, OH - 36.0 MILES

Fifty racing days down and thirteen days left to race. (They don't race the last day. Time stops at the end of day sixty-three.) Because of the shorter distance, the stage looked more like a race than the last week or so. Through twenty miles, David, Dusan, Patrick, and Ray enjoyed the cooler temperatures, light rain, little towns, and rolling hills as a group. But Manfred soon caught the lead pack and went on by, taking Patrick with him. Soon after, Koyago caught the threesome and ran with them for awhile before going on. It was around twenty-four miles that Dusan picked it up, passing Koyago at twenty-six miles. David and Ray had backed off the pace. The race, seeming like a giant game of leapfrog, changed again when David passed Koyago at thirty miles, leaving Ray on his own. In the end, the finish order was Manfred and Patrick, Dusan, followed by David and then Ray. David said he was weary today and pushing the pace would have no advantage and would only unnecessarily risk injury.

David was pleased to see a number of familiar faces today. "Lone Wolf" (a.k.a. David Blair) was waiting at the finish line ready to crew for the next several days. Regis and Diana Shivers were also there, planning to spend the Ohio days taking video and pictures and nursing David with good massages. Donald Smith was also there. Donald is a great friend of David's, and David will be serving as groomsman in his wedding the week after the Trans-Am's completion. Hope they make some men's trousers with twenty-eight or thirty-inch waists! Maybe he could use suspenders to keep his pants from falling down!

The group is staying in the basement of a Lutheran church.

Since there are no showers, any cleaning up is outside underneath a camp shower. David said he was standing under the shower outside and in the rain. But at least he got clean — we hope!

Today's results: Manfred and Patrick 5:13:05, Dusan 5:23:36, David 5:25:57, Ray 5:27:30, Koyago 5:32:55.

DAY 51 - AUGUST 6 - LEWISBURG, OH TO SOUTH VIENNA, OH - 52.65 MILES

Under the coolest skies since Georgetown, Colorado, the race began at 5:00 a.m. with the mercury hanging around sixty-three degrees. Being in the most western part of a new time zone also gave the runners the benefit of additional darkness. The group of David, Dusan, Ray, and Patrick ran together from start to finish, with David setting the pace. He felt like he was the strongest of the group and even considered taking off from the rest. However, his knee is still a concern and he does not want to take any unnecessary risk of a major injury at this point in the race. The first twenty miles were basically run in silence, although David did occasionally make comments or ask questions that would go unanswered. However, in the last twenty miles, the conversation picked up and included a variety of topics: the ease of filing lawsuits for things like spilling coffee when driving, discipline in schools, and current movies (not that any of them have seen one). When they arrived at the finish line, nothing was said, but all four crossed the line together. The four are all superb athletes, tremendously motivated, mentally tough, all with different personalities, but all winners.

As David and I talk daily, he tells me of more and more comments that are being made to him in all sincerity and as a means of encouragement. Comments like, "You've got it made now," "The hard part is over," "Now you can just cruise on in," are not being taken very well. Although he knows the excitement of the end drawing near is growing, it is felt more by the family, friends, and crew than by the runners. To the runners, seven hundred more miles of racing is still seven hundred more miles — and many more miles than most ultrarunners will race in an entire year! Injuries can crop up at any time. Runners still need to get up at 4:00 a.m. every morning, put on their shoes and "go to work."

The runners are aware that no one made them do this race, but it doesn't change the fact that the grind, physically and mentally, is almost beyond imagination. There are still consecutive days with mileage in the mid-fifties to almost sixty-one. None of them really feel like talking about the stages after they run. They are just too mentally fatigued to recount all their experiences. What they need to do is continue to take care of their bodies, eat, and sleep. However, all are concerned that they not come across as ungracious to those who are interested and those who care. The runners know they walk a fine line, and they certainly do not want to hurt anyone's feelings. This is especially of concern to David, since so many people have given of their resources to aid him in his adventure. He is looking forward to the reception to be given in his honor at Liberty University in September, where he will be able to tell a large collective body the details of his experience rather than doing it one person at a time.

David's accommodations tonight are in a hot and stuffy school gymnasium. Since the weather has turned out to be so pleasant, he set up his tent outside underneath a big tree. He thinks that sleeping out will be a welcome change from the confining walls of the gym. Now, if we can just keep lightning from striking...!

Today's results: David, Dusan, Ray, and Patrick 8:10:31, Koyago 8:30:09, Manfred 8:36:05.

DAY 52 - AUGUST 7 - S. VIENNA, OH TO REYNOLDSBURG, OH - 43.7 MILES

The stage started in the cool (sixty-five degrees) and the dark of the early morning. Running on a four-lane divided highway, the first twenty-four miles were flat. The four front-runners (David, Dusan, Patrick, Ray) were at mile four when David felt someone tap him on his shoulder. Surprised to see Manfred, he exclaimed, "What are you doing here, my friend?" and then watched him run off. The pack, wanting just to run cautiously and smart, let him go without a fight. In fact, David says that all the runners are now in a daze for at least the first twenty miles. No one talks, no one is excited about what lies ahead, but everyone knows they have to move on down the road. So, they just run with the sole aim of getting from point A to point B. Despite the silence, it was noticed that at eighteen miles, Koyago had come within a hundred yards, but was dropping back significantly at twenty miles and was not seen again. Mile twenty-four brought them into Columbus proper and led them right down Broad Street, which is in the center of downtown. Seeing all the people "dressed for success," David and Patrick commented they felt out of place: sweaty, slimy, road warriors just passing through on a three thousand-mile run. One lady did inquire if they were running a marathon. Although it took effort to be cordial, the pack quickly and politely stated, "No, we are running across America." On they went, relentlessly pursuing the goal. Up on the sidewalk, down to the road. Up on the sidewalk, down to the road. (The police would wave the runners back onto the sidewalks if they were seen running on the road.) They did enjoy perhaps the prettiest one-mile section of road for the entire race when they turned onto Park View Avenue, a stately and prestigious tree-lined street. Since the Columbus area is very urbanized, they basically had nothing but sidewalks and stoplights all the way to the end. The runners finished up at a huge and beautiful high school, with David carrying an American flag that he found all the way back at mile thirty-nine. Manfred ended up with the win, finishing thirty-two minutes in front of "The Boys." But no one really cared about the thirty-two minutes. They are glad to have finished in a reasonable time with no new injuries, saving themselves for the one hundred-seventy-two-miles that are coming up in the next three days. All the runners are very concerned about these miles and will continue to run easy.

Not contending well with flies and ants in his tent last night, David is hoping to get a better night's sleep tonight in the cool and large gymnasium. He continues his routine of icing, eating, and resting, and then repeating the sequence at least once. He had dinner at a Ponderosa restaurant tonight, still finding eating difficult and actually very painful given his blistered lips. Oh, but he was excited to have driven Donald Smith's sporty little car yesterday. He claims that he didn't hit anyone — on the road or sidewalk. Hard to believe if you know how David normally drives, let alone not having driven in eight weeks! Anyway, the evening news did not report any incidents of a deranged man behind the wheel, so I guess we'll assume that things went reasonably well.

Just a note about Nagata. As you will remember, Nagata dropped from the race and was hospitalized with possible kidney failure. He has been released from the hospital and came by the high school to report that he must return to Japan. His physical condition is so depleted that it would be impossible and very dangerous to continue his quest for New York. This must be terribly disappointing after completing over two thousand miles.

Today's results: Manfred 6:18:17, David, Dusan, Patrick, and Ray 6:50:39, Koyago 7:04:14.

Overall standings: Dusan 336:50:02, Ray +11:34:54, David +19:08:44, Patrick +31:51:23, Koyago +37:15:05, Manfred +51:01:36, Jun Onoki +86:32:15, Eiko Endo +110:28:57, Michiyoshi Kaiho +125:18:18, Don Winkley +242:08:27.

DAY 53 - AUGUST 8 — REYNOLDSBURG, OH TO NEW CONCORD, OH - 59.0 MILES - CUMULATIVE MILES - 2391.2

David is one who always seems to make connections between events, times, and places. He was quick to point out that in 1991 it took him fifty-two days, nine hours and forty-one minutes to set the speed record for the 2144-mile Appalachian Trail. Today, after fifty-two days, nine hours and fifteen minutes, David completed over 2391 miles in his Trans- America bid. The A.T. endeavor was very difficult in terms of effort, running surface, steep mountains and solitude. The Trans-Am is difficult because of the beating you get by running only on hard surfaces, as well as racing other runners on a daily basis. David has already proven his excellence in both environments.

The weather at the start was warm and humid, and the first ten miles were gradually uphill. The boys' club of Dusan, David, Patrick, and Ray were all together when a huge thunderstorm with lightning and heavy rain came up around the ten-mile mark. The downpour was at times so heavy that the runners could barely see where they were going. These conditions persisted until about mile twenty-six, forcing many of the now cold runners to don warmer clothing.

In fact, Patrick thought the rain was through at mile twenty-six and changed into dry clothes and shoes. Unfortunately for him, he got wet again, even though the rain was not quite as hard. However, this quick change wasn't quick enough to prevent the others from slipping away. With the three running on, mile thirty-four presented a big uphill climb. David decided to walk this hill, Dusan ran it, and Ray stopped to change his shoes. This effectively separated the three runners, with Dusan steadily pulling away. Ray stayed anywhere from four hundred yards to as little as fifty yards behind David, depending on if David was walking a hill, running level, or running downhill. (Ray runs all the uphills, so he would gain ground going up but lose ground going down.) At mile forty-six in a town called Zanesville, David took time to have his picture taken hugging a wooden Indian (go figure!). Ray did actually catch up but told David, "Don't let me hold you up." Shortly after that, a spectator yelled, "Go Forest!" and David responded. With the end of the rain and very comfortable weather conditions at this point, David ran on and closed in on Dusan who had previously been out of sight. He felt good throughout the run and finished in second position, just five minutes behind Dusan.

They are staying tonight at Muskingum College. The facilities are very nice at this Presbyterian school that was founded in 1837.

From the mail box:
    I can't believe it, but it will almost be over soon. I am so very curious to know what you will do the week following the completion of the race. I wonder, too, in my inquiring little mind, if this trek will change you, somehow, in some someway. You know it has been said that in times of disaster, war, famine, pestilence, or whatever, we emerge from them a "changed" person, inevitably. Sometimes it is only that we are changed mentally, other times, in other ways. Maybe you won't even notice that you have changed, but others will....
Life is change. Growth is optional. Choose wisely.
                                                    ~Linda Sledge

The town of New Concord, with a population of one thousand people, more than doubles when the eleven hundred students are in town during the academic year. The town also boasts that its favorite son is John Glenn, having been born, raised, and schooled in this mid-America town. And it is a good thing that the post office functions efficiently, because they successfully transferred all thirty-five pieces of mail into David's hands today. You can't believe what a kick he gets out of mail drop days! Thanks to all of you!

Today's results: Dusan 9:10:03, David 9:15:34, Ray 9:20:03, Manfred, Patrick, and Koyago 10:10:50

DAY 54 - AUGUST 9 - NEW CONCORD, OH TO ST. CLAIRSVILLE, OH - 52.6 MILES

No sun. No rain. Temperatures between sixty-five and seventy-five degrees. Overcast skies. Breezy. Those were the conditions the runners had for the day's stage. This helped considerably, since the course's numerous and very steep hills demanded a higher level of energy. The first twenty miles went by with David, Dusan, Patrick, and Ray all together once again. However, with David's knees, hips and Achilles hurting again and feeling all of the 2443 miles behind him, he started walking the hills. Dusan calls him the "trial walker." He really means, "trail," but his Slovenian tongue can't quite get it right. Anyway, despite his walking, David did not lose any ground overall. The only thing that irritated him was that the other guys would be talking and he couldn't quite hear what was being said until he caught up again with the pack. And we all know how David hates to miss out on a good conversation! Ten miles of the stage were on a dirt road that led them past a buffalo farm. The uphills were mostly short and steep, and no one pushed the downhills because it hurt too much. From twelve miles out, David started running all the hills with the boys, and with just two-and-one half-miles left to go, Patrick started picking it up. Today, everyone picked it up as well. At one mile to go, Patrick continued to run harder, until Dusan told Patrick in no uncertain terms, "Don't try war!" Patrick replied, "Oh, no. That's fine. We'll all finish together." David said he was a little disappointed because he wanted to see those two take it to the wire.

The runners are really wishing for a good motel, but they will have to wait several more nights. David has not been sleeping well (mainly because of his lips), and Patrick says David was talking in his sleep all night. Tonight they get to stay in a tiny room of a community rec center. There are no phones, so David and his crew, Lone Wolf, had to go to the mall to make his calls. He pulled a nearby bench over to the phone so he could sit down, only to be told by the security guard that he couldn't do that — maintenance would complain. So he took the weary runner's seat away. How cruel! They found a Bonanza Steak House for supper, so hopefully he will get his stomach refueled. His lips are so raw that it is very difficult for him to eat. That is why he is drinking two to three chocolate malts per day. Slurping the high calorie stuff through a straw is much easier than getting real food past his lips. He is so desperate that he even tried putting some Bag Balm (intended for cow teats) on his lips. It didn't help.

In asking David what he eats and drinks on these long stages, he replied that he drinks mainly Conquest™, although Mountain Dew™ is sometimes a welcome change. He likes to eat Reese's Peanut Butter Cups™, Mallo Cups™, Skor™ bars, pretzels, Power Bars™, ice cream bars after thirty miles, and cantaloupe or watermelon after forty miles. He normally will not allow himself to look at his watch until after forty miles.

All of these runners are getting seriously fatigued, mentally and physically. Please continue to pray them in across the finish line in New York. David would also be grateful for healing prayers for his lips. This condition really depresses him and makes him feel miserable.

Today's results: David, Dusan, Ray, and Patrick 8:24:58, Koyago and Manfred 8:47:19.

I am sitting here in Red Devil Stadium. Very cool, about 70 degrees. Big stadium, cinder track, beautiful field. Why would any town name their mascot a "red devil"? I wonder what the Christians around here think about that. One solitary guy was jogging around the track.... Stayed cloudy all day. I am always thankful for that. I was a little tired today. I ran pretty hard overall.

DAY 55 - AUGUST 10 - ST. CLAIRSVILLE, OH TO MONONGAHELA, PA - 60.3 MILES - 2504.1 CUMULATIVE MILES

Does the word "dogmeat" mean anything to you? I think it means plenty to David. A course of 60.3 miles on extremely steep, hilly terrain after 2504 miles means that he was one tired pup, even at the start. Under cloudy skies, the usual foursome started out together. At four miles Manfred came up from behind and kept on going. They continued at the same pace, leaving Ohio at mile ten and entering West Virginia. Somewhere around fifteen miles, Koyago caught the group and ran with them through twenty miles, at which time he said "adios" to the boys. A mile before leaving West Virginia at mile twenty-five, the hills became very steep and David wisely decided to walk. In fact, he probably walked more today than he did some of those times in the Rockies. Therefore, the trio pulled away and Dr. Dave was left alone. But, not for long. At thirty miles, Jun Onoki caught David and they started playing games with each other. If Onoki was ahead, David would quietly close in and then let out a terrific yell to scare the living daylights out of him. He did this several times, but then got his when Onoki scared David just before running off and leaving him. His parting words were, "You are one crazy runner!" Aided by crew person Lone Wolf, David managed to make it over the last twenty-four miles to the finish. He was not injured at the end of the run, just very tired. Fortunately, the next nine days average "only" forty-four miles per day with nothing over fifty. That's a bunch, but it's not as bad as sixty-mile days!

The runners are staying in the Monongahela Fire Hall tonight. It is really just one big room where the runners can spread out their stuff and try to get comfortable. Ultrarunning standout Chris Gibson and his wife are providing dinner: spaghetti, salad, bread, and the works for the entire crew. How nice! A huge article in a Pittsburgh newspaper highlighted David personally in conjunction with this race. This was encouraging to him. Although we have yet to see it, he said the writer did an excellent job of including lots of factual information and accurate details.

Today's results: Manfred 9:16:57, Koyago 10:08:20, Patrick 10:18:01, Ray and Dusan 10:20:07, Jun Onoki 10:22:39, David 10:27:25, Eiko Endo 11:08:00.

DAY 56- AUGUST 11 - MONONGAHELA, PA TO LIGONIER, PA - 43.45 MILES

The morning was warm and humid. Like so many other mornings, the quartet of David, Dusan, Patrick, and Ray took the early lead. They were joined this morning by Manfred as they ran four miles along the Monongahela River. Then a big hill reared its ugly head and David started walking while the others continued to run. You can guess what happened. At five miles Jun Onoki passed David. Then at sixteen miles, a little Japanese voice said, "You okay, David?" Eiko Endo went on by. She eventually caught and passed Ray and Patrick as well. (Ray was struggling and actually almost quit due to a bad Achilles problem today.) But David ran on and caught up to Patrick at mile twenty-three. They ran together just briefly before David went on by. Even though he was really tired, seeing Eiko up in the distance motivated him. He wished she would speed up and get out of sight. But his ego got the best of him, and he finally caught her at thirty-three miles. She did seem to pick it up with David closing in on her, but being so sweet and polite, she had a "Good job, David," as he went by. David finished up the run with sore hamstrings and feeling very weary. The terrain was extremely hilly, and everyone is showing signs of fatigue. Koyago had a good run, finishing first and gaining a minute and twelve seconds on Patrick. If Koyago continues to run strong and Patrick remains tired, there could still be a close race between fourth and fifth place.

Gary and I got up early this morning to drive to Pennsylvania. We are joining Lone Wolf on this final week into New York. We have been busy planning for David's race for such a long time — it hardly seems possible that we will finally get to see the actual thing. We are really looking forward to these eight days!

Today's results: Koyago 6:48:40, Onoki 6:52:33, Leismann 6:52:33, Mravlje 7:00:36, Horton 7:45:25.

Overall standings: Dusan 351:45:46, Ray +12:45:32, David +20:05:44, Patrick +34:01:04, Koyago + 38:14:22.

CHAPTER 20

Week 9 of the Trans-Am

It never always gets worse.

~ David Horton

DAY 57 - AUGUST 12 - LIGONIER, PA TO SHELLSBURG, PA - 37.8 MILES

If I tell you that today's course was hilly, believe me, it was hilly! David said this was even tougher than the Rockies. The first climb out of the town of Ligonier was a lousy three-and one-half-miles long with a grade up to eleven or twelve percent. Of course, this was followed by a very long descent. Then, another steep hill would follow with a downhill on the other side. (You never would have guessed, right?) This sequence was repeated over and over again. David decided to run smart and take it easy on the down-hills and walk/run the uphills. Even though his place was seventh today, he ran pretty well. This is good, since a number of good friends and family showed up to see him. It would have been a real drag had he run poorly and been in a rotten mood!

The race was also interesting from the standpoint that there was a very intense contest up front. Since Koyago was trying to make up some of the four hours that he is behind Patrick, he went out fast. It was sort of funny to see Patrick yawning and acting so nonchalant at the start and then taking off after Koyago. There was no way he was going to give up any more time to the Japanese runner. If you could have seen them charging up those hills, you would all be amazed. As it ended up, Patrick finally got a 0.7-mile lead, only to have Koyago catch him at around twenty-six miles. They fought to hold each other at bay with Koyago sprinting in and beating Patrick by one second.

Considering Jun Onoki's strong performances the last couple of days, seven men are now ahead of record pace. Eiko Endo is well ahead of the women's record. What an incredible field!

Two little fun facts that might be of interest: Eiko Endo's hus-band presents her with flowers at the close of each stage, and David will only eat the same flavor Starburst™ candies at one time. No rainbow flavors for Horton! I'm sure you all feel privileged to know this!

We are staying in a motel tonight. It is not fancy but adequate, even though the bathtub looks like it was made for vertically challenged people. There is a nice little restaurant two hundred yards down the street and a hamburger joint further down the road. David doesn't even have to do without his two or three chocolate milkshakes.

Today's results: Koyago 5:34:07, Farmer 5:34:08, Onoki 5:55:37, Mravlje 6:04:05, Bell 6:12:15, Leismann 6:21:30, Horton 6:28:17.

DAY 58 - AUGUST 13 - SHELLSBURG, PA TO MCCONNELLSBURG, PA - 41.7

The morning was overcast but humid. You could tell there were going to be at least a couple of people racing when several were warming up for the day's run by actually running. At the two-mile aid station, David was in the lead, with Patrick, Ray, and Dusan on his heels. At four miles it was still basically "The Boys" with Jun Onoki closing in. But how things changed by mile six. They came two-by-two: Patrick and Koyago, Ray and Jun, and David and Dusan. It is hard to describe how hard Patrick and Koyago run even the hills! By mile eight, Jun, who is running incredibly well and had also pulled away from Ray and Dusan, had a hundred yards on David. Koyago did manage to get an edge on Patrick by nine miles, but Patrick caught up by mile twelve. Meanwhile, David, running now in sixth position, stopped briefly for a photo-op beside a plastic four-foot ice cream cone next to a DQ™. Although David's hat was blown off his head by a passing semi, and he stopped to pick up a screwdriver and later a great dog leash (which he gave to the Bells for their dog), he maintained his position through twenty-five miles. The race up front continued to heat up, neither Patrick nor Koyago stopping even to "water the weeds" unless the other one did. Manfred, starting off slow, but really picking it up, caught and passed David on one of the incredibly steep and long hills of the course. Unfortunately, the cloud cover disappeared by twenty-eight miles and it became hot enough to start sponging David with ice water. I hardly have to mention that whenever there are uphills, there are inevitably downhills. In fact, there was very little (five percent) of the course that wasn't either up or down. Flat is not in the dictionary in this part of the state! David persisted and Manfred ran even harder, passing Ray at thirty-four miles. David stopped for another photo-op atop a wooden cow, and it was appropriate that the song on the radio at the time was a Moody Blues tune entitled "I'm Getting Closer to My Home." Ligonier resident Arnold Palmer's black Cadillac also passed us on the road. How about that?! Anyway, although emotionally on the thin side and tired, David brought it to the finish line and was greeted by a number of friends who drove up to see him. He really does appreciate the time and effort many have made to greet him along the way.

Incidentally, running his heart out in an attempt to get closer to Patrick's fourth place overall, Koyago put the hurts on Patrick and won the stage by twenty-one minutes.

The intersection of I-70/I-76 and Route 30 in Breezewood, Pennsylvania shows that not all the roads on the Trans-Am were so desolate.

Tonight's lodging is a lovely, hot, steamy, fly-infested 1934 gymnasium. Many of the runners have acquired fly swatters to get an edge on the war with the winged enemy. Some of the runners are getting a little testy about the conditions, but there are not enough hotel rooms in town to be able to do anything about it. I think that a key ingredient to surviving this race as crew or runner is to "make like a boat and go with the flow."

Today's results: Koyago 5:56:51, Patrick 6:17:20, Jun 6:23:47, Dusan 6:31:23, Manfred 6:34:24, Ray 6:39:33, David 6:55:54.

DAY 59 - AUGUST 14 - McCONNELLSBURG, PA TO GETTYSBURG, PA - 47.1 MILES

After a hard rain last night that left all those sleeping outdoors drenched, the runners had a very humid, thick start. (Getting a real break,) the runners had at least 100 yards of gradual downhill before they were treated to a steady, three mile, 14-percent grade climb to the top of a mountain. David ran halfway up and was in the lead before deciding that it just wasn't worth it and the others caught up to him. With Koyago now in the lead, Dusan quipped, "Hey, don't you think this pace is a little slow? This hill is child's play!" Whether or not it had any effect, Koyago was the first one to the top and ran the entire day like a man possessed. Patrick did run with Koyago, but a stop for "the call of nature" allowed Koyago to build a one-mile lead by mile fourteen. Koyago extended the lead to three miles by the time he entered Gettysburg and finished with a new stage record of 6:30:44.

Meanwhile, back at the ranch, David ran cautiously down the backside of the three-mile climb. During the descent he was passed by the eighth-place runner but regained his position by the ten-mile aid station. He ran consistently six-and-one-half-minutes behind Jun Onoki for much of the stage.

At the twenty-six-mile mark it was interesting to see Dusan catch Patrick, with Patrick telling his crew, "I never thought I'd be glad to see Dusan!" Although the Australian and Slovenian have had personality clashes in the past, Dusan told Patrick to run with him and he would have no problem. Patrick has problems keeping an even pace when running by himself. Dusan's steady pace was a welcome relief for about fifteen miles.

Jumping back to David, he picked up a hat around eight miles that had a profound saying. It read, "If older is getting better, then I must be approaching magnificent." Into the bag of road-kill items it went. At thirty miles, he took the time for a photo with some Lynchburg hasher friends, and at 30.5 miles he took a five-minute break. Why? Because it was here that David's two "adventures" physically crossed. In 1991, David crossed this same spot as he was traveling south to north in his record-breaking Appalachian Trail run. Now he was traveling west to east on his journey across America. He took time to record his thoughts on video and run up the trail just a bit before he resisted the cool, quiet trail and turned back to the noise and traffic of Route 30.

As the heat and humidity continued to rise, it began to take its toll. David did not slow down, but he did say at mile thirty-eight, "I'm starting to get tired." As crew, we continued to offer him lots of food and drink. He even downed a slushy pint of Ben and Jerry's™

Intersection of Appalachian Trail and Trans-America Foot Race (near Chambersburg, PA). David takes time to reflect along with his crew: Lone Wolf (David Blair) and Gary & Rebekah Trittipoe.

ice cream which was in the cooler. After working his way through the heart of tourist-ridden Gettysburg, he crossed the finish line and retired to icebags, milkshakes, lunch, and massage.

We had a nice hotel tonight, complete with swimming pool. Of course, none of the runners used it, but a few of the crew had about forty-five minutes to cool off. Kaiho, in ninth place overall, held a shoe show, laying out all seventy-five pairs of $150 Asics™ shoes. Why so many? Who knows! David only used eight pairs of shoes, Manfred five pairs, and Don Winkley is still working on his first pair!

Today's results: Koyago 6:30:44, Patrick 6:55:15, Dusan 6:58:13, Manfred 7:03:20, Jun 7:07:54, Ray 7:13:05, David 7:27:13.

DAY 60 - AUGUST 15 - GETTYSBURG, PA TO LANCASTER, PA - 49.7 MILES

To keep things in perspective, when the signs on two churches say, "It's hotter in hell," and, "You think it's hot here?" Guess what? It's hot. The temperature at 5:00 a.m. this morning was a very humid seventy-five degrees. In fact, it was so humid that it looked as if it had rained. But the runners took their mark anyway and started the task for the day. Although David had no grand plans for the day, by two miles he had a 150-yard lead on the others. By four miles, the lead had extended to about 250 yards. He was in good spirits and came into the aid station quoting a road sign he had just seen that had some significance: "Today is a special day because it is called the present." Stopping for a chance to relieve himself of excess fluid, he heard the sound of tiny little

206

pitter-pats coming up. No surprise to anyone, it was Koyago. As he ran by, David jokingly said, "Come back here, little Japanese dude. You're not allowed to pass me!" Koyago laughed, did an about face, took several steps back toward David, exchanged some light-heartedness, and promptly took off down the road. We did not see his crew for very long at each of the aid stations because he was still in the "run-your-guts-out" mode of the last week or so. He ended up finishing twenty-two minutes ahead of David. But, David was also running very well and comfortably. The pack of Dusan, Patrick, Jun Onoki, and Ray were 4:27 behind David's second position by mile sixteen. Because his knee was starting to hurt pretty badly he told us that he might back off a tad. There were a few aid stations where we measured the difference of between 3:50 and 4:04. However, the next time we compared the pack with David, the time difference was more like 4:50. He was still running smoothly and looking great. Although he got a little

Patrick and David
share time together on the road.

testy, and in frustration said, "This is stupid," his lead increased over the pack to 5:20. At the second to last aid station, Patrick called to us saying it was David's turn to buy ice cream, chocolate preferably. He finished strong in 7:31:31, although he was quite stressed mentally. As it has been the last several days, several friends and acquaintances were waiting for him at the finish.

The lodging for tonight is the private home of Will Campbell, an attorney who is on the Trans-Am board of directors. I hope they knew what they were getting into, since fifty people, give or take a few, invaded every available space of living area. The local running club is supplying the evening meal.

Two fun facts for today are as follows: when going through the city of York, there was actually a spotted firehouse dog (Dalmatian) in a firehouse. And speaking of dogs, Ray Bell not only has his whole family traveling with him, even the dog, Heidi, came along. It is the first dog ever to make the crossing!

With three racing days and one fun day on Saturday left in the 1995 Trans-America Footrace, the worst thing to say to any of the runners is, "You've got it made." The runners still have about 180 miles to run. It's not over till the fat lady sings.

Today's results: Koyago 7:09:03, David 7:31:31, Dusan, Ray, Patrick, and Jun 7:37:43.

DAY 61 - AUGUST 16 - LANCASTER, PA TO KUTZTOWN, PA - 47.5 MILES

This morning it was actually a comfortable temperature for the runners. As they started out for their 47.5 miles, David was leading the pack. From the first aid station all the way to the finish, "The Boys" (David, Dusan, Patrick, and Ray) ran as a group. Their attitude was to make the stage as pleasant as possible, without the mental and physical stress of racing. The one lone ranger of the day was Koyago, which was no surprise to anyone. By the second aid station (four miles), Koyago was in front by a third of a mile. By the end of the day, he would have just a smudge over a thirty-two-minute lead. No one really worried about that. In fact, Dusan teased him as he went by that he was not running fast enough. Dusan is of the opinion that Koyago has not yet learned that you cannot go out at a kamikaze rate all the time, everyday. This is probably why he, as well as Patrick, has suffered the most dramatic hills and valleys: Run hard, good results, breakdown. Run slow, bad results, heal. Run hard, good results, etc.

So, the "Boys Club" kept on "motoring" down the road, taking in many different views. The most colorful area was when they ran through the slums of Reading. One lady got irate because there was a flour arrow on the sidewalk outside her run-down row house. Jesse, one of the race directors, said that the police got quite a few calls complaining about the very temporary flour markings on the roads. To the delight of the Club, however, a garbage man spoke to them, recognizing them from the TV news report the evening before. He even recalled exactly how many miles had to be crossed today. Then, since the runners could advance almost as quickly as we could in the traffic, David ran up on our support truck (Lone Wolf and me) and "scared the fool" out of us. (If you're wondering, that phrase came straight out of Arkansas as taught to us by both David and Nancy Horton!) There were also a number of ice creams and popsicles given out at aid stations to provide cool refreshment on a hot day. The guys even got playful, squirting each other with their water bottles. So, the day was uneventful and stress free for David and his buds. But don't think it was totally a piece of cake. The mileage of 47.5 was still a long way, and all of them were glad to get another day behind them.

We have a motel tonight with a pool. No one except the kids and a few of the crew use it, but it's nice to have it available. We

One of 1,453 stops for crews to aid their runners.

are hoping to find a good restaurant where lots of calories can be consumed — for David's sake, of course!

Today's results: Koyago 6:49:01, David, Dusan, Patrick, and Ray 7:21:05.

DAY 62 - AUGUST 17 - KUTZTOWN, PA TO WASHINGTON, NJ - 52.15

The first thing we heard out of David's mouth this morning was "Number 62!" All the runners (and crew) are really excited to be nearing the end of this endeavor. Everyone is tired and is putting in the miles simply to get from point A to B. Everyone, that is, except for Koyago. He is still running for his own pride and tearing up the course. He had his sixth stage win in a row, but it looks like his fifth place overall standing will remain. He has closed the gap on Patrick, but barring a major catastrophe, Patrick should hold onto fourth place.

As far as David's run today, he, Dusan, Patrick, and Ray ran together as a pack. By six miles, Koyago took the lead and never relinquished it. However, by twelve miles, Ray began having some problems and Jun Onoki, an abdominal surgeon currently studying tropical disease in London, joined the pack. It was at twenty-six miles that Jun also fell off the pace leaving the second position to David, Dusan, and Patrick. The traffic was heavy into the Allentown, Bethlehem, and Easton areas, but the directors routed the course through previously uncharted territory. We all found ourselves on a one-way, very narrow road through the woods that took us over railroad tracks. As we were waiting, a freight train began to pull out and we placed a quarter on the track to be smashed as a souvenir for David. It squished! But after that excitement, the course continued through the country as the sun rose higher and hotter in the sky. The course passed by the Larry Holmes Training Center and shortly thereafter into New Jersey. Some guys at the corner gas station cheered the runners on saying, "Only seventy-five miles to New York City. It's just over the top of the hill!" How appropriate. David is always using lines like "just over the mountain" or "just around the next bend." Despite the crew getting temporarily misplaced, we saw the runners through the last twelve miles. It was sunny, ninety-one degrees, and one runner (who shall remain nameless) was pretty tense and irritable. (It was not David or Dusan!) Anyway, although it was hard work and not fun, David, Dusan and Patrick crossed the line more as comrades than competitors.

For your information, several of the Moonbat people ran twenty-six miles today — just to see what it was like. All but one had never run even recreationally before. It just goes to prove that you can do nearly anything you want if the desire is there. Now, there is no guarantee that you'll be able to walk the next day, but that's life.

Today's results: Koyago 7:31:53, David, Dusan, Patrick 8:08:10, Jun 8:24:58.

DAY 63 - AUGUST 18 - WASHINGTON, NJ TO S. ORANGE, NJ - 49.4 MILES - 2872.75 CUMULATIVE MILES

In terms of significance, this was it: the last day of competitive running. The attitude at the start was a little different from other mornings. Once they woke up, I think everyone realized that the end was near — finally. After sixty-two days of steady running through desert, over the Rockies, across the wide open plains, over more mountains, toward the coast, and on toward NYC, the runners are more than ready to actually enjoy the thirty-mile journey tomorrow. Saturday's stage signifies the culmination of a tremendous physical and mental challenge; a task that many would say should be impossible. But ten runners will get up in the stillness of the morning and set out to finalize the race. Thirty miles, run as a group, will lead them to their destination of Central Park. But there is not one who would disagree that truly it was the journey and not the destination that was the most important.

Nevertheless, today's miles still had to be run, and the course was difficult with rolling hills and some steep, long climbs. Everyone knew that Koyago would be blasting through the course. In fact, he told race director Michael Kenney that he knew he couldn't overtake Patrick for fourth place overall, but that he wanted to run as fast as he could for as long as he could. He did.

He won the stage by fifty-two minutes, setting a fifth straight stage record.

The plan was for David, Dusan, Patrick, Ray, Jun, and Manfred to run together as a group. The plan worked except for Ray. He had an injury flare up and started falling back as early as mile four. He finished, but was eighty-two minutes back from the pack. The weather was cool this morning, but heated up with the rising sun, although the humidity was not a problem. The runners did not particularly enjoy the hills, but they saw it through to the finish line, each carrying their country's flag. Lone Wolf slipped David the beautiful floral bouquet he had us purchase between aid stations, and he presented it to Nancy, his wife. David was very happy to have Nancy, Charlie and Nancy Hesse, Muffy and Pastor Wayne and Doris McCraw also join the traveling band for the impending finale.

Today's results: Koyago 6:47:30, David, Dusan, Patrick, Manfred, Jun 7:40:17.

From the mailbox:

I imagine by now your mind has been dulled to many things and only concentrating on each day — perhaps each mile — and I am sure in some cases, every step. I can only imagine how you and the others are doing this. To put so much out of your mind — and to be in this race for so long — is, to me, a challenge in itself — and may be the toughest. I want you to know I pray for your mind to stay clear and focused. As you run along, negative thoughts can creep in and create problems. So, remember as you run that I and many others are praying for you…. You are not running alone, not at all.

~Sam Lanham

Runner and support crews take time to pose in Kutztown, Pennsylvania.

CHAPTER 21

The Final Day

I press toward the mark for the prize of the high calling of Jesus Christ.
~ Phil. 3:14

DAY 64 - AUGUST 19 - S. ORANGE, NJ TO NYC, NY - 33.3 MILES - TOTAL MILES - 2906.05

This was the day all the runners had dreamed about. This was the day that would seal the enormous nature of the summer's challenge. What would they feel like? Would they run effortlessly? Would the time fly by as they took in the sights and the sounds of the race's last stage? Would they be overcome with emotion during the run? What about at the finish? Each runner awoke with certain expectations. Were they fulfilled? Although we cannot report on all the runners, David did relate how this day went down in his own personal history.

He really wasn't sure what to expect when he came down from his room. Although the stage was to start at 5:30 a.m., he awoke at his normal time of 3:55 a.m., got dressed, and went in search of breakfast. He reports not feeling anything different. Just the same old same old. Don Winkley and the injured Ray Bell were to start at 4:00 a.m. so that the pack, running at a leisurely eleven minutes per mile pace, would catch them and they would finish in the proper order. The start of these two men was delayed, so at 4:17 a.m. David wandered outside and saw them begin the last leg to the sounds of the song "New York, New York." It was only then that David was hit with a tidal wave of emotion as he realized just how close he was to achieving his goal. The tears flowed as the two comrades shuffled off into the darkness of the morning.

David returned to his breakfast and the chores of gathering his gear for the day. The morning was cool and dry. As the final starting buzzer was sounded, he and the other seven runners were in good spirits. Laughter and light-hearted joking could be heard as they made their way down the street. There were two vehicles

David and Eiko Endo, the only woman entrant in 1995 and women's record holder, on the George Washington Bridge entering New York City.

assigned to crew the group as they made their way into the city. Meanwhile, the other crews, family, and friends waited until 8:00 a.m. to form a caravan into Central Park.

David reports there was quite a bit of chatter for the first fifteen miles. But after that, even the miles of that final day became more difficult. The group fell silent, and it actually became a struggle to keep the group together at such a slow pace. Ray had gotten lost, but managed to catch the pack. He was so relieved to have caught the pack that he lost concentration, stumbled on a curb and fell, hitting his ribs. The others runners rushed to his side, finding him in immense pain and hardly able to breathe. He finally convinced everyone he could move a little bit and encouraged the pack to go on. Other than that incident, Koyago seemed to be the one who was holding up the group the most. Apparently the hard running of the previous week finally caught up to him. However, as the George Washington Bridge came into sight, the mood lifted once again. The emotions of some of the runners could not be contained as they crossed the river. Manfred spontaneously threw his hat off the bridge, others laughed, and some cried. David was carrying a one-time use camera and took many pictures of his friends. At the end of the bridge, they began to run in the order of their overall finish. Unfortunately, David's turn sheet flew out of his pack on the bridge, floating down into the river. Those remaining six miles were not well marked, and David began to fear that he was lost. However, he instinctively made his way into the city and found himself running down the last half mile of his journey. Reid Lanham (Muffy) met him with an American flag, and he finished to the cheers of many people, carrying high his country's flag and a bouquet of flowers that had also been handed to him. He ran into the arms of Nancy, his wife, and basked momentarily in the flood of congratulations, pictures, and TV cameras. However, the moment of glory was short lived, as the very obnoxious and rude NYC Road Runner members who had set up the finish line shoved him out of the area. Still, many friends who applauded his achievement surrounded him. David certainly enjoyed the moment, but it actually seemed anticlimatic when compared with what he felt at 4:17 a.m. and as he crossed the bridge.

The first priority for David after finishing was to get some food. His last aid was given with six miles to go, and he was really hungry.

David crosses the finish line in Central Park.

So, he grabbed a hot dog, sandwich, ice cream, and soda for starters. After we all made our way to the hotel, he took his two-minute shower, got dressed, and led the way for all of us as a friend, Steve Feller, gave us a personal tour of some NYC sites. We walked, ate, rode the subway, rode a bus, and bought cheap T-shirts before returning to get cleaned up for the awards dinner at Mickey Mantle's restaurant. The meal was great, and it was so good to see David receive the third place finisher's award. The

David and wife, Nancy, reunited in Central Park following the finish of the 1995 Trans-America Foot Race.

fifty-plus summer friends, both runners and crews, exchanged pictures, hugs, and good wishes. As we left, we knew we may never see most of these people again, but the memories of the times spent together will last a lifetime.

DAY 0 - AUGUST 20 - THE DAY AFTER

David slept in this morning — until 5:45 a.m. Reid, David, and I met in the lobby at 6:00 a.m. for a run in Central Park. It was a great way to celebrate together. We ran for one hour at a leisurely pace, David initiating short conversations with runners, walkers, and cyclists that we passed. He felt a little slow but okay. He loved running for the joy and camaraderie rather than for the racing. We returned to the hotel, showered, and left the city at about 8:00 a.m. The ride back was light-hearted and the time passed quickly. Only when he and Nancy pulled into their drive-way did David realize that the hardest challenge of his life was over. What would tomorrow bring? They unlocked the kitchen door and went in. Only time would tell.

FINAL RESULTS

1. Dusan Mravlje, SLO	427:59:00
2. Ray Bell, FL	+16:50:31
3. David Horton, VA	+21:27:51
4. Patrick Farmer, AUS	+33:14:50
5. Nobuaki Koyago, JPN	+34:25:58
6. Manfred Leismann, GER	+53:32:18
7. Jun Onoki, JPN	+89:07:04
8. Eiko Endo, JPN	+123:46:01
9. Michiyoshi Kaiho, JPN	+141:54:26
10. Don Winkley, TX	+307:37:43

CHAPTER 22

From Racing to Recovery

My life is a gift from my Creator.
What I do with my life is my gift back to the Creator.

- Billy Mills

I had said before I ever left for the Trans-Am that I intended to run the four-mile "mall loop" on the Monday following my return with my running buddies from Liberty. Traveling home on Sunday and experiencing no real soreness, I did not think there would be much of a problem with Monday's run. So, ready to run, I was disappointed to discover that none of my friends were to be found. However, Rebekah did come up to run and we started off down the road. After planning this reuniting run in my mind for so long, it was anticlimactic not to have the jesting and laughing amongst the usual pack of "boys." However, about halfway through the run, we intercepted Kim Graham, LU's assistant athletic director at the time, and ran the rest of the way with him. I had wanted to start telling everyone stories, and now I only had one person to tell. In a way, I really didn't feel like getting into it. It was depressing. Where would I start and what would I say? The three of us made small talk, finished the run, and went our separate ways.

I remember feeling trashed after the A.T. ordeal, but I did recover within the relatively short period of two or three months. I thought my recovery would be the same after my cross-country trek. I took off Tuesday and Wednesday of that first week and then ran just a few miles on Thursday, Friday, and Saturday. I felt horrible.

The next week I ran Monday through Thursday and discovered that my hip joints were extremely sore. I got a massage from my muscle therapist, Jim McFarland, took off Friday, and then proceeded to do what any normal person would do on a beautiful Saturday — run twenty miles with Dennis Herr. Although I enjoyed running through the woods and down the Blue Ridge Parkway, I did feel beat up, and the downhills really hurt.

I started to worry a little when I was still feeling pretty bad the next week. I even decided not to run long that weekend. The following weeks became a series of "I feel horrible," to "I feel a little bit better," and back to "I feel horrible." My hips seemed to give me the most trouble, but I basically ignored the symptoms and continued to run. I did enjoy a couple of fun runs in the mountains with friends, but it just wasn't what it was in the past.

Rick Hamilton had asked me earlier that summer if I was prepared for the consequences of the racing — physically and mentally. He queried, "What if you are injured to the point of never running as good again? Are you willing to risk that?" At the time, I said, "Yes, of course." However, now there was that nagging doubt in my mind, and a big pain in my hip suggested there really had been some damage done over the last three thousand miles. I even went as far as getting examined by my orthopedist and having x-rays taken of my joints. The films failed to answer the question of why I was having pain. It was so frustrating! Why wasn't I coming around? I certainly did not want Rick to be right. In fact, I wanted to prove him wrong. I wanted to show everyone that I was just as tough and fast as before. I formulated a plan. I would train and race as hard as I could at the famous JFK 50-Miler in November. I'll show all those nay-sayers, I thought!

At ten weeks out from the finish in New York, I ran a 107-mile week. My training had started in earnest for the JFK. I had also been asked to be on a team for the race — five runners, top three times count. The team members made a true "dream team" — Eric Clifton, Courtney Campbell, Mike Morton, Chris Gibson, and me. I did not want to embarrass myself. I did not want to be weak. So, I continued to train.

On November 18th, race day arrived and found me at the starting line. The conditions were tough, as an early storm dropped thirteen inches of snow on the trail and there were countless blowdowns all along the infamous twenty-six-mile long section of towpath. However, out of 575 runners, I placed sixth with a time of 6:54. Not my best time, by any means, but one that was good for the conditions and "counted" toward a first place team award.

Unfortunately, I cannot report to you that everything was fine from that point on. My wife tells me I was very moody and depressed for months. I had trouble sleeping and would have nightmares. Good runs were hard to come by. The only race since then in which I feel I ran well was at Hardrock in 1996. I continued to have severe hip pain in the twelve to fifteen month time period after the Trans-Am. "Something" was missing from my running. "Something" may still be missing. I don't know for sure.

Some people have suggested that my age (presently forty-seven) is the explanation for losing the edge. If it is, I don't want to admit to that. I will admit that I probably trained too hard, too soon after the race. I believe even now I have to deal with the deep-down physical consequences of the trans-continental race. But I want to race well. I want to be strong. I want to be a force with which to be reckoned. The Lord willing, I will continue on in my quest for adventure.

▲

Sent to David by Rebekah Trittipoe:
"Far better it is to dare mighty things, to win glorious triumphs, even though checkered by failure, than to take rank with those poor spirits who neither enjoy much nor suffer much, because they live in the gray twilight that knows not victory or defeat."   - Theodore Roosevelt

▼

1995 Trans-America Footrace Statistics

DAVID HORTON: 2906 MILES

Stage	Date	Finish Point	Mileage	Time	Place	Pace
1	6/17	Rancho Cucamongo,CA	52.8	7:41	2	8:44
2	6/18	Victorville, CA	44.6	6:56	2	9:20
3	6/19	Barstow, CA	36.9	5:06	2	8:19
4	6/20	Ludlow, CA	52.9	7:22	3	8:22
5	6/21	Amboy, CA	28.5	3:44	4	7:52
6	6/22	Kelso, CA	39.5	5:50	4	8:52
7	6/23	State Line, NV	49.5	7:04	3	8:53
8	6/24	Las Vegas, NV	35.5	4:50	4	8:11
9	6/25	Moapa, NV	55.05	8:44	1	9:31
10	6/26	Mesquite, NV	36.5	5:05	4	8:22
11	6/27	St. George, UT	47.8	7:18	5	9:11
12	6/28	Cedar City, UT	51.5	8:32	4	9:58
13	6/29	Beaver, UT	54.5	8:26	4	9:17
14	6/30	Monroe, UT	50.7	8:28	3	10:02
15	7/1	Salina, UT	28.55	4:17	5	9:01
16	7/2	Meadow Gulch rest area	32.9	6:14	6	11:23
17	7/3	Eagle Canyon Overlook	29.5	5:24	7	10:59
18	7/4	Green River, UT	44.95	7:44	7	10:20
19	7/5	Cisco, UT	47.6	7:58	6	10:03
20	7/6	Fruita, CO	44.15	7:14	4	9:51
21	7/7	Parachute, CO	56.35	9:16	4	8:48
22	7/8	Glenwood Springs, CO	40.3	6:28	6	9:39
23	7/9	Eagle, CO	36.9	5:42	5	9:17
24	7/10	Frisco, CO	37.9	6:18	4	10:00
25	7/11	Georgetown, CO	34.9	5:55	3	10:11
26	7/12	Denver/Aurora, CO	34.7	5:11	5	8:59
27	7/13	Byers, CO	46.2	6:55	4	9:00
28	7/14	Anton, CO	53.5	8:06	5	9:06
29	7/15	Joes, CO	31.0	4:18	5	8:21
30	7/16	St. Francis, KS	51.1	7:12	5	8:28
31	7/17	Atwood, KS	41.45	5:57	4	8:37

32	7/18	Norton, KS	60.6	9:07	5	9:02
33	7/19	Kensington, KS	47.4	7:01	5	8:54
34	7/20	Mankato, KS	43.3	6:11	3	8:34
35	7/21	Cuba, KS	41.5	5:54	4	8:32
36	7/22	Marysville, KS	43.6	6:09	5	8:28
37	7/23	Hiawatha, KS	59.9	9:09	4	9:10
38	7/24	Elwood, KS	36.5	5:16	5	8:41
39	7/25	Hamilton, MO	48.65	7:10	4	8:50
40	7/26	Brookfield, MO	49.9	7:18	5	8:35
41	7/27	Clarence, MO	45.65	6:45	5	8:53
42	7/28	Hannibal, MO	49.7	7:18	4	8:50
43	7/29	Pittsfield, IL	33.2	4:34	5	8:17
44	7/30	New Berlin, IL	53.5	7:48	1	8:45
45	7/31	Decatur, IL	55.7	8:44	1	9:25
46	8/1	Newman, IL	37.9	5:39	3	8:58
47	8/2	Rockville, IN	55.9	8:48	4	9:27
48	8/3	Indianapolis, IN	52.5	8:10	4	9:20
49	8/4	Dublin, IN	56.6	8:44	1	9:16
50	8/5	Lewisburg, OH	36.0	5:25	4	9:03
51	8/6	South Vienna, OH	52.65	8:10	1	9:19
52	8/7	Reynoldsburg, OH	43.7	6:50	2	9:24
53	8/8	New Concord, OH	59.0	9:15	2	9:25
54	8/9	St. Clairsville, OH	52.6	8:24	1	9:36
55	8/10	Monongahela, PA	60.3	10:27	7	10:24
56	8/11	Ligonier, PA	43.45	7:45	5	10:43
57	8/12	Schellsburg, PA	37.8	6:28	7	10:16
58	8/13	McConnellsburg, PA	41.7	6:55	7	9:58
59	8/14	Gettysburg, PA	47.1	7:27	7	9:30
60	8/15	Lancaster, PA	49.7	7:31	2	9:05
61	8/16	Kutztown, PA	47.5	7:21	2	9:17
62	8/17	Washington, NJ	52.15	8:08	2	9:22
63	8/18	South Orange, NJ	49.4	7:40	2	8:55
64	8/19	NYC, NY	33.3	6:02	2	10:52